W9-BYR-958

Fourth
Generation
Evaluation

I know of no safe depository of the ultimate
powers of the society but the people themselves;
and if we think them not enlightened enough
to exercise their control with a wholesome
discretion, the remedy is not to take it from
them, but to inform their discretion.

—Thomas Jefferson
Letter to William Charles Jarvis
September 28, 1820

Evaluation is an investment in people and in progress.

Contents

Foreword

It is our hope that you, the reader, will find this book dramatically different from any other book about evaluation that you have ever read. We do not describe the field of evaluation as it has emerged historically, although we touch upon selected historical facts here and there. We do not treat the many different models for the doing of evalution that abound in the literature, although we briefly reference selected models from time to time. We do not treat evaluation primarily as a technical process of inquiry, with the concomitant emphasis upon techniques, particularly statistical techniques, that one might expect in such a work, although we certainly deal with process matters, including the proposing of criteria of goodness that seem to us to be applicable. Perhaps most startling, we do not treat evaluation as a *scientific* process, because it is our conviction that to approach evaluation scientifically is to miss completely its fundamentally social, political, and value-oriented character.

7

It is our intention to define an emergent but mature approach to evaluation that moves beyond mere science—just getting the facts—to include the myriad human, political, social, cultural, and contextual elements that are involved. We have called this new approach *fourth generation evaluation* to signal our construction that this form moves beyond previously existing generations, characterizable as measurement-oriented, description-oriented, and judgment-oriented, to a new level whose key dynamic is *negotiation*. This new form has some interesting properties.

First, it takes the position that evaluation outcomes are not descriptions of the "way things really are" or "really work," or of some "true" state of affairs, but instead represent meaningful constructions that individual actors or groups of actors form to "make sense" of the situations in which they find themselves. The findings are not "facts" in some ultimate sense but are, instead, literally *created* through an interactive process that *includes* the evaluator (so much for objectivity!) as well as the many stakeholders that are put at some risk by the evaluation. What emerges from this process is one or more *constructions* that *are* the realities of the case.

Second, it recognizes that the constructions through which people make sense of their situations are in a very major way shaped by the values of the constructors. Of course, if all of the constructors share a common value system, there are few problems. Indeed, it may well appear, under such circumstances, that the commonly shared construction *is* the true state of affairs, and little harm is done by engaging in such a delusion. But virtually every modern society (including those putatively "primitive" societies found in, say, Third World countries) turns out to be value-pluralistic. Then the question of whose values are to be taken into account, and how different value positions might be accommodated, becomes paramount. It is immediately clear that a methodology that claims to be value-free will probably have little utility in such cases.

Third, it suggests that these constructions are inextricably linked to the particular physical, psychological, social, and cultural contexts within which they are formed and to which they refer. The context provides the "surround" within which the persons forming the constructions live and of which they try to make sense. At the same time, the surround remains formless until the constructions of the people in it endow it with parameters, features, and limits. In a very literal sense the context gives life to, and is given life by, the constructions that people come to form and hold. Since these same people form part of the context for one another, it is not surprising that shared constructions emerge over time; those who inhabit a particular context come to consensus about its nature. Consensus does not imply a greater degree of reality for whatever is agreed upon, however; it simply means that those in agreement have come to share a construction that has reality for them. Furthermore, the consensus is the product of human conceptual exchange in a *particular* setting; it is thus unlikely that this same consensus would necessarily help other persons make sense of *their* settings. Finally, precisely because they are the product of human thought, consensual constructions are subject to human error; none can be considered "true" in an absolute sense, nor even an approximation of "truth."

Fourth, this emergent form of evaluation recognizes that evaluations can be shaped to enfranchise or disenfranchise stakeholding groups in a variety of ways. Clearly there can be selective involvement of these stakeholders in the design and implementation of the evaluation. If only the evaluator and the client are privileged to decide on the questions to be asked, the instrumentation to be employed, the mode of data analysis and interpretation to be used, and the like, other stakeholders will be denied the opportunity to pursue their own legitimate interests. Given the "cozy relationship" (we thank Michael Scriven for the term) that often exists between evaluator and client, it is not surprising that evaluations tend to reveal ineffectiveness or malfeasance in groups *other* than the clients (for example, teachers being held accountable for the putative poor state of the schools) or that the objectives of the client are given priority over those of other stakeholders (for example, evaluating alternative police procedures for intervening in domestic disputes on the criterion of reduced recidivism, a condition that police aspire to because it reduces their risks, paperwork, court appearances, and the like, rather than on the criterion of reduced wife-battering, which has little immediate impact on police work load). Stakeholders can be empowered or disempowered through the selective dissemination of evaluation findings. If information is power, then information withheld is power reduced. If clients have the final word on what information will be released, to whom, when, and by what means, the process is clearly tilted toward the maintenance and even enhancement of power for those who already possess it, while depriving the relatively powerless of even that little that they have.

Fifth, it suggests that evaluation must have an action orientation that defines a course to be followed, stimulates involved stakeholders to follow it, and generates and preserves their commitment to do so. Evaluators, perhaps in the image of their senior brethren, the "pure" scientists, appear inclined to relegate follow-up, the applied aspect of the evaluation, to others. That this follow-up does not often occur is well documented in the current hue and cry for evaluation utilization. The profession is aghast over nonuse, alternately blaming the clients for perverse failure to act despite the compelling rationality of the recommendations and themselves for failing to "market" the evaluation product satisfactorily. Indeed, in a recent (1987) address to the American Evaluation Association, incoming President Michael Quinn Patton urged the members to adopt the postures and techniques of the salesperson, although cautioning that the first requisite for successful selling is to "have a product you can believe in." Very often the evaluation "product" is a set of recommendations that suits only the purposes of the evaluator and the client, pays little attention to the legitimate interests of other stakeholders, displays unconcern for the questions and issues raised by other groups, and reflects only one (their own) of the multiple sets of values that inhere in the situation. If there is to be a course of action with which most stakeholders can agree, it can only be arrived at through *negotiation* that honors the separate sets of values and makes it possible for individuals to find a reason to support it, work at it, and feel good about it. If that goal is to be achieved, the evaluator must play a larger role by far than simply that of technician-gathering-infomation; instead he or she must be the orchestrator of the negotiation process, which in the final analysis is the guts of the evaluation.

Finally, fourth generation evaluation insists that inasmuch as an evaluation involves humans (as clients, as stakeholders, as information sources, and in many other ways), it is incumbent on the evaluator to interact with those humans in a manner respecting their dignity, their integrity, and their privacy. Of course, conventional evaluators have been careful about ethics; canons respecting fully informed consent, harm, deception, and privacy/confidentiality are well understood, and mostly practiced. But the full meaning of the phrase "respecting their dignity, their integrity, and their privacy" goes well beyond such standard protections. It reaches to the level of *full participative* involvement, in which the stakeholders and others who may be drawn into the evaluation are welcomed as equal partners in every aspect of design, implementation, interpretation, and resulting action of an evaluation—that is, they are accorded a full measure of *political parity* and *control*. It means further that human participants are accorded the privilege of sharing their constructions and working toward a common, consensual, more fully informed and sophisticated, *joint* construction—they are accorded a full measure of *conceptual parity*. And, of course, it means that the participants continue to be treated as humans, *not* as subjects of experimentation or objects of study.

If the intentions and promise of this emergent conception of evaluation are to be fulfilled, a means of carrying out an evaluation must be found that recognizes the constructed nature of findings, that takes different values and different contexts (physical, psychological, social, and cultural) into account, that empowers and enfranchises, that fuses the act of evaluation and its follow-up activities into one indistinguishable whole, and that is fully participative in that it extends both political and conceptual parity to all stakeholders. It is our contention that the mode of fourth generation evaluation that we propose meets this challenge, at least to a first level of approximation. Of course, further development is very much needed.

Fourth generation evaluation, as we shall show, rests on two elements: *responsive focusing*—determining what questions are to be asked and what information is to be collected on the basis of stakeholder inputs— and *constructivist methodology*—carrying out the inquiry process within the ontological and epistemological presuppositions of the constructivist paradigm.[1]

Historically, evaluations have been focused in many ways: by attending to the collection of scores and norms from available tests, usually standardized; by determining the congruence of performance with prespecified objectives; by analyzing decisions to be made and collecting information needed to inform them; by determining an evaluand's cost-benefit utility; by assessing the effects of an innovation or intervention, whether intended or not; by ascertaining the degree to which previously unmet needs are fulfilled or ameliorated; and in other ways. All of these approaches are based on the premise of an intensive collaboration between evaluator and client (who specifies—or at least ratifies—the tests to be used, the objectives to be achieved, the decisions to be serviced, the cost-benefit ratios to be achieved, the intervention or innovation to be tested, the needs to be responded to, and so on) which tends to ignore other actors in the situation and, particularly, their values and constructions. Responsive evaluation was so named by its originator, Robert Stake, to signal the idea that all stakeholders put at risk by an evaluation have the right to place their claims, concerns, and issues on the table for consideration (response), irrespective of the value system to which they adhere. It was created as the antithesis of preordinate evaluation, which assumes that the evaluator and client together possess sufficient information and legitimation to design and implement an evaluation completely, without the need to consult other parties (although in practice such consultation often occurs for political reasons).

The second element supporting fourth generation evaluation is constructivist methodology. In the past, the methodology employed in evaluations has been almost exclusively scientific, grounded *ontologically* in the positivist assumption that there exists an objective reality driven by immutable natural laws, and *epistemologically* in the counterpart assumption of a duality between observer and observed that makes it possible for the observer to stand *outside* the arena of the observed, neither influencing it nor being influenced by it. Given these assumptions the evaluator can claim to have produced findings that represent "the way things really are" and "the way things really work," with no possibility of being influenced by the evaluator, the client, or anyone else.

The posture of fourth generation evaluation is quite different. It begins with the assumption that realities are not objectively "out there" but are constructed by people, often under the influence of a variety of social and cultural factors that lead to shared constructions. But socially shared constructions are not equivalent to the positivist's "reality"; there *is no reality* except that created by people as they attempt to "make sense" of their surrounds. Obviously such socially constructed realities are not only *not* independent of the "observer" (read, "constructor") but are absolutely dependent on him or her for whatever existence they may have. A methodology of evaluation that reflects such assumptions must be grounded in an inquiry paradigm radically different from scientific positivism. We believe that such a paradigm exists in what we have come to call the constructivist paradigm (also called, with different shades of meaning, the *interpretive* or the *hermeneutic* paradigm and, sometimes—erroneously, we believe—the *qualitative* paradigm). This paradigm rests on a relativist rather than a realist ontology, and on a monistic, subjective rather than dualistic, objective epistemology. Its exercise unites the evaluator and the stakeholders in an interaction that *creates* the product of the evaluation, utilizing a hermeneutic dialectic approach aimed at establishing that interaction and maintaining it within quality bounds. Moreover, the product of the evaluation is not, in sharp contrast to conventional methodology, a set of conclusions, recommendations, or value judgments, but rather an *agenda for negotiation* of those claims, concerns, and issues that have not been resolved in the hermeneutic dialectic exchanges.

These are substantial claims, introduced in this Foreword in the skimpiest of fashion, and totally unsupported. Their explication and justification is, of course, the aim of this book. In writing it, we have in mind several distinct audiences—and also some audiences we would urge *not* to read this book.

First and foremost, we address ourselves to evaluators as a professional group. That evaluation is a profession has become apparent over the past decade, if it had not been apparent before. First, two independent professional associations were formed, the Evaluation Network and the Evaluation Research Society, which within the past three years merged into a single group, the American Evaluation Association. Further, multiple standards for guiding the work of evaluators (while also informing clients and users) have been devised, the most prominent of these being the Joint Committee *Standards for the Evaluation of Educational Programs, Projects, and Materials (1981)* and the counterpart *Personnel Evaluation Standards (1988)*. Finally, multiple journals have come into existence, such as *Evaluation Practice, Evaluation Review, Educational Evaluation and Policy Analysis,* and the series *New Directions in Program Evaluation,* by means of which a meaningful literature is rapidly being built up. It is our experience that more and more of these professionals are becoming disaffected with conventional approaches to the doing of evaluation. Such persons will find in this book both a theoretical philosophic basis for an alternative, and practical suggestions for carrying it out. Researchers and policy analysts who may not regard evaluation as central to their interests may nevertheless find in this volume materials and concepts of use in the reconstruction of their own guiding inquiry paradigms.

We are also writing for stakeholders, those persons who, sometimes willy-nilly, are drawn into an evaluation because they are put at risk by it. That there are always stakeholders whose claims, concerns, and issues deserve to be identified and honored may be taken as axiomatic. Included in their number are the *agents* that devise, operate, manage, fund, oversee, or otherwise contribute to the development, establishment, and operation of the evaluand; the putative *beneficiaries* (often called "targets") that profit, or are expected to profit, from the evaluand, and secondary beneficiaries related to them, for example, spouses of persons undergoing alcoholism rehabilitation, parents of children who are receiving remediation in school, and the like; and *victims,* persons who directly or indirectly are injured or deprived of some good by the implementation of the evaluand, including forgone opportunities. Stakeholders are often unaware that an evaluation affecting them is going on, or that information that might be important to them is being withheld, or that only those questions that concern some other, perhaps rival, group are being asked. Stakeholders often have no concept of the role they might play in an evaluation, or even of the legitimacy of their claim to involvement. We hope to provide such stakeholders with insights about the roles they might play and the questions they might ask, as well as to confirm them in the belief that they have the right to become full partners in the evaluation enterprise, politically and conceptually.

We hope also to interest evaluation clients or sponsors, that is, those persons who commission evaluations and/or provide the funds and other resources needed to carry them out. Most clients or sponsors do not have a very clear idea of what to expect from an evaluation; we hope that this book will provide some clarification. But we particularly hope to persuade clients or sponsors that the conventional mode of evaluation, which effectively reserves power and decision-making authority to them, is not only morally and ethically wrong but also politically naive and conceptually narrow. Conventional evaluations rarely coalesce public opinion behind some course of action that clients and sponsors believe to be wise; indeed, quite the opposite—evaluations tend to persuade stakeholders that the whole point of an evaluation is to collect information that rationalizes and legitimates some decision already made "behind the scenes." Public input is often solicited but rarely honored. If this book can lay bare some of the reasons for the failure of conventional evaluation not only to produce useful information but also to achieve political consensus, we will regard it as having achieved our hopes.

While we hope to influence these three broad audiences with what we have to say, there are some persons who, we believe, would not profit from reading this book. We will characterize them as "true believers," persons who are persuaded that they already have *the* way to manage an evaluation. Michael Quinn Patton tells of an experience he had while conducting an evaluation in a Caribbean village. His inquiry took him one day to a sugarcane field, where, in the hottest part of the summer, a group of villagers were busily cutting down cane—surely one of the most physically demanding tasks anyone could imagine. In their effort to keep as cool as possible, the villagers, men and women alike, had stripped to the barest of loincloths. Suddenly, as if on a signal, the women dropped their machetes, hurried to the edge of the field where they had left their belongings, and quickly put on shirts, Mother Hubbards, or whatever else they had to cover their bare breasts. Patton had no sooner noticed this when he discovered the reason for their odd behavior. The local village priest was driving up in his Jeep, which the sharp-eared villagers had heard and identified long before Patton became conscious of it. Knowing that the priest would find their bare-breastedness a sufficient reason for at least a diatribe and perhaps for imposing penances, the women had wisely decided to cover up. But as soon as the priest had gone, they once again divested themselves of their outer clothing and returned to their task.

Patton points out that, since the cane cutters embraced not only Catholicism but also voodooism and possibly other beliefs, it did not disturb them to put on their coverings—or to take them off—as seemed appropriate to the circumstances. The priest, on the other hand, was a true believer, and he could not brook the notion that practices not condoned by his belief system could be anything but bad, deserving condemnation and punishment.

We believe it is so with true believers in positivism. Convinced that there exists some single, true reality, driven by natural laws, open to discovery and harnessing by the methods of science, positivists reject all relativist views, of which constructivism is one, as not only seriously in error but pernicious and repugnant. Advocates of such a view, they feel, rank but a notch above con men and snake-oil salesmen. True believers are not likely to find anything in this book that will change their minds on that score. On the other hand, the relativist constructivist, while not agreeing with the positivist formulation, can nevertheless accept it as one of many possible constructions. The constructivist may find the positivist view ill-informed and unsophisticated, but not *wrong* or *untrue.*

We do not argue that this book provides the "real" or "final" answer to the questions we raise, either of what evaluation is or how it should be done. We regard our work as simply another construction. We hope the reader will find it reasonably informed and sophisticated, but it is certainly far from universal truth. Indeed, there *is no universal truth* to which our construction is a more or less good approximation. We trust that continuing dialectic dialogue about what we have to say will lead to reconstructions of greater power and worth but not of greater truth. In the final analysis, all of these constructions, those we now have and those yet to come, are the constructions of *human minds,* and hence are subject to all of the errors and foibles that always bedevil human enterprises. If we have a moral imperative embodied in our work, it is simply this, that we will continue to make every effort to seek out and take account of every reaction and criticism that we can, and will attempt to deal with them, even if that means completely abandoning our present construction and embracing an utterly different one (which is what we believe is meant by the phrase, "paradigm revolution").

To that end, we welcome meaningful exchanges with anyone regardless of their present belief system, *provided only* that they are committed to a hermeneutic dialectic that leaves them open to other constructions, willing to change as their knowledge and sophistication grows and to move in whatever directions such an exchange may identify as fruitful. We in turn pledge ourselves to that same stance.

We have argued that no accommodation is possible between positivist and constructivist belief systems as they are now formulated. We do not see any possibility for accommodation if that accommodation is to occur by having one paradigm overwhelm the other by the sheer power of its arguments, or by having the paradigms play complementary roles, or by showing that one is simply a special case of the other. We *do* see the possibility that, through a hermeneutic dialectic process, a new construction will emerge that is not "better" or "truer" that its predecessors, but simply more informed and sophisticated than either. Such an exchange represents, we believe, the finest meaning of phrase "the academic marketplace of ideas."

In this spirit we hope that no one will read this book with the intent of finding a "formula" for doing evaluation. We do not wish anyone to conclude that now, finally, we know what to do and how to do it. Mary Hesse (1980) has aptly noted that just as all scientific theories have sooner or later proven to be false, so will every theory that we now entertain. We are not proposing a new orthodoxy, and we do not want readers to use our book to such an end.

Let us take a moment to describe briefly the contents of the book. Chapter 1 takes a historical view of the development of evaluation through what we construct as its first three generations, analyzes the major criticisms that have been brought to bear on those earlier approaches, and argues that responsive evaluation, as proposed by Robert Stake, overcomes most of these problems. Fourth generation evaluation is introduced as a form that can usefully incorporate responsive techniques.

Chapter 2 is devoted to a discussion of the need for a new paradigm. The problems of positivist philosophy are briefly examined, and the constructivist paradigm is proposed as a useful alternative. Chapter 3 develops the paradigm in detail, contrasts its basic belief system with that of positivism, and cites arguments and evidence supporting the rejection

of positivism and the acceptance of constructivism in its place. A variety
of ways that have been proposed as means for reaching an accommodation between the two paradigms are examined and rejected.

Chapter 4 takes up the questions of the role of ethics and politics in
evaluation. Ethical and political problems are examined from the van-
tage point of both paradigms, with the conclusion that, while each
paradigm is subject to difficulties in these arenas, the constructivist
paradigm offers multiple advantages, including as not the least the
empowerment and enfranchisement of all stakeholders.

Chapter 5 moves to a detailed examination of the hermeneutic dialectic process. It begins with a discussion of constructions as created realities,
and asks how constructions are formed, challenged, changed, and compromised. The conditions for a productive hermeneutic dialectic are
described, and the process steps are considered in detail.

Chapter 6 deals with the question of whether paradigms influence
methodologies. Methodologies, or the overall strategies for the use of
tools and techniques (methods), are often confused with the methods
themselves; it is for this reason, for example, that the constructivist
paradigm is sometimes called the "qualitative" paradigm, as though it
were defined entirely by a preference for qualitative methods. The
chapter distinguishes between "naturalistic (constructivist) evaluation of
the 1st kind," which is no more than qualitative evaluation within the
positivist paradigm, and "naturalistic (constructivist) evaluation of the
2nd kind," which proceeds from the basic belief system of constructivism
and hence calls for a very different methodology. The methodologies of
both conventional and constructivist paradigms are explored in some
detail, in order to make this distinction clear.

Chapter 7 moves on to the delineation of the preferred methodology
for the doing of fourth generation evaluation. The reader is taken
through every implementation step from initial contracting, through the
identification of stakeholding groups and their several claims, concerns,
and issues, through a hermeneutic dialectic interchange in which the
constructions of each group are exposed to critique and reaction from all
other groups, through the development of an agenda for negotiation and
the process for moving through that agenda, to final reporting.

Chapter 8 examines the question of criteria of goodness or quality. If evalutions in the new mode are to be taken seriously as disciplined inquiries, it is imperative that they can be shown to meet certain criteria. The problem, of course, is to specify what criteria are *appropriate* to fourth generation evaluation. Two sets of standards are proposed: the so-called *trustworthiness* criteria, which we developed as counterparts paralleling those usually specified for positivist inquiries (hence often called "parallel" or "counterpart" criteria), and the so-called *authenticity* criteria, which are generated from the basic belief system of the constructivist paradigm itself. Emphasis is also placed on the hermeneutic dialectic process as its own quality control.

Finally, Chapter 9 reviews and highlights the consequences of adopting the fourth generation mode of evaluation: the consequences for *evaluation as a process,* for example, it is a sociopolitical process, continuous, recursive, and divergent; the consequences for the *role of the evaluator,* for example, a shift from technician, describer, and/or judge to collaborator and negotiator; and the consequences for *evaluation outcomes,* for example, certain principles that the fourth generation evaluator may wish to keep in mind while pursuing this emergent form of evaluation.

Note

1. In our previous writing we have most often used the terms *naturalistic* and *naturalist* to label the inquiry process we espouse and the person engaged in such a process. For a variety of reasons—for example, that those terms conjure up nineteenth-century British naturalism with which we have nothing in common, that they suggest a realist ontology that we specifically reject, that they imply a claim to legitimacy for our work (Nature's Way) that is unwarranted, and that we are espousing inquiry in natural settings as *the* solution to paradigm dilemmas—we feel those terms are no longer appropriate. Further, we have come to appreciate that the central feature of our paradigm is its ontological assumption that realities, certainly social/behavioral realities, are mental constructions. Thus we have elected to use the terms *constructivism* and *constructivist* to label the paradigm and the person engaged in carrying it out, respectively. This convention is followed in most places in this book, except in instances where we refer to earlier work, sometimes quoting from it. We have endeavored in those instances to remind readers of the new conventions.

Acknowledgements

We gratefully acknowledge permission to quote from the following sources:

Joe David Bellamy
Ruth Bleier
J.R. Brown
Lee J. Cronbach
P.C.W. Davies
A. Michael Huberman
Joint Committee on Standards
    for Educational Evaluation
H. Earle Knowlton
Matthew B. Miles
Marion Namenwirth
Michael Q. Patton
Peter Reason

Shulamit Reinharz
John Rowan
Graham D. Rowles
J. Sanders
Thomas A. Schwandt
Thomas Skrtic
Robert E. Stake
Robert M.W. Travers
J. Wagner
David D. Williams
B. Worthen
Gary Zukav

1   *The Coming of Age of Evaluation* ⋆

If this is to be a book about *evaluation,* it would seem reasonable to begin with a definition of what we shall mean by that term. But to propose a definition at this point, aside from being arbitrary and preemptive, would be counterproductive to the book's central themes. For we will argue that there is *no* "right" way to define *evaluation,* a way that, if it could be found, would forever put an end to argumentation about how evaluation is to proceed and what its purposes are. We take definitions of evaluation to be human mental constructions, whose correspondence to some "reality" *is not* and *cannot* be an issue. There is no answer to the question, "But what is evaluation really?" and there is no point in asking it.

⋆AUTHORS' NOTE: Much of the material in this chapter is drawn from our paper "The Countenances of Fourth Generation Evaluation: Description, Judgment, and Negotiation" (pp. 70-80 in *Evaluation Studies Review Annual,* Volume 11, Newbury Park, CA: Sage, 1986). A slightly different version appears in *The Politics of Evaluation* (Dennis J. Palumbo, editor, Newbury Park, CA: Sage, 1988).

Instead we will begin by sketching briefly the changed meanings that have been ascribed to evaluation for the past hundred years, ascriptions that have reflected the existing historical context, the purposes that people had in mind for doing evaluations, and the philosophic assumptions that evaluators, theoreticians, and practitioners alike have been willing to make. We will argue that, over time, the construction of evaluation has become more informed and sophisticated, until, at this present time, we are in a position to devise a radical new construction, which we characterize as fourth generation evaluation. There is, of course, no consensus about this form of evaluation, as there has not been on earlier forms—a state of affairs that a brief glance through any standard text on evaluation quickly verifies. But we offer it as a construction that we believe counters, or at least ameliorates, the imperfections, gaps, and naiveté of earlier formulations.

We do not believe that we have stumbled upon the ultimately correct formulation. We *are* prepared, however, to argue that the construction that we have labeled fourth generation evaluation is more informed and sophisticated than previous constructions have been. But like those earlier forms, this form will sooner or later also prove to be inadequate in some way, and will require revision, refinement, extension, and probably even complete replacement. Indeed, we take it to be our obligation to seek out aspects of evaluation that this form does *not* handle well, in a continuing effort at *re*construction.

On that note, we may begin.

The First Generation: Measurement

Evaluation as we know it did not simply appear one day; it is the result of a developmental process of construction and reconstruction that involves a number of interacting influences.

Chief among the early influences is the measurement of various attributes of schoolchildren. School tests had been utilized for hundreds of years, to determine whether students had "mastered" the content of the various courses or subjects to which they were exposed. Appropriate content was defined by reference to authority, whether Aristotle, the Bible, or, most recently, the findings of science. The major purpose of the

school was to teach children *what was known to be true*; children demonstrated mastery of those "facts" by regurgitating them on what were
essentially tests of memory. The earliest school tests were administered
chiefly orally, one student at a time, and required, had they been written
down, "essay-type" answers.

It is thus not surprising that the first published example of educational
research, "The Futility of the Spelling Grind" (Rice, 1897), depended on
test scores for its data. Joseph Mayer Rice was appalled at the fact that *all*
school time was devoted, at least in American schools, to what we would
nowadays call the "basics." Rice felt that, if schools could be made more
efficient, that is, if the same basic learning could occur in *less* time, the
curriculum could be expanded to include art, music, and other subjects
that he wanted to see included (the "frills"). After an abortive effort to
attack the problem curriculumwide (which failed because he could not
establish adequate field controls for so vast an enterprise), Rice focused
on spelling as a prime example. He devised a spelling test that he himself
administered in multiple schools widely scattered geographically, also
collecting from each school data about the amount of time devoted to
the teaching of spelling. His subsequent analysis indicated that there was
virtually no relationship between time spent studying spelling and subsequent achievement on the test. The scores achieved by pupils were taken
as concrete evidence of the degree of their achievement.

Another application of testing that was to have major import occurred
in France. The French national minister of education, harried by
teachers demanding that he find some way to screen out mentally
retarded youngsters, who, it was said, were making it impossible to teach
"normal" children (a kind of reverse mainstreaming, as it were), asked a
psychologist, Alfred Binet, to devise a test for that purpose. Binet tried first
to utilize the psychometric measurement techniques that had been
perfected in England by Francis Galton (whose staff member, Karl
Pearson, had earlier invented the product-moment correlation coefficient
as a means to analyze data) and in Germany by Wilhelm Wundt. When
these techniques did not prove to be successful, Binet devised a new
approach, based on the commonsense observation that mentally retarded
youngsters would not be able to cope with simple life situations such as
counting money or identifying household objects as well as their normal

counterparts. Binet was ultimately able to organize his tasks according to the age of subjects typically able to complete them, coining the term "mental age" in the bargain. By 1912 it had become commonplace to divide the achieved mental age by the subject's chronological age to determine the "intelligence quotient." The Binet test leaped across the Atlantic in 1910 via a translation by Henry Goddard; when, in 1916, Louis Terman revised and renormed the Binet (now called the Stanford-Binet) for use with American children, the IQ test had become a permanent part of the American system.

The utility of tests for school purposes was well recognized by leadership personnel. The National Education Association appointed a committee in 1904 to study the use of tests in classifying children and determining their progress; the association appointed three additional committees by 1911. In 1912, the first school district Bureau of Research was established in New York City; its mandate was to conduct a continuing survey of the system, using the "new measurement techniques." Similar bureaus were soon established in other major cities; the directors of these bureaus, who often held titles such as assistant superintendent, began to meet annually in conjunction with the American Association of School Administrators; later they organized themselves more formally into the American Educational Research Association.

Probably the single most important influence leading to the rapid advance and acceptance of mental tests was the need to screen personnel for induction into the armed services in World War I. Military leaders enlisted the support of the American Psychological Association to devise an appropriate instrument. The APA appointed a committee, chaired by Arthur Otis, to undertake this task, which they accomplished in remarkably short time as well as with distinction. This first *group* intelligence test, the Army Alpha, was successfully administered to more than 2 million men. Encouraged by this success, Otis undertook to revise and adapt the instrument for use in the schools.

Several factors that appeared to be only indirectly related to testing were also destined to play major roles in the development of this first generation of evaluation. The first of these contextual factors was the legitimation provided by the phenomenal rise of *social* science. When John Stuart Mill called in 1843 for the application of "the science approach" to the study of human/social phenomena, a call based on the enormous successes of that approach in the physics and chemistry of the late eighteenth and early nineteenth centuries and on the lack of a systematic base for "human" studies, he could scarcely have foreseen the enthusiasm with which his suggestion would be greeted, or the far-reaching consequences that its adoption would have. The first major efforts to be "scientific" were stimulated by Darwin's thesis that even small differences in animal or plant structure could, when accumulated over long time periods, have very significant functional consequences for the species. If that is so, social scientists began to reason, then perhaps small differences in humans might also be a key to understanding major developmental patterns in humans. It was for this reason, among others, that the already mentioned psychometric laboratories were established by Galton, in 1873, and by Wundt, in 1879. Findings such as that individual differences in reaction times were typical of human subjects suggested that these investigators were on the right trail. Psychology in particular became wedded to the new scientific approach, attempting to emulate the physical sciences as closely as possible. Of course, this intent was well served by the apparently precise quantitative measurements that tests were yielding. When, by the mid-1920s, Ronald Fisher, working as statistician for the British cotton industry, had devised the basic analytic tools together with the mathematical tables needed to interpret their results, the social sciences, including education, were treading closely in the footsteps of their much-admired hard science counterparts.

A second contextual factor stimulating testing was the emergence of the scientific management movement in business and industry. If human beings are the major element in the production of goods and services, the task of the manager is to make their work as effective and efficient as possible. Beginning before World War I but coming into full flower in the 1920s, the movement relied heavily on time and motion studies to determine the most productive methods of working and on piecework wage rates to make the workers willing to submit themselves to such an arduous and personally unrewarding discipline. By the time that view was critically challenged by the Hawthorne Studies (Roethlisberger & Dixon, 1939), the ethos of scientific management had also penetrated the schools. Pupils were seen as "raw material" to be "processed" in the school "plant," which was presided over, appropriately enough, by the school "superintendent." Tests played a key role in the unfolding of this metaphor; they were seen as the means for determining whether pupils measured up to the "specifications" that the school had set, specifications that at this time in history were mainly college-preparatory in nature. All of these influences culminated in a remarkable proliferation in school tests during the 1920s and 1930s. School achievement tests, which had been pioneered in 1908 with the publication of the *Stone Reasoning Test in Arithmetic,* were now produced in many forms. The 1922 publication of the *Stanford Achievement Battery* provided an instrument that, for the first time, permitted the simultaneous assessment of a student's relative standing across multiple school subjects. Gertrude Hildreth of the University of Minnesota undertook to publish a list of available tests good enough to warrant adoption; her 1933 bibliography of mental tests and rating scales contained more than 3,500 items. Her third and final bibliography, appearing in 1945, contained more than 5,200. And, during this period of time, the terms *measurement* and *evaluation* came to be used interchangeably. Books dealing with these topics often had both terms in their titles—although *measurement* invariably appeared first.

Thus, the first generation of evaluation can legitimately be called the *measurement generation.* The role of the evaluator was technical; he or she was expected to know the full panoply of available instruments, so that any variable named for investigation could be measured. If appropriate instruments did not exist, the evaluator was expected to have the expertise necessary to create them. And, it is terribly important to note, this first generation or technical sense of evaluation persists today, as evidenced, for example, by the frequent practice of requiring pupils to pass tests as part of their high school graduation or college admission procedures, by the use of such tests in many states to rank schools and even individual teachers for effectiveness, and by the continuing publication of texts that use the phrase *measurement and evaluation* in their titles (see, for example, Gronlund, 1985).

The Second Generation: Description

The second generation of evaluation was spawned by a serious deficiency of the first generation, namely, its targeting of *students* as the objects of evaluation. For, shortly after World War I, it became evident that school curricula needed to undergo dramatic revision, and an evaluation approach that could not provide other than student data could not serve the purposes for evaluation now contemplated.

Soon after the war the secondary schools of American began experiencing an influx of students who had rarely gone beyond the elementary level in earlier times. These students exhibited needs and aspirations that could not be met adequately by the prevailing college-preparatory curricula. Many of these students saw the secondary school as an opportunity to acquire the skills needed to rise above the social and economic status of their parents, but the schools were ill equipped to provide such teaching. Moreover, efforts to devise curricula that were more appropriate were defeated before they could receive a fair trial, because the secondary schools were inextricably locked into the Carnegie unit system (which specified the types and numbers of units required for graduation). The chief obstacles in the path of altering this requirement were, not surprisingly, the colleges and universities, which feared that if the Carnegie unit were abolished as the basis for accumulating secondary school credits, they would be forced to accept high school graduates who were ill prepared to cope with their standard collegiate curricula.

The Eight Year Study launched in 1933 was intended to determine the validity of that position. Thirty public and private secondary schools were given license to develop more responsive curricula with the understanding that their graduates would be admitted to cooperating colleges without necessarily having met Carnegie requirements. The purpose of the Eight Year Study was to demonstrate that students who were trained by these unorthodox curricula would nevertheless be able to succeed in college. The time period of eight years was selected to permit at least one cohort of such students to complete four full years each of secondary school and college work.

An immediate problem confronting the designers of the study was to devise a means for assessing whether the developing new curricula were working as intended. It would, after all, not be a fair test if students failed in college not because the curricula were *in principle* inadequate but only because they were so *in practice*. By a serendipitous coincidence, Ralph W. Tyler, a member of the Bureau of Educational Research at Ohio State University,[1] the campus on which the Eight Year Study was headquartered, had for several years been working with selected Ohio State faculty to develop tests that would measure whether or not the students learned what their professors *had intended them to learn*. These desired learning outcomes were labeled *objectives*. Tyler was engaged to carry out the same kind of work with the Eight Year Study secondary schools, but with one important variation from conventional evaluation (measurement): the purpose of the studies would be to *refine the developing curricula* and *make sure they were working*. Program evaluation was born.

As the participant secondary schools began devising their new curricula, Tyler collected information about the extent of achievement of their defined objectives by the pupils in the programs. This information, together with an analysis of the strengths and weaknesses that thereby became apparent, was utilized to guide refinements and revisions—a process we today would call *formative* evaluation, except that the results were not available until *after* rather than *during* a trial. This process was reiterated over successive course offerings until the curriculum was found to produce an appropriate level of achievement.

Thus there emerged what we now choose to call second generation evaluation, an approach characterized by *description* of patterns of strengths and weaknesses with respect to certain stated objectives.[2] The role of the evaluator was that of *describer*, although the earlier technical aspects of that role were also retained. Measurement was no longer treated as the equivalent of evaluation but was redefined as *one of several tools* that might be used in its service. When the report of the Eight Year Study was published in 1942, the third volume, which described the evaluation activities of the project (Smith & Tyler, 1942), drew widespread attention. Like Lord Byron, Tyler awoke one morning to find himself famous. Later he was to be recognized as the "Father of Evaluation" (Joint Committee, 1981).

The Third Generation: Judgment

The objectives-oriented descriptive approach had some serious flaws, although they were not very noticeable until the post-Sputnik period (1957). Then it proved inadequate to the task of evaluating the federal government's response to the putative deficiencies of American education that had allowed the Russians to gain a march in space exploration: the course content improvement programs of the National Science Foundation (BSCS Biology, Project CHEM, PSSC Physics, and SMSG Mathematics) and of the then Office of Education (Project English and Project Social Studies). When evaluators appointed to these project staffs insisted that they could not begin working until they had project objectives in hand, they were dismissed by the program developers (who, it should be recalled, were practicing physicists, chemists, biologists, and mathematicians in the earlier NSF projects, *not* science educators or mathematics educators) as irrelevant. These developers feared to commit themselves to objectives until they had a clearer picture of what they were doing, and they did not want to state even provisional objectives that might later be found to have closed off their creativity prematurely. Moreover, they could not brook an evaluation strategy that would not produce results until after the program had been completely developed; if an evaluation then showed deficiencies it was in many ways too late to do anything about them (recalling especially the sense of national crisis under which they worked). These problems are well documented in Cronbach's now classic "Course Improvement Through Evaluation" (1963).

But the dissenter from what had by this time become *the* accepted mode of evaluation had another even more important criticism to level. Since it was essentially descriptive in nature, second generation Tylerian evaluation neglected what Robert Stake in his earlier-cited 1967 paper called the *other* countenance or face of evaluation: *judgment*. Stake noted:

> The countenance of evaluation beheld by the educator is not the same one beheld by the specialist in evaluation. The specialist sees himself

as a "describer," one who describes aptitudes and environment and accomplishments. The teacher and the school administrator, on the other hand, expect an evaluator to grade something or someone as to merit. Moreover, they expect that he will judge things against external standards, on criteria perhaps little related to the local school's resources. Neither sees evaluation broadly enough. Both description and judgment are essential—in fact, they are the two basic acts of evaluation. (cited in Worthen & Sanders, 1973, p. 109)

The call to include judgment in the act of evaluation marked the emergence of third generation evaluation, a generation in which evaluation was characterized by efforts to reach *judgments*, and in which the evaluator assumed the role of *judge*, while retaining the earlier technical and descriptive functions as well. This call, widely echoed in the profession, notably by Michael Scriven (1967), exposed several problems that had not been dealt with adequately in earlier generations. First, it required that the objectives *themselves* be taken as problematic; goals no less than performance were to be subject to evaluation. As a wag pointed out, something not worth doing at all is certainly not worth doing well. Further, judgment, as Stake pointed out, requires *standards* against which the judgment can be made. But the inclusion of standards that must, by definition of the genre, be value-laden into a scientific and putatively value-free enterprise such as evaluation, was repugnant to most evaluators. Finally, if there is to be judgment, there must be a judge. Evaluators did not feel competent to act in that capacity, felt it presumptuous to do so, and feared the political vulnerability to which it exposed them. Nevertheless, they were urged to accept that obligation, largely on the ground that, among all possible judge candidates, the evaluators were without doubt the most objective (Scriven, 1967).

In the final analysis the call to judgment could not be ignored, and evaluators soon rose to the challenge. A bevy of new evaluation models sprang up in 1967 and thereafter: neo-Tylerian models including Stake's own Countenance Model (1967) and the Discrepancy Evaluation Model (Provus, 1971); decision-oriented models such as CIPP (Stufflebeam et al., 1971); effects-oriented models such as the Goal Free Model (Scriven, 1973); neomeasurement models in the guise of social experimentation (Boruch, 1974; Campbell, 1969; Rivlin & Timpane, 1975; Rossi &

Williams, 1972); and models that were directly judgmental, such as the Connoisseurship Model (Eisner, 1979). All of these post-1967 models agreed on one point, however: Judgment was an integral part of evaluation. All urged, more or less explicitly, that the evaluator be judge. There were differences in the extent to which evaluators were represented as appropriate judges, ranging from the tentativeness of decision-oriented models—whose proponents hesitated to advocate an aggressive judgmental role because that seemingly co-opted the very decisionmakers whom the evaluations were ostensibly to serve—through DEM advocates—who saw their role as helping the client determine standards for judgment—to the assertiveness of the advocates of judgmental models in which the evaluator was chosen precisely because of his or her connoisseurship qualities. Nevertheless, it seems fair to say that during the decade and more following 1967, judgment became the hallmark of third generation evaluators.

Pervasive Problems of the First Three Generations

Although the preceding discussion of the first three generations of evaluation has been brief, it is sufficient to demonstrate that each succeeding generation represented a step forward, both in the range of substance or content included in the construction held as well as in its level of sophistication. Collection of data from individuals was not systematically possible until the development of appropriate instruments of the sort that characterized the first generation. But evaluation would have stagnated at that level had not the second generation shown the way to evaluate the many nonhuman evaluands as well—the programs, materials, teaching strategies, organizational patterns, and "treatments" in general. The third generation required that evaluation lead to judgment, both about an evaluand's merit—its inner or intrinsic value—and about its worth—its extrinsic or contextual value (Guba & Lincoln, 1981). But all three generations, as a group, have suffered and continue to suffer from certain flaws or defects sufficiently serious to warrant raising the question whether additional refinements—or even a complete reconstruction—may not now be needed. We believe there are at least three such major flaws or defects: a tendency toward managerialism, a failure to accommodate value-pluralism, and overcommitment to the scientific paradigm of inquiry. We consider each briefly below; we shall return to these themes frequently throughout this book.

A *tendency toward managerialism.* The term *manager* includes a variety of individuals, but most often it will denote the clients or sponsors who commission or fund an evaluation as well as the leadership personnel to whom the agents responsible for implementing the evaluand (not the evaluation) report. The latter category includes, for example, the school board members, the superintendent, and the principals (sometimes) in whose schools a curricular innovation is being tried; the administrator of a hospital and the director of nursing services in a hospital in which new care modes for oncology patients are being instituted; or the manager of a social agency in which several new programs intended to provide leisure opportunities for the disabled are being compared. It is the manager(s) with whom the evaluator typically contracts for an evaluation, to whom he or she defers in setting parameters and boundaries for the study, and to whom he or she reports. This traditional relationship between managers and evaluators is rarely challenged; yet it yields a number of highly undesirable consequences.

First, given such an arrangement, the manager is effectively *saved harmless.* Insofar as the manager *stands outside* the evaluation, his or her managerial qualities and practices cannot be called into question, nor can the manager be held accountable for what the evaluand does or does not produce. If there is a failure, the evaluation will necessarily point the finger of blame elsewhere.

Second, the typical manager/evaluator relationship is *disempowering* and *unfair.* The manager has the ultimate power to determine what questions the evaluation will pursue, how the answers will be collected and interpreted, and to whom the findings will be disseminated. Of course, these matters are often settled in consultation with the evaluator, but in case of disagreement, the final decision is the manager's. The only recourse the evaluator has is to refuse to conduct an evaluation under conditions not to his or her liking. This state of affairs in effect disempowers stakeholders who may have other questions to be answered, other ways of answering them, and other interpretations to make about them. It is difficult if not impossible to conduct an evaluation in any of the first three generation modes open to inputs from other stakeholder groups. The entire process is patently unfair to those other groups, whose potential inputs are neither solicited nor honored, while the manager is elevated to a position of greatest power.

Third, the typical manager/evaluator relationship is *disenfranchising*. Frequently the manager retains the right, contractually, to determine if the evaluation findings are to be released, and, if so, to whom. It has not been uncommon for evaluators to trade information release power for the right to produce whatever report the evaluators see fit. It seemed a reasonable exchange: the evaluator protected his or her integrity by retaining editoral prerogatives, while the manager in turn decided on dissemination issues. But those stakeholders who remained ignorant of the findings were effectively prevented from taking whatever actions those findings might have suggested to them, including, and most important, the protection of their own interests. They were denied privilege of information and hence their rights.

Finally, the typical manager/evaluator relationship is very likely to become a *cozy* one. To concede to the manager the right to determine the form of an evaluation is, in a very real sense, to enter into collusion with him or her. There are obvious advantages to both manager and evaluator to engage in such collusion. On the manager's side, an evaluation conducted in ways that save the manager harmless, while disempowering and disenfranchising possible rivals, is clearly preferable to one that holds the manager accountable and makes it possible for rivals to assume some modicum of power. On the evaluator's side, an evaluation done in ways that gain the manager's aproval is likely to lead to other contracts and ensure a steady source of income. Henry M. Brickell once noted that an evaluator perforce engages in a delicate balancing act: "Biting the hand that feeds you while appearing only to be licking it." That balance is maintained more easily if the evaluator decides not to bite at all. While the vast majority of evaluators probably would hesitate to engage consciously in collusion, it was nevertheless all too easy to slip into such a state of affairs in any of the first three generations.

Michael Scriven has written extensively on the problem of managerialism (1983); his solution to the problem is to engage in a form of evaluation that asks questions of putative interest to the *consumer* and that reports to that group. He projects evaluations that parallel the kinds of analyses found in *Consumer Reports*. That approach does represent an important step forward in that it recognizes some group other than managers as important. But there is no compelling reason to *exclude* managers simply to avoid the possibility of managerialism; there are better ways to deal with that problem, as we shall show. Consumerism does add *one* stakeholding audience to the mix; others, including managers, remain that are not included in the consumerism approach.

Failure to accommodate value-pluralism. It is common to believe that societies share values, that there is some value set that characterizes members of a society to which all members are acculturated and subscribe. The concept of the "great melting pot" that assimilated immigrants and somehow turned them into Americans is an example. Another is that schools are expected to teach "our heritage," a phrase that includes the idea that our heritage is shared. A third: It is commonly asserted that our moral system is based on the "Judeo-Christian ethic."

It has been only during the past twenty years that we have come to understand that *this* society, *our* society, is essentially value-pluralistic. Lessons about value pluralism were brought home to all of us in the latter 1960s, which witnessed not only traditional rivalries as between political parties but also ethnic, gender, and, alas, even generational conflicts that seemingly could not be resolved.

The call to judgment in evaluation first came at about the same time that an appreciation of value-pluralism emerged. Of course, values had been implicit in evaluation since its first use; indeed, the very term *evaluation* is linguistically rooted in the term *value*. But it was easy to overlook the fact that even the development of an "objective" instrument involved value judgments, or that the delineation of objectives implied value agreement, so long as the question of value differences was not raised. But once raised it could not be stuffed back into its container. The question of *whose values* would dominate in an evaluation, or, alternatively, how value differences might be negotiated, now emerged as *the* major problem.

It had long been argued that, despite the existence of value differences, the findings of an evaluation could be trusted because the methodology used is scientific and science is demonstrably value-free. The whole point of demanding objectivity is to obviate the question of value influence. Of course, it was admitted, the evaluator has no control over how evaluation findings are used; if persons with different values choose to interpret the factual findings in different ways, the evaluator can hardly be held accountable. But, as we shall see, the assertion that science is value-free can be seriously challenged. *If* science is *not* value-free, then it is the case not only that findings are subject to different interpretations but that the "facts" themselves are determined in interaction with the value system the evaluator (probably unknowingly) brings to bear. Then *every act of evaluation becomes a political act.* Indeed, every act of inquiry, whether evaluation, research, or policy analysis, becomes a political act in this sense.

The assertion of value-freedom for evaluations is completely resonant (reinforcing) with the managerial tendency already described. If values make no difference, then the findings of an evaluation represent states of affairs as *they really are;* they must be accepted as objective truths. The fact that the manager sets the boundaries and parameters for the study would then be relatively inconsequential, as would be the fact that he or she controls the questions asked, the methodology, and the findings.

The claim of value-freedom is not tenable, as we shall show. And if *that* is the case, then the value-pluralism of our society is a crucial matter to be attended to in an evaluation. None of the evaluation approaches of the first three generations accommodates value differences in the slightest.

Overcommitment to the scientific paradigm of inquiry. As we have noted, practitioners of the social sciences have followed Mill's advice to emulate the methods of the physical sciences with conviction and enthusiasm. There are multiple reasons for this strong positive response, among them the spectacular successes that have been enjoyed in the physical sciences, the desire of social scientists to be rational and systematic, in the spirit of Descartes ("I think, therefore I am") and of positivism generally, and the need to achieve legitimation as a profession by following as rigorously as possible the methodology that characterized their hard science counterparts.

The premises of the scientific method were themselves siren songs, since they seemed so self-evidently true. There is an objective reality "out there" that goes on about its business regardless of our interest in it; this reality operates according to certain immutable natural laws. It is the business of science to describe that reality and to uncover those laws. Once that is done, science can be used to exploit nature to humankind's advantage; we become able to predict and control at will. Each act of inquiry brings us closer to understanding ultimate reality; eventually we will be able to converge on it. But in order to understand reality and its laws fully, the investigator must be able to stand outside (a neutral distance from) the phenomenon being studied, so as not to influence it (which would keep us from seeing things as they really are and work) or be influenced in our judgment by it. We must also be mindful that nature is tricky and has many tactics to obfuscate the search for truth. The buzzing, bumbling confusion of nature-in-the-raw must be carefully controlled to avoid the confounding of results that will otherwise surely occur. Thus the investigator must control the phenomenon, either through manipulation, as in a laboratory, or statistically, as is the case in most human studies. To yield control is to ensure spurious results.

Virtually every first, second, or third generation evaluation model uses the scientific paradigm to guide its methodological work (an exception is the Eisner Connoisseurship Model, which purports to follow a humanistic paradigm). But this extreme dependence on the methods of science has had unfortunate results. First, it has led to what some have called "context-stripping," that is, assessing the evaluand as though it did not exist in a context but only under the carefully controlled conditions that are in force after a design is implemented. Such conditions are instituted in the hope that irrelevant local factors can be swept aside, and more generalizable results obtained (it unfortunately being the case that many evaluations are commissioned to determine the generalizable qualities of the evaluands). We shall argue later that the motivation for such context-stripping is in any event mistaken, in that generalizations are *not possible*. But for now let us note that, when attention is paid only to general factors, the local situation, existing as it does in the original unstripped context, cannot be well served by the evaluation results. Moreover, the resources needed to institute and maintain controls offset other uses to which the inquiry might have been put; thus the range of available information is truncated. Surely this effort to derive general truths through context-stripping (control) is one of the reasons why evaluations are so often found to be irrelevant at the local level, leading to the much lamented nonuse of evaluation findings about which we, as a profession, seem so fond of complaining. No one of the first three generations deals with this problem.

Second, commitment to the scientific paradigm inevitably seems to lead to an overdependence on formal quantitative measurement. The rigor that that paradigm appears to promise rests on the "hardness" of the data that are fed into the process. Hard data implies quantifiable data, data that can be measured with precision and analyzed with powerful mathematical and statistical tools. Quantifiable data also ease the problems associated with prediction and control; they can easily be inserted in formulas especially designed for those tasks. After a time these measuring instruments take on a life of their own; while initially intended as "operationalizations" of scientific variables, they become, in the end, the variables themselves. It follows that what cannot be measured cannot be real. No one of the first three generations deals with this problem.

Third, since the methods of science promise to provide us with information about the way things really are, they claim a certain authority that is hard to resist. Hannah Arendt (1963) has noted this "coerciveness of truth." Truth is nonnegotiable. As evaluators using the scientific method, we can assure our clients that nature herself has provided us the data we in turn present; there is no arguing with them or denying them. None of our values, the client's, or anyone else's can have influenced the outcome. We as evaluators can take on the authority with which nature has clothed us as her lawful messengers. If the status quo reflects nature's own laws, it exists by a kind of divine right. It is easy, then, to see how the scientific method reinforces and supports the managerial tendencies we noted earlier. Anything being evaluated that is supported by positivistic (scientific) evaluation is locked in as the right thing to do. And we evaluators, as messengers, are not accountable for what nature has decreed. *Both* manager and evaluator are rendered unassailable. No one of the first three generations deals with this problem.

Fourth, use of the scientific method closes out alternative ways to think about the evaluand. Since science discloses the truth about things, any other alternatives must be in error. Evaluators, clients, and stakeholders alike are all forced to be "true believers," because science has that authority that comes with being able to discover how things really are and really work. The worst thing that can be said about any assertion in our culture is that there is no scientific evidence to support it; conversely, when there *is* scientific evidence, we must accept it at face value. Perfectly reasonable alternatives cannot in good conscience be entertained. There are no negotiations possible about what is true. No one of the first three generations deals with this problem.

Finally, because science is putatively value-free, adherence to the scientific paradigm relieves the evaluator of any moral responsibility for his or her actions. One cannot be faulted for just telling the truth, for giving the facts, for "callin 'em as we sees 'em," or for "letting the chips fall where they may." It is easy to argue that the evaluator cannot control how evaluation findings are used. It is also easy to assert that the evaluator has no responsibility to follow up on evaluation; his or her role ends when the report is delivered. In any event, the evaluator (messenger) cannot be held responsible for findings (the message) that simply reflect what exists in nature. No one of the three generations holds the evaluator morally responsible for whatever emerges from the evaluation or for the uses to which the findings may be put.

An Alternative Approach

We hope to have made it clear that an alternative approach to evaluation—indeed, in the very meaning of the term—is desperately needed. We shall propose one, which we designate by the perhaps clumsy but nevertheless highly descriptive title of *responsive constructivist evaluation*. The term *responsive* is used to designate a different way of *focusing* an evaluation, that is, deciding on what we have been calling its parameters and boundaries. In the models included in the first three generations, parameters and boundaries have been established a priori; their specification, usually accomplished through negotiations between client and evaluator, is part of the design process. Robert Stake coined the term *preordinate evaluation* as a way of signaling this a priori quality. Responsive evaluation, also first proposed by Stake (1975), determines parameters and boundaries through an interactive, negotiated process that involves stakeholders and that consumes a considerable portion of the time and resources available. It is for this reason, among others, that the design of a responsive evaluation is said to be emergent.

The term *constructivist* is used to designate the methodology actually employed in doing an evaluation. It has its roots in an inquiry paradigm that is an alternative to the scientific paradigm, and we choose to call it the *constructivist* but it has many other names including *interpretive* and *hermeneutic.* Each of these terms contributes some specific insight into the nature of this paradigm, and we shall use them all at different places in this book. In this section we introduce a few of the leading ideas that characterize, respectively, a responsive mode of focusing and a constructivist mode of doing. Each is explored in much greater detail as the book unfolds.

The responsive mode of focusing. The algorithm for any evaluation process must begin with a method for determining what questions are to be raised and what information is to be gathered. In the case of first generation evaluation, certain variables are identified, and the information to be gathered consists of individual scores on instruments that putatively measure those variables (frequently, in school settings, achievement scores). In the case of second generation evaluation, certain objectives are identified; the information to be collected consists of assessment of the congruence between pupil performance and the described objectives. In the case of third generation evaluation, various models call for different information; thus decision-oriented models such as CIPP require information that services the decisions to be made in a timely manner (usually that implies collecting comparable information for each of the decision alternatives); goal-free models call for information about experienced "effects"; the connoisseurship model calls for judgments in relation to certain critical guideposts internalized by connoisseur/critics through training and experience; and the like. These focusing elements—variables, objectives, decisions, and the like—may be called "advance organizers"; the organizer that an evaluator is using becomes apparent as soon as the evaluator raises such questions as "what are your objectives?" or "what decisions must this evaluation inform?" and the like.

Responsive evaluation has its advance organizer as well: the *claims, concerns,* and *issues* about the evaluand that are identified by stakeholders, that is, persons or groups that are put at some risk by the evaluation. A *claim* is any assertion that a stakeholder may introduce that is *favorable* to the evaluand, for example, that a particular mode of reading instruction will result in more than a year's gain in standard test reading scores for every year of classroom use, or that a particular mode of handling domestic disturbance calls by police will materially reduce recidivism in offenders. A *concern* is any assertion that a stakeholder may introduce that is *unfavorable* to the evaluand, for example, that instruction in the use of a computer materially reduces pupils' ability to do computations by hand, or that use of the evaluand will result in a great deal more "homework" time for teachers. An *issue* is any state of affairs about which reasonable persons may disagree, for example, the introduction of education about AIDS into the elementary schools, or the use of school property to conduct classes in religion. Different stakeholders will harbor different claims, concerns, and issues; it is the task of the evaluator to ferret these out and to address them in the evaluation.

There are always many different stakeholders. In *Effective Evaluation* (Guba & Lincoln, 1981), we identified three broad classes, each with some subtypes:

1. The *agents*, those persons involved in producing, using, and implementing the evaluand—these agents include:
   a. the developers of the evaluand
   b. the funders, local, regional, and national
   c. local needs assessors who identified the need that the evaluand will putatively ameliorate or remove
   d. decision makers who determined to utilize or develop the evaluand locally
   e. the providers of facilities, supplies, and materials
   f. the client for the evaluation itself (the contractor)
   g. the personnel engaged in implementing the evaluand, such as classroom teachers, halfway house staff, police officers, nurses, and the like
2. The *beneficiaries*, those persons who profit in some way from the use of the evaluand—these beneficiaries include:
   a. the direct beneficiaries, the "target group," the persons for whom evaluand was designed
   b. indirect beneficiaries, persons whose relationship with the direct beneficiaries is mediated, eased, enhanced, or otherwise positively influenced

c. persons who gain by the fact that the evaluand is in use, such as publishers of the materials, contractors who provide needed services, and the like

3. The *victims*, those persons who are negatively affected by the use of the evaluand (which may include, because of some failure in the evaluand, one or more putative beneficiary groups)—these victims include:

   a. groups systematically excluded from the use of the evaluand, such as "normal" youngsters excluded from special programming for the gifted

   b. groups that suffer negative side effects, such as students, and their parents, who are bused to a distant school so that disadvantaged youngsters may occupy their places in the original school

   c. persons who are politically disadvantaged by the use of the evaluand, such as those suffering losses in power, influence, or prestige

   d. persons who suffer opportunity costs for forgone opportunities as a result of the use of the evaluand, such as persons who would have elected to devote the necessary resources to some other venture, or publishers of rival materials

Responsive evaluation is not only responsive for the reason that it seeks out different stakeholder views but also since it responds to those items in the subsequent collection of information. It is quite likely that different stakeholders will hold very different constructions with respect to any particular claim, concern, or issue. As we shall see, one of the major tasks of the evaluator is to conduct the evaluation in such a way that each group must confront and deal with the constructions of all the others, a process we shall refer to as a hermeneutic dialectic. In that process some, perhaps many, of the original claims, concerns, and issues may be settled without recourse to *new* information, that is, information that is not already available from one or more of the stakeholding groups themselves. As each group copes with the constructions posed by others, their own constructions alter by virtue of becoming better informed and more sophisticated. Ideally, responsive evaluation seeks to reach consensus on all claims, concerns, and issues at this point, but that is rarely if ever possible. Conflicts will remain whose resolution requires the introduction of outside information, which it becomes the evaluator's task to obtain. When this information (as much of it as is feasible) has become available, the evaluator prepares an *agenda for negotiation*, taking the leadership in setting up and moderating a negotiation session. Representatives of all relevant stakeholders join with the evaluator in a joint effort to resolve what remains on the table. The final conclusions and recommendations that emerge from such a negotiation (as well as those reached earlier in the hermeneutic dialectic) are thus arrived at *jointly*; they are never the unique or sole province of the evaluator or the client. Those agenda items that cannot be resolved remain as points of contention, of course, but at the very least each of the stakeholders will understand what the conflict is and where other groups stand in relation to it. The stage is set for recycling the evaluation. Such iteration and reiteration is typical of responsive evaluation; evaluations are never complete but are suspended for logistical reasons, such as the timing of a mandated decision or because resources are exhausted.

Responsive evaluation has four phases, which may be reiterated and that may overlap. In the first phase, stakeholders are identified and are solicited for those claims, concerns, and issues that they may wish to introduce. In the second phase, the claims, concerns, and issues raised by each stakeholder group are introduced to all other groups for comment, refutation, agreement, or whatever reaction may please them. In this phase many of the original claims, concerns, and issues will be resolved. In the third phase, those claims, concerns, and issues that have *not* been resolved become the advance organizers for information collection by the evaluator. The precise form of information collection will depend on whether the bone of contention is a claim (information may be gathered to test the claim, for example), a concern (information may be gathered on the extent to which the concern is justified), or an issue (information supporting or refuting each side—and there may be more than two sides—may be gathered). *The information may be quantitative or qualitative.* Responsive evaluation does not rule out quantitative modes, as is mistakenly believed by many, but deals with whatever information *is* responsive to the unresolved claim, concern, or issue. In the fourth phase, negotiation among stakeholding groups, under the guidance of the evaluator and utilizing the evaluative information that has been collected, takes place, in an effort to reach consensus on each disputed item. Not all such items will be resolved; those that remain become the core for the next evaluation that may be undertaken when time, resources, and interest permit.

Constructivist methodology. Constructivist methodology is the approach that we propose as a replacement for the scientific mode that has characterized virtually all evaluation carried out in this century. It rests in a belief system that is virtually opposite to that of science; a kind of belief system that is often referred to as a *paradigm.* As Michael Quinn Patton (1978, p. 203) has put it,

> A paradigm is a world view, a general perspective, a way of breaking down the complexity of the real world. As such, paradigms are deeply embedded in the socialization of adherents and practitioners: paradigms tell them what is important, legitimate, and reasonable. Paradigms are also normative, telling the practitioner what to do without the necessity of long existential or epistemological considerations. But it is this aspect of paradigms that constitutes both their strength and their weakness—their strength in that it makes action possible, their weakness in that the very reason for action is hidden in the unquestioned assumptions of the paradigm.

It is not possible to prove or disprove a paradigm in an absolute sense, as it is not possible, say, to prove the existence of a deity, or to prove the value of the adversarial system in use in the courts, or to prove the judgmental system that characterizes literary criticism. We shall, however, show that questions can be raised about the positivist paradigm that has characterized contemporary science that are so fundamental as to suggest that the positivist paradigm needs to be replaced.

We believe that the constructivist paradigm is appropriate to that task. It resembles science hardly at all, particularly in its basic assumptions, which are virtually polar to those of science. For *ontologically,* it denies the existence of an objective reality, asserting instead that realities are social constructions of the mind, and that there exist as many such constructions as there are individuals (although clearly many constructions will be shared). We argue that science itself is such a construction; we can admit it freely to the pantheon of constructions provided only that we are not asked to accept science as the *right* or *true* construction. And we note that if realities are constructions, then there cannot be, except by mental imputation, immutable natural laws governing the constructions, such as cause-effect laws. *Epistemologically,* the constructivist paradigm denies the possibility of subject-object dualism, suggesting instead that the findings of a study exist precisely because there is an *interaction* between observer and observed that literally creates what emerges from that inquiry. *Methodologically*, and in consequence of the ontological and epistemological assumptions already made, the natural-istic paradigm rejects the controlling, manipulative (experimental) ap-proach that characterizes science and substitutes for it a *hermeneutic/dialectic process* that takes full advantage, and account, of the observer/observed interaction to create a constructed reality that is as informed and sophisticated as it can be made at a particular point in time.

The reader should not fail to note the *resonance* between an inquiry paradigm that proposes a hermeneutic/dialectic methodology and an evaluation model that depends exactly on such a process to substantiate its claim of responsiveness. Responsive focusing calls out for a constructi-vist methodology, and constructivist methodology fits exactly the inquiry process needs of responsive evaluation.

The consequences of utilizing constructivist methodology are star-tlingly different from those we have come to expect from scientific inquiry. We shall argue that both are forms of *disciplined* inquiry, in the sense of that term proposed by Cronbach and Suppes (1969), which is that within both methodologies it is possible to submit for public inspec-tion and verification "both the raw materials entering into the argument and the logical processes by which they were compressed and rearranged to make the conclusions credible." Within that framework we shall argue for something very different than scientific assumptions would suggest, for example (Guba, 1987):

- "Truth" is a matter of consensus among informed and sophisticated constructors, not of correspondence with an objective reality.
- "Facts" have no meaning except within some value framework; hence there cannot be an "objective" assessment of any proposition.
- "Causes" and "effects" do not exist except by imputation; hence accountability is a relative matter and implicates all interacting parties (entities) equally.

- Phenomena can be understood only within the context in which they are studied; findings from one context cannot be generalized to another; neither problems nor their solutions can be generalized from one setting to another.

- Interventions are not stable; when they are introduced into a particular context they will be at least as much affected (changed) by that context as they are likely to affect the context.

- Change cannot be engineered; it is a nonlinear process that involves the introduction of new information, and increased sophistication in its use, into the constructions of the involved humans.

- Evaluation produces data in which facts and values are inextricably linked. Valuing is an essential part of the evaluation process, providing the basis for an attributed meaning.

- Accountability is a characteristic of a conglomerate of mutual and simultaneous shapers, no one of which nor one subset of which can be uniquely singled out for praise or blame.

- Evaluators are subjective partners with stakeholders in the literal creation of data.

- Evaluators are orchestrators of a negotiation process that attempts to culminate in consensus on better informed and more sophisticated constructions.

- Evaluation data derived from constructivist inquiry have neither special status nor legitimation; they represent simply another construction to be taken into account in the move toward consensus.

Assertions such as those above—and others we might have made and will make elsewhere in this book—at first glance seem so unreasonable as to be rejected out of hand. Yet there seems to be a powerful move in the direction proposed in this paradigm—often, and mistakenly, termed the qualitative paradigm. While perhaps not everyone—or even many— would agree that the naturalistic paradigm should be the paradigm of choice, it is surprising to note the variety of fields in which issue is being taken with scientific positivism and proposals for redirection are being made.[3] In that context our proposal to realign evaluation with a different paradigm than the scientific does not seem so unusual.

The Trade-Offs in Accepting
Responsive Constructivist Evaluation

Acceptance of the responsive constructivist mode of conceptualizing and doing evaluation involves gains and losses—although what counts as a gain or a loss is a matter of the perspective from which you happen to be speaking.

Certainly proponents of more conventional forms of evaluation are likely to consider a shift to responsive constructivist evaluation as unfortunate, incurring many losses. For one thing, there is the implicit admission that there can be no certainty about states of affairs; there is no objective truth on which inquiries can converge. One cannot find out how things really are or how they really work. That level of ambiguity is almost too much to tolerate. If evaluations cannot ferret out the truth, what use can there be in doing them?

Shifting to responsive constructivist evaluation also implies giving up control over the process, given that stakeholders play equally definitive roles at all stages with the evaluator and the client. Such loss of control has both methodological and political consequences. On the one hand, if persons who are not typically expert in methodological issues become major decision makers, exercise of their prerogative may seriously threaten the technical adequacy of the study. Further, if these persons are given the power to make methodological decisions, they are simultaneously dealt a political hand as well; methodology may become the object of a tug-of-war between politically dissident groups.

Third, a commitment to responsive constructivist evaluation means abandoning the hope that interventions (treatments, programs, materials, strategies, and the like) can be found that, on evaluation, prove widely equal to whatever task they were intended to accomplish, such as ameliorating alcoholism, remediating underachievers, reducing recidivism, or whatever. If there were no basis for assuming generalizability of interventions, or of devising such interventions on the basis of well-established cause-effect relationships, there can be little reason to believe, conventionalists would aver, that society can finally cope with the many problems that patently beset it. To accept the basic premises undergirding responsive constructivist evaluation is virtually to abandon hope that solutions to social problems can ever be found. If everything must be tailored to specific mores and a specific context, culture, economic level, and so on, society will soon be overwhelmed by this impossibly large and difficult task.

But, answer the proponents of responsive constructivist evaluation, all these fears—about the loss of absolutes on which to pin our hopes, about intolerable ambiguity, about the loss of experimental and political control, about our inability to find widely useful solutions to our pressing problems—are themselves only *constructions* in which their constructors are trapped because of their rigid adherence to assumptions that have patently outlived their utility and their credibility. It is precisely because of our preoccupation with finding universal solutions that we fail to see how to devise solutions with local meaning and utility. It is precisely because of our preoccupation with control that we fail to empower the very people whom we are putatively trying to serve.

The replacement of the certainty that appears to be invested in conventional methodology with the relativism characteristic of responsive constructivist evaluation does not lead to an "anything goes" posture. Instead, that change focuses special attention on the question of how one can compare one construction with another to determine which is to be preferred. Conventionally such a comparison is made on the basis of which construction better approximates reality. But when the possibility of an objective reality is denied, that standard disappears, and other more subtle and sophisticated distinctions are called for. The moral imperative of the responsive constructivist evaluator is continuously to be on the alert for—indeed, to seek out—challenges to the prevailing construction (however much it may be supported in consensus), and to stand ready to refine, change, or even reject that which is currently believed in favor of something else that, on examination, seems more reasonable and appropriate to those in the best position to make that judgment. If nothing else, commitment to responsive constructivist evaluation replaces the arrogance so easily assumed by the conventionalist, convinced that he or she has found out about "reality," with a humility appropriate to the insight that one can *never* know how things "really" are; that one's construction about how things are is *created* by the inquiry itself and is not determined by some mysterious "nature." To substitute relativity for certainty, empowerment for control, local understanding for generalized explanation, and humility for arrogance, seems to be a series of clear gains for the fourth generation evaluator. You, the reader, will have to decide for yourself how you wish to count the gains and losses.

Notes

1. By a curious twist of fate, one of us had the privilege of directing this same bureau (which had been renamed the Bureau of Educational Research & Service) from 1961 to 1965.

2. We have chosen the term *description* to characterize this generation because it is the term used in the now classic article by Robert Stake (1967). This generation could equally well have been termed the *objectives generation*.

3. Here are some examples, the first 11 drawn from the field of education and the final 12 drawn from other social science fields: Garrison, James W., Some principles of postpositivistic philosophy, *Educational Researcher, 15,* (1986), 12-18; Rockhill, Kathleen, Researching participation in adult education: The potential of the qualitative perspective. *Adult Education, 33* (1982), 3-19; Ettinger, Linda F., Styles of on-site descriptive research: A taxonomy for art educators, *Studies in Art Education, 28* (1987), 79-95; Smith, Mary Lee, Naturalistic research. *The Personnel and Guidance Journal, 59,* (1981), 585-589; Dillon, J. T., The problems/methods/solutions of curriculum inquiry. *Journal of Curriculum and Supervision, 1* (1985), 18-26; Kantor, K. J., Kirby, D. R., & Goetz, J. P., Research in context: Ethnographic studies in English education. *Research in the Teaching of English, 15* (1981), 293-309; Driscoll, Marcy P., Alternative paradigms for research in instructional systems. *Journal of Instructional Development, 7* (1984), 2-5; Harste, Jerome C., Reading research: Portrait of a new paradigm. In R. J. Spiro (Ed.), *Reading Research in the 90's,* Hillsdale, NJ: Erlbaum, 1985; Spector, Barbara S., Qualitative research: Data analysis framework generating grounded theory applicable to the crisis in science education. *Journal of Research in Science Teaching, 21,* (1984), 459-67; Stainback, Susan, & Stainback, William, Broadening the research perspective in special education, *Exceptional Children, 9,* (1984), 400-409; Jax, Judy, Ethnography: An approach to using interpretive science in vocational education research, *Journal of Vocational Research, 9,* 1984, 8-19; Cochran, Daniel S., & Dolan, Janet A., Qualitative research: An alternative to quantitative research in communication, *Journal of Business Communication, 21,* (1984), 25-33; Piore, Michael J., Qualitative research techniques in economics. *Research Techniques in Economics, 24,* (1979), 560-568; Hollinger, David A., T. S. Kuhn's theory of science and its implications for history, *American Historical Review, 78,* (1973), 370-393; Harris, Janet C., Hermeneutics, interpretive culture research, and the study of sports, *Quest, 33* (1981), 72-86; Grover, Robert, & Glazier, Jack, Implications for application of qualitative methods to library and information science research, *Library and Information Science Research, 7* (1985), 247-260; Duffy, Mary E., Designing nursing

research: The qualitative-quantitative debate, *Journal of Advanced Nursing,* 10 (1985), 225-232; Morgan, Gareth, & Smircich, Linda, The case for qualitative research, *Academy of Management Review,* 5 (1980), 491-500; Rogers, Joan C., Order and disorder in medicine and occupational therapy, *American Journal of Occupational Therapy,* 36 (1982), 29-35; Gergen, Kenneth J., The social constructivist movement in modern psychology, *American Psychologist,* 40 (1985), 266-275; Haworth, Glenn O., Social work research, practice, and paradigms, *Social Service Review,* 58 (September 1984), 343-357; Bramson, Leon, Subjectivity in social research, Chapter 7 in Leon Bramson, (Ed.), *The Political Context of Sociology.* Princeton, NJ: Princeton University Press, 1961. This listing is in no sense either representative or exhaustive (a much more complete assessment of this paradigm-related literature may be found in Lincoln, 1989), but it does illustrate the point that dissatisfaction with the conventional inquiry paradigm is widespread, detected in many fields, with a variety of alternatives being proposed.

2 What Is Fourth Generation Evaluation? Why Should We Choose to Practice It?

Fourth generation evaluation is a form of evaluation in which the claims, concerns, and issues of stakeholders serve as organizational foci (the basis for determining what information is needed), that is implemented within the methodological precepts of the constructivist inquiry paradigm. What warrant is there for using claims, concerns, and issues as organizers, and for adopting the constructivist paradigm as the guiding format? We shall address each of these questions in turn in this chapter, and then shall briefly introduce the steps involved in carrying out this proposed form.

Why Use Stakeholder Claims, Concerns, and Issues as Organizers?

As we saw in Chapter 1, a wide variety of organizers for evaluations have been invoked, including, most prominently, objectives, decisions, and effects. Each has something to recommend it; in all events, these organizers are patently reasonable, evocative, heuristic, and pragmatic. Nevertheless, we have asserted that a strong case can be made against the use of any or all of these, including their susceptibility to managerial ideology, their presumption of value consensus, and their commitment to a realist ontology. But even if these problems with more traditional organizers are overlooked, compelling arguments in favor of using stakeholder claims, concerns, and issues can be made; among them are the following:

(1) *Stakeholders are groups at risk.* Stakeholder groups are those that, by definition, have something at stake in the evaluand—the entity being evaluated. As we saw in Chapter 1, there are always many groups of stakeholders. Their stakes may be placed at hazard or in jeopardy by the evaluation, as the evaluand is assessed with respect to some set of standards. In that sense stakeholder groups are at risk, that is, they may lose their stakes should the evaluation result—in their view—in negative findings.

Both the nature and the size of stakes may vary considerably from group to group. Stakes may be counted in terms of money, status, power, face, opportunity, or other coin, and may be large or small, as constructed by the groups in question. Nevertheless, the existence of a stake, whatever its form or size, is sufficient warrant in an open society for a stakeholder group to expect, and to receive, the opportunity to provide input into an evaluation that affects it and to exercise some control on behalf of its own interests. A group at risk ought to have the opportunity to make whatever claims, or raise whatever questions, it deems appropriate, and to have those inputs honored. Anything else is patently unfair and discriminatory.

The problem is particularly acute when different stakeholders may bring different value standards to bear. It is bad enough to be at risk of losing one's stake when the basis for the loss is a value judgment with which one must in principle agree, because the judgment reflects one's own values. If the judgment reflects some other group's values, however, the loss is much harder to bear. Unlike in the courts, a rule of double jeopardy may seem to apply—a disagreeable judgment is made for seemingly wrong reasons. Stakeholders must be able to feel that they have some defense against that level of risk.

(2) *Stakeholders are open to exploitation, disempowerment, and disenfranchisement.* Evaluation is a form of inquiry whose end product is information. Information is power, and evaluation is powerful.

The power of an inquiry can be used in a variety of ways inimical to the interests of stakeholder groups. At one level, the information obtained in an evaluation can be used *against* the groups from whom it is solicited. The most obvious example is the use of information collected from a sample of the individuals to whom a product may be marketed (including any of the variety of innovations or interventions touted as providing relief from extant problems) to persuade the potential market that it has a need for the product, or that it is well served by investing in it. Needs assessments too often identify just those needs that the sponsor's product happens to be capable of fulfilling, to which the sponsor happens to be capable of providing a response, or which the sponsor's values dictate ought to exist as needs of the target group.

At another level, power can also be withheld by the expedient of not making information available except to selected stakeholder groups— usually those who already hold power. The effect is disempowerment, but carried out in a rather subtle form, because stakeholders who do not possess information cannot be aware of its political significance. Several reasons may be advanced in defense of the proposition that it is not feasible or desirable to share information, as for example, not all stakeholders are technically capable of understanding it or using it wisely, different stakeholders bear different levels of risk so that not all deserve to have access to the same level of information or to have it at the same point in time, or stakeholders may misuse the information to further their own political interests. But these arguments all have the ring of preserving the status quo, of maintaining power in whatever hands currently hold it, of giving higher priority to the interests of those presently in control. It seems clear that an open determination of who should have what information and when might lead to a very different resolution of the power issue. Without such open determination it is inevitable that disempowerment will occur.

At yet another level, disempowerment brings with it a dark companion: disenfranchisement. This is so even when the trappings of open decision making are in evidence. For it is not simply voting that counts but voting from a position of knowledge, that is, of power (to close the logical circle). Even apparently open societies can seriously impede informed decision making by arranging for differential allocation of information, or by withholding information entirely from certain involved stakeholders. Blame can be assigned where it is politically expedient to do so, and, indeed, even the blamed can be maneuvered into accepting their culpability ("blame the victim" is a commonly played game in today's world).

It is not likely, given modern social and technical complexities, that meaningful involvement of stakeholders in deciding how an evaluation is to be focused, what information is to be collected, and how interpretations are to be made will guarantee that those stakeholders will not be exploited, disempowered, or disenfranchised to some degree. But it *is* likely that stakeholders *will* suffer these misfortunes in much greater degree so long as they are denied such inputs.

(3) *Stakeholders are users of evaluation information.* Probably no issue has so dominated discussion at recent meetings of professional evaluators as that of the putative nonuse of evaluation findings. As we have already noted, Michael Patton, the 1988 president of the American Evaluation Association, urged members to think of themselves as salespersons, and to use techniques that have proven successful in selling other "products" to gain acceptance of their own.

There are many reasons for nonuse. First, there is the very real possibility that evaluators have failed to provide information whose technical quality *warranted* its use. Second, more than a decade ago, Carol Weiss (1973) warned evaluators that evaluation information had to take its place within a political arena of decision making; scientific validity could not and would not be the sole basis for determining whether to pay attention or not. Third, the fact that evaluation typically did not yield unequivocal information, or that competing evaluations sometimes yielded conflicting information, also detracted from uncritical acceptance of the results.

But certainly one of the more important reasons for nonuse is the fact that evaluators tend to provide information that they—that is, the cult of evaluators—believe to be relevant but hardly anyone else does. Or evaluators tend to provide information that they have agreed upon with the sponsors or funders of the evaluation, that does not speak to the interests of other concerned parties. Another way to put this state of affairs is to say that the focus of evaluation tends to be much too narrow. If only objectives (whose?), decisions (made by whom about what when?), or effects (specified as important by whom?) are used as organizers, it seems clear that many other possible foci will be ignored.

So long as one remains impervious to the risks to which such a narrow focus exposes stakeholders, or to the consequences of using information in ways that exploit, disempower, or disenfranchise stakeholders, none of these considerations is terribly important. The issue of use/nonuse can then be conceived as one affecting solely sponsors, funders, or a few selected (and powerful) stakeholding groups. The problem clearly becomes one of persuading (selling?) these users that they ought to place higher priority on evaluation information than they do. But as Weiss suggests, evaluation information is likely to play second fiddle to such more important matters as control, money, opportunity, or even preservation of the status quo, when it takes its place in a decision-making arena where large numbers of claims, concerns, and issues can, from a political point of view, be safely ignored.

But stakeholders *are* users of information that they see as clearly responsive to the claims, concerns, and issues that *they* have. Given an opportunity to have input into the evaluation process, and having those inputs honored, they also see a way to flex *their* political muscles and, perhaps more important, to be able to do it from a base of informational legitimation that they would not have otherwise. To eschew use under such circumstances is, as everyone will quickly recognize, tantamount to giving up power. We remain unaware of any group that would voluntarily take such a step. Use is virtually guaranteed.

(4) *Stakeholders are in a position to broaden the range of evaluative inquiry to the great benefit of the hermeneutic/dialectic process.* When

evaluations are focused on a few preordinate objectives, decisions, or effects, their results must necessarily be limited and formally quite predictable. Indeed, it is this very predictability that makes it possible to predesign an evaluation (or other conventional) inquiry. But when one does not know in advance what information is to be collected, it is literally impossible to design an inquiry that will provide it. Open-endness (an "emergent" design) is called for.

The utilization of stakeholder inputs (claims, concerns, and issues) as foci for organizing an evaluation forces a degree of open-endedness well beyond that usually contemplated in an evaluation. As we shall see later, a considerable amount of the evaluator's time and energy must be expended, in a fourth generation evaluation, simply to identify the several stakeholders and to interact with them sufficiently to understand what their claims, concerns, and issues are. Further, the numbers and kinds of such claims, concerns, and issues are typically beyond those contemplated by the evaluator him- or herself or by the sponsor, funder, or other client. Claims, concerns, and issues, we shall see, arise out of the particular construction(s) that a stakeholder group has formulated, and reflect their particular circumstances, experiences, and values. Often the nature of their claims, concerns, and issues is completely unpredictable by anyone not him- or herself a member of the group.

That state of affairs assuredly complicates the evaluation process. Indeed, it may seem to render fourth generation evaluation impractical. We shall deal with that objection in later chapters. But here we note that this seeming fault of fourth generation evaluation is also one of its greatest strengths, in that it forces stakeholders to confront and deal with the constructions of other groups that they would otherwise not have conjured up in their wildest imaginings.

The effect of this confrontation must be witnessed to be appreciated, since it produces rapid change in the constructions of virtually *all* groups, and, if it does not lead to consensus, it at the very least exposes the several positions with electric clarity. If a major purpose of evaluation is to refine and improve (in addition to judge), then the fact that a wide variety of stakeholders is given entrée into the process quickly focuses the energies of the group on those matters about which there is disagreement. If each of the groups, moreover, is provided with some political clout in the process, movement inevitably occurs. Hermeneutic/dialectic principles are rarely better served.

(5) *Stakeholders are mutually educated by the fourth generation process.* Evaluation findings, even when utilized, are rarely accepted by everyone. Insofar as evaluation renders judgment (even in those cases in which the intent of the judgment is improvement or refinement), there are always those, perhaps with values different from those on which the judgment was based, who disagree. It is always possible to attack evaluation findings. Usually someone (another professional evaluator?) can be found to cast doubt on the technical adequacy of the evaluation (an inappropriate or weak methodology was used). Failing that, it is always possible to challenge interpretations, since they are clear extrapolations from the "facts" that have putatively been scientifically established. It is unlikely that either side (or more likely none of the several sides) learns anything from this exchange; each is simply reinforced in its belief in the validity of its own interpretation and in its judgment about the intransigency and stubbornness of the other(s).

The involvement of stakeholders in fourth generation evaluation implies more than simply identifying them and finding out what their claims, concerns, and issues are. Each group is required to confront and take account of the inputs from other groups. It is not mandated that they accept the opinions or judgments of others, of course, but it is required that they deal with points of difference or conflict, either reconstructing their own constructions sufficiently to accommodate the differences or devising meaningful arguments why the others' propositions should not be entertained.

In this process a great deal of learning takes place. On the one hand, each stakeholder group comes to understand *its own* construction better, and to revise it in ways that make it more informed and sophisticated than it was prior to the evaluation experience. Later we shall hold this outcome to be one of the major goals of the fourth generation process and judge the process to be deficient if this reconstruction does not take place (see Chapter 8). On the other hand, each stakeholder group comes to understand the constructions of other groups better than before. Again we stress that that does not mean coming to agreement, but it does mean gaining superior knowledge of the elements included in others' constructions and superior understanding of the rationale for their inclusion. We also hold this outcome as a goal for the fourth generation process and judge it to be deficient if this increased appreciation of others' constructions does not occur (Chapter 8).

These five arguments seem to us to be compelling reasons for insisting upon the use of stakeholder claims, concerns, and issues as focal organizers for evaluation: the fact that stakeholders are placed at risk by an evaluation and, thus in the interest of fairness, deserve to have input into the process; the fact that evaluation exposes stakeholders to exploitation, disempowerment, and disenfranchisement so that they, in the interest of self-defense, are entitled to some control of the process; the fact that stakeholders represent a virtually untapped market for the use of evaluation findings that are responsive to self-defined needs and interests; the fact that the inclusion of stakeholder inputs greatly broadens the scope and meaningfulness of an inquiry and contributes immeasurably to the dialectic so necessary if evaluation is to have a positive outcome; and the fact that all parties can be mutually educated to more informed and sophisticated personal constructions as well as an enhanced appreciation of the constructions of others. When these arguments are laid alongside those developed in Chapter 1—the need to escape from a managerial ideology, the need to take account of pluralistic values, and the need to rethink the ontological bases of evaluative interpretations—we believe that an overwhelming case is formed that mandates serious consideration of fourth generation evaluation.

Why Change Guiding Methodological Paradigms?

It is one thing to argue for the wisdom of changing advance organizers for an evaluation, but it is quite another to insist that the basic paradigm—the basic belief system—that guides inquiry must also be changed. After all, the conventional paradigm has had a long and distinguished history, not only in the social sciences but in the physical and life sciences as well. Indeed, it was largely because of the extraordinary success that scientific method enjoyed in those senior sciences that social scientists were persuaded to adopt scientific methodology in the first place. Is it really necessary to throw out the baby with the bath?

A variety of considerations can be brought to bear in dealing with this question, some of them rooted in more applied matters and others in philosophical issues. Many of these considerations will be referred to over and over again in this book; the present discussion should be regarded only as an introduction. Let us begin with the more applied matters.

(1) *Conventional methodology does not contemplate the need to identify stakeholders and to solicit claims, concerns, and issues from them.* In conventional methodology the propositions or questions to be investigated are determined a priori by whatever theoretical considerations the investigator (evaluator) chooses to bring to bear. Since we exist, it is believed, in a "real" world driven by natural laws, the aim of science must be to describe that world and to discover the natural laws that determine it. A given inquiry is directed by those descriptions and laws of which we are already reasonably sure, by building on them, extending them, or applying them in new situations. These descriptions and laws are matters of fact, not of opinion, and can be determined by conventional methodology. Further, once described or discovered these facts can be used to predict and control subsequent events.

Given such a construction, conventional evaluators see no need to discover who the persons or groups are who may have constructions about states of affairs, or what they believe to be the case. Certainly their unique interests can hardly qualify them to direct an inquiry. Their constructions are at best matters of perspective. While postpositivist inquirers would agree that one cannot know the "real" world in a definitive way but can come to see it only from a variety of perspectives (as the blind men came to know the elephant in different ways because each of them was able to contact only one part of it), they do not doubt that each perspective is, in its own way, an approximation of reality as it truly exists. If different stakeholders have different constructions (perspectives), the task of the inquirer is not to deal with each of these in *its own right* but to discover which construction (perspective) comes closest to reality, that is, which is the "best" construction. It is this equation of construction and perspective that obviates the need for close work with stakeholders.

To suggest that each construction has equal *validity* (if that is even the right word) with all others that are as well informed and sophisticated goes far beyond the ken of the conventional paradigm. To suppose that elements of such different constructions might be used to focus an inquiry, including an evaluation, is to be utterly inconsistent with the realism, naive or critical, which conventional methodology, positivist or postpositivist, embraces.

There is thus no point whatever, in the conventional view, in soliciting stakeholder constructions as the basis for focusing an inquiry. It is not surprising that conventional methodology does not explicitly provide for such solicitation—the proper source for discovering foci is in the accumulated knowledge that the body of science comprises. Only a paradigm that treats constructions as equally meaningful "realities" can contemplate and legitimate such a step.

(2) *Conventional methodology cannot solicit claims, concerns, and issues except by adopting a "discovery" rather than a "verification" posture, but only the latter is served by the positivist or postpositivist paradigm.* Scientists have long known that progress in science is not always orderly (compare Kaplan's 1964 distinction between *reconstructed logic* and *logic-in-use*), but depends heavily on intuitions, flashes of insight, "vibes," or mental experiments to provide the propositions that can then be tested in authentic scientific fashion. This prescientific phase is often termed the "discovery" phase. Discovery is clearly a creative process and cannot be guided by a series of steps or rules. It is ironic that the constructivist paradigm is often seen as appropriate to discovery by conventionalists, who argue that the conventional paradigm should take over to guide the inquiry once the discovery process has culminated in something capable of being dealt with scientifically (a question that can be answered or a hypothesis that can be tested). We shall maintain that the constructivist paradigm is appropriate to *both* discovery *and* verification, while making the point that the distinction between the two is meaningless in this emergent approach (Chapter 6). In any event, it seems clear that conventional approaches do *not* deal with discovery, relegating it to a role *outside* scientific inquiry. But if the solicitation of claims, concerns, and issues—clearly a discovery activity—is to be a central and systematic part of fourth generation evaluation, a paradigm that *disclaims* such activity as appropriate to its own axiomatic structure cannot be the paradigm of choice.

(3) *Conventional methodology does not take account of contextual factors, except by physically or statistically controlling them.* Within the belief structure that undergirds conventional methodology, the world of nature is viewed as consisting of a buzzing, bumbling confusion of variables. If one wishes to describe reality and to uncover the laws that drive it, it is important to focus an inquiry very specifically on the variables to be investigated, controlling all other variables—the confounding variables—that may mimic, mask, or overwhelm them. If one wishes to test the proposition that all bodies fall with equal speed when dropped, it is necessary to conduct the study in a vacuum, given that otherwise light bodies with larger areas, a sheet of paper, say, will fall more slowly than compact heavy bodies such as a cannonball. Controls can be instituted either physically, as in the cannonball case; through replication at different levels of the variable(s) to be controlled, as for example, replicating a learning experiment with high, medium, and low intelligence groups of subjects; or statistically, as through an analysis of covariance in which the effects of the covariate(s) are statistically taken into account via a correlation/prediction procedure.

But to undertake investigations in this way effectively *strips away the context* and yields results that are valid only in other contextless situations. To put the matter another way, excessive preoccupation with internal validity makes it less and less likely that the results will be externally valid (to use the terms common to the conventional paradigm although not to the constructivist; see Chapter 8). Context-stripping is a recognized problem even for those with continuing allegiance to the conventional paradigm; the frequent calls to conduct research in more "natural" settings is one reflection of this concern. But within the fourth generation evaluation approach this failing is more than a mere technical problem—it is absolutely counter-productive to the aims of that form of evaluation. Constructions held by people are born out of their experience with and interaction with their contexts. Indeed, the tie is so close that one can easily argue, as we shall, that constructions *create* the context that the constructors experience and are in turn given life by that erected context. A methodology that deliberately sets out to strip context in the name of controlling confounding variables cannot be the paradigm of choice.

(4) *Conventional methodology does not provide a means for making evaluative assessments on a situation-by-situation basis.* The methodology of conventional inquiry is geared toward the identification and harnessing of factors (variables) that will act in predictable ways in a variety of situations. Indeed, the end product of inquiry is, ideally, a *generalization* which is a time- and context-*free* assertion, not a *specification,* which is a time- and context-*bound* assertion. Ironically, one of the criticisms often made of constructivist inquiry is that it cannot lead to generalizations, and hence is not worth doing. Why would anyone wish to engage in inquiry that had applicability only in a specific case?

What is at issue here is often termed the *nomothetic/idiographic dilemma.* Generalizations—nomothetic statements—have little utility for local understanding or prediction—idiographic application. Consider the case of the physician confronted with a patient's recital of her symptoms. He or she might say, "Well, 80 percent of patients presenting these symptoms have cervical cancer. I will therefore immediately schedule *this* patient for a total hysterectomy." Surely the patient would find it reasonable to ask that she be examined and *the particulars of her case determined* before such a serious diagnosis is made and such a radical treatment prescribed. Similarly, a teacher confronted with a group of children cannot teach simply on the basis of certain general laws of learning. He or she must begin, as the saying goes, where the child (not children) is. That mode of teaching requires individual observation and individual teaching tactics. Michael Scriven (1987) has similarly made a compelling case that general research findings cannot, legally, ethically, or rationally, serve as the basis for individual teacher evaluations.

Now evaluands certainly possess features that can be assessed once and for all, that is, in a generalized way. For example, one can determine that a proposed new curriculum is internally coherent, inclusive of modern concepts, and appropriately sequenced. But one cannot determine that this curriculum will *fit* into and *work* in a given setting without trying it in that setting. To use our earlier language (Guba & Lincoln, 1981), it may be possible to assess an evaluand's *merit* in a general way, but one cannot assess its *worth* except in the individual case. Conventional methodology does not contemplate that application; indeed, many conventional evaluations are aimed precisely at providing a "seal of approval" for an evaluand that in effect warrants it for universal application.

(5) *Conventional methodology's claim to be value-free makes it a dubious instrument to use in an investigation intended to lead to a judgment about some entity (an evaluand).* Science's claim to be value-free (an aspect of its putative objectivity) is well known. We shall show later that this claim, ironically, the reader should note, a value claim in itself, cannot be maintained, but for the moment we are simply considering whether the conventional inquiry paradigm is, *in its own terms,* an appropriate vehicle to guide fourth generation evaluation. For if it is value-free, it *is* indeed a curious tool to use when attempting to come to some value judgment.

Value is the very root of the term *evalua*tion. As we saw in Chapter 1, the obligation of evaluation to lead to value judgments was not clearly apprehended until the advent of third generation evaluation, for which the task of valuing became central. Indeed, it became the evaluator's *duty* to exercise judgment, if for no other reason than that he or she could be counted on to be most objective.

But value judgments cannot be made in the absence of value standards. Whether everyone agrees on the standards or not (and we have argued that in today's society, values are almost always pluralistic), it is difficult to see how the establishment of values and their application can be incorporated into a process that disclaims values from the start. Some third generation evaluators attempted this difficult task by collecting value data from a variety of sources (usually not then called stakeholders) and presenting those value data along with the "factual" data to the client or sponsor. In effect, values were turned into just another set of facts. Others attempted to deal with the issue by defining *two* processes: *assessment*—the collection of factual evidence—and *evaluation*—the interpretation of those factual data within the value framework brought to the task by the individual or group designated (empowered?) to carry it out. But neither solution can escape the logical disjunction that follows from attempting to use putatively value-free tools in the service of a value-laden task.

At an applied level, then, we argue that the use of the conventional paradigm is inappropriate to fourth generation evaluation, because conventional methodology does not and cannot contemplate direct work with stakeholders and their constructions (that much of the methodology is simply missing); because the conventional paradigm is tied to the verification mode and cannot deal with discovery processes; because the conventional paradigm strips contextual factors rather than taking them into account; because conventional methodology is aimed at generalizations and not at specifications; and because the value-free posture assumed within the conventional paradigm is logically disjunctive with evaluation's goal of making value judgments. But there are also, and in our view, more serious issues that can be raised at the philosophical level. Among the more salient are these:

(1) *The theory-ladenness of facts, and the factual underdetermination of theory.* It is the claim of adherents of the conventional paradigm that they can, in a neutral, objective way, put questions directly to nature and receive nature's undistorted responses, by virtue of science's objective methodology. That claim rests on the possibility of performing *independent* empirical tests. To put the matter more precisely, the claim rests on the possibility that there can exist *separate* observational and theoretical languages: the theoretical language within which propositions can be cast, and the observational language within which they can be empirically tested. The results of such tests are the "facts" that determine the truth or falsity of the propositions at issue. The whole point in insisting on *operational* definitions of concepts is to assure that such a distinction will exist. Otherwise, the test may be biased and may result in a tautology—a circular argument. The major reason for the formation of the Vienna Circle of Logical Positivists in the early part of this century was to devise a system of doing science that was independent of the concepts used by scientists to cast their ideas into propositional or theoretical form.

Philosophers of science have come increasingly to believe, however, that the effort to establish separate observational and theoretical languages is doomed to failure. Facts can be facts, they aver, *only within* some theoretical framework (see, for example, Hesse, 1980). That is, facts and theories are so intricately intertwined that it is impossible to imagine an empirical language that does not depend heavily on theoretical assumptions and formulations for its meaning. Separate observational and theoretical languages are *in principle* impossible to formulate. And if that is so, then empirical tests cannot be relied upon to provide unimpeachable evidence about nature or the laws that putatively drive it. Those aspects and those laws are, in effect, generated by and have meaning only within the basic belief system out of which theories are themselves generated.

There is an interesting reverse aspect to the problem of theory-ladenness, and that is the problem of factual underdetermination of theory (sometimes called the problem of induction). Any body of "facts" is not uniquely interpretable in terms of only one theory. Indeed, in principle, there is a very large if not an infinite number of theories all of which can account for a given array of "facts" equally well. No theory is ever uniquely determined, for, if it could be, theories could be proven. The fact that no theory has ever been finally proven is eloquent testimony to the principle of underdetermination.

The conventional paradigm thus loses its basis for claiming to be able to produce findings that represent nature "as it really is" or "as it really works," since the "facts" can represent only those aspects contemplated by and accounted for by the theory within which the investigation is conducted. Empirical tests lose their validity. Inquiry can produce findings only about how things and actions are *constructed* by human beings.

It is exactly the posture of the constructivist paradigm that there is no single, "real" reality, but only multiple realities constructed by human beings. To be sure, constructions may be and often are shared, and shared widely. It should not astonish us that physicists, for example, should tend to agree on an essentially unitary construction (although anyone familiar with the frontiers of modern physics is well acquainted with the widespread and volatile disagreements that exist among even, or perhaps especially, world-class physicists). Given that the constructivist paradigm replaces the realist ontology of the conventional paradigm with a relativist ontology that admits and honors multiple constructions (not perceptions!), it seems the obvious choice for anyone contemplating engaging in fourth generation evaluation.

(2) *The value-ladenness of facts.* We have already noted that the claim of value-freedom made on behalf of the conventional paradigm would, if valid, render that paradigm a dubious choice for the conduct of a valuing enterprise such as evaluation. But the claim of value-freedom is itself undergoing serious challenge. And if the conventional paradigm is

not value-free, then its utility for guiding fourth generation evaluation is not, as one might at first suspect, enhanced, but is even further diminished.

That the conventional paradigm is not value-free is now widely recognized. Values permeate every paradigm that has been proposed or might be proposed, for paradigms are *human* constructions, and hence cannot be impervious to human values. Values enter an inquiry through such channels as the nature of the problem selected for study or the evaluand to be evaluated, the choice of paradigm for carrying out the inquiry (as the discussion of this chapter aptly illustrates), the choice of instrumentation and analysis modes, the choice of interpretations to be made and conclusions to be drawn, and the like. Thus nature cannot be viewed as it really is (even if one starts with the assumption that there exists a real nature out there to be assessed) but only as seen (constructed) *through some value window.* Further, if values do enter into an inquiry, then the questions of what values and whose values become paramount. If the findings of studies or evaluations can vary as a function of the value system brought to bear, then the arbitrary choice of a *particular* value system tends to empower certain individuals and to disempower and disenfranchise others, that is, those with other values.

It is in this sense that the conventional paradigm is labeled by some as an instrument of the status quo, or, worse, as an instrument of repression. Critical theorists such as Henry Giroux (1983), neo-Marxists such as Brian Fay (1987), advocates of participatory inquiry such as Paulo Freire (1970), and, in Europe, Peter Reason and John Rowan (1981), and feminist researchers such as Evelyn Fox Keller (1985) and Sandra Harding (1987), call for a radical revision in the conventional paradigm to take account of different value positions, particularly those of oppressed minorities.

If these critiques are taken seriously, it becomes clear that the conventional mode of inquiry—and indeed any mode of inquiry—can properly be called a *political* activity. If that is so, fourth generation evaluators are well advised to select the constructivist paradigm that, by virtue of the hermeneutic/dialectic inherent in its methodology, elicits political input and takes it into account. If one of the aims of responsive evaluation is to protect against exploitation while empowering and enfranchising less

powerful groups, the constructivist paradigm, which openly acknowl-
edges and seeks out political input, is vastly superior to a paradigm that
denies any possibility of political input because of its putatively value-
free nature.

(3) *The interactive nature of the knower-known dyad.* The conventional paradigm is based on a premise often called "subject-object
duality," that is, it presupposes that the inquirer (subject) can assume and
maintain a detached, objective stance in relation to the inquired-into
(object). It is believed that, if the inquirer can adopt such a stance, the
findings cannot be other than characteristics of the object. Archimedes is
reputed to have boasted, once he had formulated the law of the lever,
that if he had a long-enough lever and a place on which to stand (the
fabled "Archimedean point"), he would be able to move the earth. By
analogy, conventional inquirers seem to feel that if they have an objective enough methodology, and a detached-enough place on which to
stand, they will be able to wring nature's secrets from her.

The premise that such a duality can exist has been sharply rejected in
the physical sciences. More than a half century ago Heisenberg enun-
ciated his now-well-accepted Uncertainty Principle, which asserted that
the actions of the investigator, while facilitating certain observations (for
example, determining the mass of a particle) made it impossible to make
certain other observations (for example, determining that particle's veloc-
ity). The Bohr Complementarity Principle, proposed about the same
time, argued that the results of any study depended upon the interaction
between inquirer and object (a proposition, as if to illustrate the fact that
not all constructions are shared even in the physical sciences, that was
sharply resisted by Einstein until his death). That is, the findings
depended as much on the nature of the questions asked (theory-laden, of
course) and on the order in which they were asked, as on any intrinsic
properties of a "real" reality "out there." More recent findings in physics
(for example, Bell's Theorem) and mathematics (for example, Godel's
Incompleteness Theorem) attest to the intrinsic and ineluctable interconnectedness of all phenomena, human or otherwise (Lincoln & Guba,
1985; Zukav, 1979).

If such interrelatedness exists even in the physical sciences, where the
"object" half of the dyad is usually some inert substance or body, it is

certainly absurd to stake an inquiry in the human sciences on the proposition that an objective dualism is possible. Where the inquired into (we hesitate to call a human an "object") is a human, or a human characteristic, the existence of interconnectedness is inescapable, even if only at so primitive a level as the well-known phenomenon of reactivity. Further, to suppose that it is possible for a human investigator to step outside his or her own humanness, for example, by disregarding one's own values, experiences, and constructions, is to believe in magic.

If these arguments are taken seriously, it is plain that *knowledge* emerges as a product of an interaction between humans or (in the physical sciences) between humans and nonhuman objects. Different interactions will yield different findings. Strange as it may sound to ears socialized to the conventional paradigm, the results are *literally*—we stress *literally—created* by that interaction; they are not "discovered" as if they had always been "out there." To put it in our own terminology, *knowlege is a human construction,* including, we might add, all theories and methodologies. Hence they cannot be taken as ultimate or objective truths but suffer, and will continue to suffer, from human foibles. As Mary Hesse (1980) so well reminds us, just as every theory ever espoused has sooner or later proven to be inadequate, every theory that we now espouse (including, of course, the constructivist paradigm) will so prove also.

In the face of these arguments, we find an ovewhelming case in favor of using the new paradigm to guide fourth generation evaluation. That form of evaluation rests on the premise that different stakeholders will have different constructions, which, while perhaps differing in the scope of already constructed knowledge accounted for and in their level of sophistication, are nevertheless legitimate to hold and worthy to honor. That does not mean that those constructions cannot be challenged or refined; indeed, as we have already asserted, *unless* fourth generation evaluation will result in the attainment of more informed and sophisticated personal constructions by all stakeholders, and in a higher level of appreciation of constructions held by others, we will regard the process as having been deficient. Our essential point is simply this: *If* knowledge exists essentially in the form of human constructions, then a paradigm that recognizes and accepts that premise from the start is to be preferred to one that does not. And *if* fourth generation evaluation stresses differences in constructions, and has as its central process a hermeneutic dialectic that requires constructors to confront one another's constructions and to deal with them, then the constructivist paradigm ought surely to be the paradigm of choice.

The Problematic Nature of Human Knowledge

We cannot stress too strongly the assertion that human knowledge consists of a series of constructions, which, precisely because they are humanly generated, are problematic, that is, indeterminate, unsettled, and ambiguous. That fact is easily lost sight of in the arena of science; science is widely regarded as *the* way to discover truth, and its products are widely accepted as true. To say that there is scientific evidence supporting such and such a proposition is tantamount to saying that it is indubitably and forever true.

We are fond of an (apocryphal?) story of Moses descending from the Mount with not two but *three* tablets. The first two, as is well known, contained the Ten Commandments, while the third, equally authoritative, carried the inscription,

KNOW YE THEN THAT THE METHOD OF SCIENCE IS THE TRUE WAY; HE [sic] THAT FOLLOWETH IT WILL SURELY FIND FOREVER DEPENDABLE KNOWLEDGE.

The tablet then went on to outline the well-known steps of the scientific method.

While it is the case that Moses recalled the steps, and could give us his personal assurance that the scientific approach did bear the official imprimatur, he was unfortunately unable to substantiate that claim. For, you see, he was not especially adept at mountain ascending or descending, particularly not while carrying three heavy pieces of stone. As it happened, he *stumbled* on the way down, furiously juggling the tablets all the while. Finally, despite a heroic effort that left him with a lame back for the rest of his days, he *dropped* the crucial third tablet. To make matters worse, it slipped through a crevasse, careened for more than a thousand feet, and finally shattered itself on an outcropping of granite. As Pogo might have put it, "Sic transit gloria mundi," which is to say (*very* loosely translated), "There goes the ball game." Ever since we have had to treat science as a human construction.

But it is a mistake to think that such a conclusion was immediately and widely accepted. By and large, scientists were wont to believe in the *un*problematic nature of the knowledge they had "discovered." The journal *American Scientist* commissioned the well-known biologist and popular scientific writer Stephen Jay Gould (1986) to write a *festschrift* on the occasion of the 100th anniversary of the death of Charles Darwin. The piece was to assess Darwin's career and single out that one greatest contribution that he had made. Now there are many things that Gould might have written about Darwin, who was clearly one of the most gifted and creative thinkers that ever lived. His theory (construction?) of evolution radically altered thought not only in his own discipline but in virtually every area of human activity. Its influence continues to be strongly felt, and while there is much argumentation about whether or not he was "right" (a question that could never have arisen within a constructivist framework), there is no doubt about the overall value of his contributions.

Gould thus seemed to be faced with a monumental task—how to sort out from the welter of Darwinian contributions that one that he could defend as "the greatest of them all." Gould did not seem to have much trouble in solving that problem, however; he quickly came to the conclusion that Darwin's greatest contribution is that *he made history problematic.* He led the world to see the indeterminate, unsettled, and ambiguous nature of history, even natural history that could have, presumably, been settled once and for all by the methods of science.

Gould points out that, prior to Darwin's work, naturalists had assumed, implicitly, to be sure, that the world they studied had been in exactly that same form since "the beginning," however one might construe what the beginning was. The forms of plant and animal life were what they always had been, as were the mountains, rivers, oceans, glaciers, and other geologic features as well. None had been added or subtracted. Darwin in one flash of insight realized how inappropriate that assessment was. At once the *history* of a life form or geologic form took on an importance that it had never had before (indeed, the very concept of natural history made little sense given the earlier presuppositions). To understand how things are now and why they are so you must understand how and where they *have been*. It was precisely because that history was problematic that contention could arise and could continue until this moment. No doubt that contention will continue. The struggle of the constructivist is to persuade reformed science *not* to ask the question, "Which construction (theory, concept, interpretation) is *right?*" but rather, "Which construction seems to take best account of that knowledge constructed to date—itself changeable—in the most sophisticated way?" And of course the constructivist struggles to remind him- or herself—as well as all others—that what may appear best now, today, may not only not appear best tomorrow but may be utterly rejected. For if knowledge is problematic, the ultimate moral imperative for inquirers must be to seek out constructions that challenge that one (or those) that currently hold the spotlight. It has been said that research means doing one's damnedest with one's mind; it also means doing one's damnedest to prove oneself in error.

All human constructions are problematic. We cannot expect them to be ultimately true, or to remain constant for a long period of time—except by stagnation. It is no accident that the period of history most characterized by strict adherence to *one (the)* set of "truths" is called "The Dark Ages."

Constructions represent the efforts of people to *make sense* out of their situations, out of the states of affairs in which they find themselves. They are *interpretations* based primarily on experience—to "see it with my own eyes" or to "hear it with my own ears" is the best evidence that anyone can muster to demonstrate to him- or herself the validity of his or her own constructions. We all learn by experience, and, indeed, one may well ask whether there is any *other* way to learn. It is in part because of their rootedness in experience that constructions are so hard to relinquish or to revise. Insofar as some of that experience is tacit (we all know a great deal more than we can say, for example, about how to ride a bicycle), it is personally unique. That feature makes constructions difficult to share fully with others, and explains in part why rational arguments are not always sufficient to change people's minds. "What you say makes sense, I suppose, but it just doesn't seem (or feel or sound or look or smell) right to me."

Constructions are nevertheless extensively shared. At the broadest level most of us share certain cultural mores, often without being aware of the fact. We are socialized to behave in certain ways, to feel certain emotions, to hold certain values, and, if we may say it without appearing coy, to practice certain paradigms. Some of the constructions we may share are *disciplined constructions,* attempts collectively and systematically to come to common agreements about state of affairs. Science, we suggest, is one such effort at formulating a disciplined construction, and it is widely shared. Constructivism is another, although one not so widely shared as some of us would like.

The nature of a construction that can be held about anything depends on two things: the range or scope of information available to a constructor, and the constructor's sophistication in dealing with that information. "Primitive" persons cannot share "civilized" constructions because of vast differences in available information and sophistication—but it is equally true that "civilized" persons cannot share "primitive" constructions for the same reasons. We shall deal later with the question of how constructions change, and what account needs to be taken of information already held (even if not always fully shared) and of the level of sophistication that various constructors (who may be organized into different stakeholder groups) possess. But we want to be very clear at this point in asserting that *all* knowledge is problematic, that it consists of constructions that are more or less shared, and that those constructions are formulated and reformulated on the basis of available information and sophistication. The implications of these assertions for doing fourth generation evaluation will come later (see especially Chapter 7).

The Process of Fourth Generation Evaluation

We have seen that fourth generation evaluation is a process for doing evaluation that meets two conditions: It is organized by the claims, concerns, and issues of stakeholding audiences, and it utilizes the methodology of the constructivist paradigm. In this chapter we have provided a rationale for each of these conditions. Given that background we can now proceed to list, in very brief form, the several purposes for doing fourth generation evaluation, purposes that will in later chapters be translated into specific process steps. We wish to be clear, however, that neither the purposes we are about to list nor the process steps that emanate from them should be considered to be linear in character; it is not only *not* essential that Purpose (or Step) 1 precede Purpose (or Step) 2 and so on but probably dysfunctional to insist that they do so. It is most useful to think of fourth generation evaluation as a form that embraces many purposes and activities, all of which go on more or less simultaneously and interactively. It is only for purposes of exposition that we lay them out in what appears to be a linear format. We shall repeat this caveat from time to time in this book because we believe it to be crucial to an understanding of what the fourth generation evaluator is obliged to do.

Essentially the fourth generation evaluator is responsible for the following:

(1) *Identifying the full array of stakeholders who are at risk in the projected evaluation.* As many of these audiences as possible should be identified before the hermeneutic/dialectic process (to be explicated in later chapters) begins, but the way must always be open to the inclusion of new stakeholders whenever and however they come to the evaluator's attention.

(2) *Eliciting from each stakeholder group their constructions about the evaluand and the range of claims, concerns, and issues they wish to raise in relation to it.* This elicitation must take place in an open-ended way, to guarantee that it is an *emic*—an insider's—view that emerges rather than an *etic*—an outsider's—view.

(3) *Providing a context and a methodology (the hermeneutic/dialectic) through which different constructions, and different claims, concerns, and issues, can be understood, critiqued, and taken into account:*

    a. First, carrying out this methodology *within* each stakeholder group, so that a group construction (or several, if there are within-group conflicts) can emerge and decisions can be reached about which claims, concerns, and issues should be pursued.

    b. Second, cross-fertilizing each group with the constructions, claims, concerns, and issues arising from other groups so that those items must be confronted and dealt with. This cross-fertilization may also include constructions drawn from the literature, from other sites, or from the experience of the evaluator. *Any* construction, claim, concern, or issue may properly be introduced *so long as it is open to critique and reconstruction.*

(4) *Generating consensus with respect to as many constructions, and their related claims, concerns, and issues, as possible.* Attempts to generate consensus may be undertaken *within* groups as part of 3a above and *between* groups as part of 3b. If consensus can be achieved with respect to an item, it can be eliminated from further consideration, although not necessarily from further action, which must be agreed upon in the consensus seeking process.

(5) *Preparing an agenda for negotiation on items about which there is no, or incomplete, consensus.* Failure to reach consensus implies the continuation of competing constructions, which, as we have argued, can be changed only through new information or increased sophistication. The evaluator's task is to identify the information needed. Because more information may be required than it is possible to obtain, given constraints of time and/or resources, the evaluator must devise some means (preferably also through a hermeneutic/dialectic) for prioritizing the unresolved items. Stakeholder inputs are essential in this determination, lest this need be taken as an opportunity to disempower selected stakeholders.

(6) *Collecting and providing the information called for in the agenda for negotiation.* That needed information *can* be provided cannot be guaranteed, but the evaluator must make every good faith effort to do so. Further, if stakeholders lack the sophistication to deal with obtained information, training is implied. That is also the evaluator's responsibility to arrange.

(7) *Establishing and mediating a forum of stakeholder representatives in which negotiation can take place.* Unresolved differences in construction, as well as unresolved claims, concerns, and issues, are reviewed in light of the new information and/or level of sophistication, in the hope that their number can be considerably reduced. It is likely that some items will remain unresolved, thereby setting the stage for another, later round of evaluation activity. Outcomes of this forum must include action steps if the negotiation is to be regarded as successful.

(8) *Developing a report, probably several reports, that communicate to each stakeholder group any consensus on constructions and any resolutions regarding the claims, concerns, and issues that they have raised (as well as regarding those raised by other groups that appear relevant to that group).* We believe that the most useful format for such a report is the case study, which we shall be at some pains to explicate later (see Chapter 7). If constructions are devised on the basis of experience, a most effective way to change them is to provide new or additional experience. That experience need not, however, be direct; it may well be vicarious. We agree with Stake's (1986) judgment that "the role of the evaluator can be to provide narrative accounts that provide vicarious experience." The case report seems to be an ideal form for that purpose (Zeller, 1987).

(9) *Recycling the evaluation once again to take up still unresolved constructions and their attendant claims, concerns, and issues.* In addition, new aspects may be explored that may have emerged as a result of changes made on the basis of the first-round evaluation. Fourth generation evaluations are never completed; they pause until a further need and opportunity arise.

This then is a capsule version of the fourth generation process. Much of this book will be devoted to making clear what each of these purposes and their process steps involve.

Making the Switch

It seems to us possible that a reader, having come this far, may be persuaded that fourth generation evaluation may be a useful alternative to try. But making the switch, even to someone committed to a good faith effort, is not nearly so easy as it may appear on purely rational grounds.

There are two mental switches that must be made. The first, and by far the easier, is to adopt stakeholder claims, concerns, and issues as useful foci for organizing an evaluation. Historically we have witnessed a steady progression in this direction. Earlier forms of evaluation were guided by considerations that related directly to *client* wants. Thus tests and measurements were introduced because clients thought that the information so generated would be useful in the scientific management of schools, particularly in providing insights about the "raw material"—students—that the schools were expected to process. The switch to objectives as the central organizer, while reorienting evaluation to *program* in a significant way, did little to overcome this client orientation, for it was clearly the client's objectives that called the tune. Decision models focused even more directly on servicing client needs (as defined by the client) directly.

Given this state of affairs, it was easy for evaluation to degenerate into the managerial ideology that Scriven (1983) so protested. His solution was to reorient evaluation to *consumer* needs, by insisting that evaluands should be judged on the basis of the effects, intended or unintended, that they produced, and how those effects related to consumer needs. His continuing reference to *Consumer Reports* as a model of such evaluation is instructive.

But Scriven's solution simply harnessed evaluation in the service of a different stakeholder group than the one that had traditionally been served. It simultaneously eliminated that traditional group from consideration; Scriven's formulation inevitably placed evaluator and client in adversarial roles. Further, the consumer-oriented evaluation urged by Scriven took no account of other stakeholder groups; they had no more input into his process than they had had traditionally.

The move to broaden the base of stakeholders who *do* have input into the evaluation process thus seems to be a "natural" progression, if not an inevitable one. It makes sense to take account of the interests of all groups that are put at risk by an evaluation. It also makes sense to protect the interests of the less powerful from encroachment by the more powerful as an integral part of the process. Thus the shift from client to consumer to stakeholder-oriented evaluation is not so dramatic as one might at first be led to believe, absent some sense of the history of the development of evaluation as a discipline. The shift may make evaluation a more complex and messy process but not an essentially different one.

The much more difficult shift that must be made is that from the conventional paradigm of inquiry as guide to the constructivist paradigm. We believe the reasons we have advanced not only for the wisdom but also for the necessity of such a shift are compelling. Nevertheless, what we are asking for is a rejection of a *basic belief system,* not just a kit of tools. And therein lies the rub.

First, we have been socialized our entire lives to believe in the scientific method as *the* way to discover truth. Most aspects of our environment reinforce us in that belief. We do not flinch when a claim is challenged by the question, "But is there any scientific evidence for that belief?" And if the answer is "yes," we feel compelled to accept the judgment, whatever it is. When we began learning in school, even in the early grades we were taught that the scientific method was the way to approach *any* problem. Even the problems posed in our social studies classes were putatively amenable to analysis and solution using the scientific approach. *Mr. Wizard* amused and amazed us on television, and we came to see how powerful and all-embracing science was. We learned we could not trust our common sense; only science could, in the end, provide conclusive answers.

This early learning might recede, however, were it not for the continual reinforcement it receives in our very language structure. A useful metaphor is our sexist language. By now everyone understands that our language reflects our gender stereotypes. And progress is being made. We have learned to replace *man* with *person,* *he* with *he* or *she, lady* by *woman,* and so on. But we have a long way to go to become equally conscious of the fact that the language we use to couch our thinking and expression about inquiry is biased by positivist terminology. Who can think about inquiry for more than a few minutes without using such terms as *variable, design, control, cause, generalize, discover, identify, correlate,* and the like, all of which are in one sense or another inappropriate to the constructivist view? All of these terms are grounded in positivist assumptions, particularly, as we shall see, in the realist ontology that is basic to that way of viewing the world. Until we have a well-developed set of counterterms (and note the bias of that expression, as though the new paradigm would necessarily have terms that *paralleled* the old), our very language will remain a major impediment to a full appreciation and understanding of the new belief system.

Probably no one has given more thought to what may be required to train individuals in new paradigm ways of thinking than Shulamit Reinharz (1981). She writes:

The socialization of a new paradigm researcher can be represented by the convergence of personal attributes, traditional training, and exposure to alternative ideas within a context of sufficient support. (p. 417)

The model for socialization, she suggests, can be conceptualized as consisting of four phases, although she is careful to point out that "there is much movement back and forth between stages of development" (Reinharz, 1981, p. 417). These four stages (the italicized phrasings are Reinharz's own) are these:

(1) *Immersion in the dominant paradigm.* One cannot understand what is done in the name of the new paradigm without understanding something about what has been done in the name of the old. This suggestion seems to be in line with Gould's earlier cited critique of Darwin in which Gould named as Darwin's most important contribution that he made history problematic. If one wishes to understand how things are now, and why, one needs to know a good deal of how they were. The new paradigm did not spring afresh from the brow of Zeus; while it would be a mistake to think of it simply as a *reaction* to the old, there is enough of reactivity in it to make it crucial to know what is being reacted to.

(2) *Exposure to or awareness of problems in the dominant paradigm, leading to conflict about methods and crisis of commitment.* Such an awareness can come by dint of a *disillusioning personal experience* with old paradigm inquiry, *personal study* or *exposure to a specific training program, role conflict* between the structure of research and other experience (a problem we shall later refer to as paradigm dissonance), or *traumatic personal or political experiences.*

(3) *Resolution of conflict in the form of enumerating specific criticisms, demystification, strengthening of commitment through receipt of support, developing an innovative stance, and learning of new paradigm alternatives.*

Reinharz comments:

By grounding oneself in specific criticism of the dominant paradigm, the process of demystification with the "scientism" of the dominant paradigm can continue. Each criticism is a crack in the edifice of belief. As the cracks accumulate there is a psychologically perceived crumbling of the entire structure of research practices, and a sense that our knowledge based on current methods is untrustworthy. (p. 421 in S. Reinharz, "Implementing New Paradigm Research: A Model for Training and Practice," in P. Reason & J. Rowan, editors, *Human Inquiry,* copyright 1981 by John Wiley; used by permission—the same applies to the quotation below)

Such grounding takes place best in "a nurturing personal and intellectual environment [that] converts mere conflict into a growth-inducing process" (p. 424). But there is a danger:

> New paradigm researchers choose to innovate; their response to conflict is to analyze and create an alternative. The danger is that to compensate for the risk they have taken, innovators become converts, embracing the new "truth" while being defensive or unaware of its shortcomings, in other words, mystified anew. This can be seen when methodological ideas are treated as so precious that they almost cannot be communicated. They then acquire the status of a secret cult or batch of private notions. If instead, the researcher has internalized a dialectic form of thinking, s/he will continuously seek and be aware of criticism of the new paradigm and its methods. (p. 425)

All of this activity needs to be carried out in an atmosphere of support: "A supportive environment builds commitment and tolerance for continued conflict" (p. 426). Also needed is a "distinctive training environment with as much dialogue, confirmation of experience . . . , and sharing of responsibility, as possible" (p. 420).

(4) *Carrying out new paradigm research within a developing model of research practice and living; retaining one's commitment through a cycle of feedback, revisions, and continuous communication with others who share one's outlook.* In order to fix the results of the previous three phases, it is necessary to undertake new paradigm inquiry, preferably in the company or in the context of other like-minded individuals, to practice it and make its methods an established part of one's repertoire. Clearly we would argue that to carry out fourth generation evaluation is one of the best ways to engage in such practice.

The shift will not be easy, but it will certainly be worthwhile.

3   *What Is This Constructivist Paradigm Anyway?*

If it is the case that several compelling arguments were mounted in Chapter 2 for the proposition that fourth generation evaluation is best served by adhering to the methodology of the naturalistic paradigm, it is now time to move to a more detailed examination of that approach. We shall spend a great deal of effort to compare and contrast the emergent paradigm with the conventional, in the spirit of the idea that history is problematic and knowing history is essential. But it is also the case that no paradigm can be successful simply because it takes a position that counters what is usually done. If the new paradigm did not have some strong virtues of its own, quite independent of its relationship to positivism, it would probably not be worth pursuing. We shall endeavor, therefore, to make these added virtues clear also.

Paradigms as Basic Belief Systems

It is useful, by way of introduction, to think of a paradigm as a basic set of beliefs, a set of assumptions we are willing to make, which serve as touchstones in guiding our activities. We daily operate out of many paradigms. For example, our court system is guided by an adversarial paradigm, our churches are guided by a variety of theological paradigms, Wall Street is guided by certain economic paradigms, and so on. Now the crucial thing to note here is that these paradigms are basic *belief* systems; they cannot be proven or disproven, but they represent the most fundamental positions we are willing to take. If we could cite reasons why some particular paradigm should be preferred, then those reasons would form an even more basic set of beliefs. At some level we must stop giving reasons and simply accept wherever we are as our basic belief set—our paradigm.

We have found it useful to use as a metaphor for belief systems and their consequences that branch of mathematics commonly called Euclidean geometry. It is a useful metaphor because it is a familiar example; virtually every person who has been in a secondary school has been exposed to it. Now geometry, as the name implies, originally had to do with the measurement of the earth. It had been a respected art for millennia before Euclid's time (circa 300 B.C.), developed because of the need to resurvey the Nile Valley each year after the annual overflow wiped out existing boundary markers. Surveyors had developed a number of rules of thumb that gave consistently "good" results. What surveyors did *not* have was any sort of proof that their rules of thumb were valid. Euclid, working in Alexandria, set out to provide that missing element.

Euclid decided that he could devise the needed proofs by showing that the rules of thumb were logical derivatives deduced from a self-evident set of axioms or assumptions. By accepting as given four statements that no reasonable person could disagree with, he set the base for demonstrating each of the "theorems" (i.e., the rules of thumb) that he wanted to prove. His statements were innocent anough; surely no one would have quarreled with their self-evident nature (Hofstadter, 1979):

(1) A straight line segment can be drawn joining any two points.
(2) Any straight line segment can be extended indefinitely in a straight line.
(3) Given any straight line segment, a circle can be drawn having the segment as radius and one end point as center.
(4) All right angles are congruent.

Starting with the simplest rule of thumb that he could work with, Euclid showed that it was indeed consistent with the axioms. Having proved that theorem enabled him to use it as part of the next proof, and so on. He was able to work his way through no fewer than 28 of the theorems, but then, with the 29th, he failed. Try as he would he could not find the proof he sought. Finally, to be able to get on with his work, Euclid simply set this theorem aside, adopting it pro tem as another axiom. It was certainly not self-evident and would surely occasion a great deal of objection if it were advanced on that basis. To state it in more modern language than Euclid employed, the axiom read (Lincoln & Guba, 1985):

(5) Given a line and a point not on the line, it is possible to construct only one line through the point that is parallel to the given line.

It was surely Euclid's intent to return to this fifth axiom and to prove it in terms of the first four, but he was never able to do so. Mathematicians tried for two millennia to concoct the proof before it was finally shown that the fifth axiom could *not* be proved. But in the process of trying to do so, some mathematicians fell back on the so-called indirect method of proof. If you wish to prove X, say, but are having difficulty, start instead with the premise of non-X. Then show that non-X leads to absurd results, thereby providing some evidence for X after all. But far from leading to absurd results, these efforts led to the discovery and development of a series of so-called *non*-Euclidean geometries.

One such geometry, for example, was devised by a Russian mathematician, Nikolai Ivanovich Lobachevsky, who started with this "absurd" restatement of the fifth axiom:

(5) Given a line and a point not on the line, it is possible to construct a bundle of lines through the point *all of which* are parallel to the given line.

One interesting consequence of this restatement is that, whereas Euclid showed that all triangles had to have a sum of angles of 180°, Lobachevsky's formulation led to the conclusion that triangles have a sum of angles that *approaches* 180° as triangles become "small." Now that our earth experience supports Euclid is not surprising since Euclid was working within a construction devised by earth surveyors. But astronomers find utility in the Lobachevskian version as they deal with the very large distances of outer space (Lincoln & Guba, 1985).

From this metaphor we (Lincoln & Guba, 1985, p. 36) earlier drew the following conclusions:

(1) Axioms (basic beliefs) are arbitrary and may be assumed for any reason, even if only for the "sake of the game."

(2) Axioms are *not* self-evidently true, nor need they appear to be so; indeed, some axioms appear to be very bizarre on first exposure.

(3) Different axiom systems have different utilities depending on the phenomena to which they are applied. These utilities are *not* determined by the nature of the axiom system itself but by the *interaction* between the axioms and the characteristics of the area of application. . . .

(4) A decision about which of several alternative axiom systems to use in a given case is best made by testing the "fit" between each system and the case, a process analogous to testing data for fit to assumptions before deciding which statistic to use in analyzing them.

We have already begun to argue, in Chapter 2, that the constructivist paradigm provides the best "fit" whenever it is human inquiry that is being considered. We hope to be persuasive on this point even though the basic belief system of constructivism—analogous to the axioms of geometry—may well seem bizarre or even absurd. This basic system is explicated in the next section.[1] Later, we shall extend the geometry metaphor by proposing certain theorems that can be derived from the system, contrasting these with analogous theorems that can be drawn from the conventional paradigm as the axiom set.[2] It will be the reader's rask to judge which belief system, and which set of theorems, provides the best fit for his or her own life space.

The Basic Belief Systems of the
Conventional and Constructivist Paradigms

We begin by laying out the basic beliefs in contrasting form in Table 3.1. The table is arranged in three levels, which reflect the three basic questions that philosophers have put to themselves for millennia as they have struggled to understand how we come to know what we know:

(1) *What is there that can be known?* This is usually called the *ontological* question. Ontology is that branch of philosophy (specifically, of metaphysics) that is concerned with issues of existence or being as such. Another way to phrase the question is this: "What is the nature of reality?"

(2) *What is the relationship of the knower to the known (or the knowable)?* This is usually called the *epistemological* question. Epistemology is that branch of philosophy that deals with the origin, nature, and limits of human knowledge. Another way to phrase the question is this: "How can we be sure that we know what we know?"

(3) *What are the ways of finding out knowledge?* This is usually called the *methodological* question. Methodology is a more practical branch of philosophy (especially of philosophy of science) that deals with methods, systems, and rules for the conduct of inquiry. Another way to phrase the question is: "How can we go about finding out things?"

It would be a mistake to presume that there are only a few ways in which these questions can be answered. Beginning with Aristotle (and probably earlier), different formulations have been proposed that are in effect different paradigms or basic belief systems (Lincoln & Guba, 1985). It must be clear that there is no way to answer these questions in an unambiguous and certain way or in a way that is capable of proof. The set of answers one gives *is* the basic belief system or paradigm.

One set of answers has been dominant for the past several hundred years—the one that we have called the conventional paradigm but can also be called, with equal legitimacy, the positivist or scientific paradigm. The constructivist paradigm, also called the naturalistic, hermeneutic, or interpretive paradigm (with slight shadings in meaning), has been in existence for several hundred years as well, but has not been widely ac-

Table 3.1 The Contrasting Conventional and Constructivist Belief Systems

CONVENTIONAL BELIEFS	CONSTRUCTIVIST BELIEFS
Ontology:	
A REALIST ONTOLOGY asserts that there exists a single reality that is independent of any observer's interest in it and which operates according to immutable natural laws, many of which take cause-effect form. Truth is defined as that set of statements that is isomorphic to reality.	A RELATIVIST ONTOLOGY asserts that there exist multiple, socially constructed realities ungoverned by any natural laws, causal or otherwise. "Truth" is defined as the best informed (amount and quality of information) and most sophisticated (power with which the information is understood and used) construction on which there is consensus (although there may be several constructions extant that simultaneously meet that criterion).
Epistemology:	
A DUALIST OBJECTIVIST EPISTEMOLOGY asserts that it is possible (indeed, mandatory) for an observer to exteriorize the phenomenon studied, remaining detached and distant from it (a state often called "subject-object dualism"), and excluding any value considerations from influencing it.	A MONISITIC, SUBJECTIVIST EPISTEMOLOGY asserts that an inquirer and the inquired-into are interlocked in such a way that the findings of an investigation are the *literal creation* of the inquiry process. Note that this posture effectively destroys the classical ontology-epistemology distinction.
Methodology:	
AN INTERVENTIONIST METHODOLOGY strips context of its contaminating (confounding) influences (variables) so that the inquiry can converge on truth and explain nature as it really is and really works, leading to the capability to predict and to control.	A HERMENEUTIC METHODOLOGY involves a continuing dialectic of iteration, analysis, critique, reiteration, reanalysis, and so on, leading to the emergence of a joint (among all the inquirers and respondents, or among etic and emic views) construction of a case.

cepted or understood, particularly in English-speaking countries. It has nevertheless now emerged as a serious competitor to the conventional paradigm. It is our contention that the conventional paradigm is undergoing a revolution in the Kuhnian sense (Kuhn, 1970), and that the constructivist paradigm is its logical successor. The reader may wish to consult our earlier work for references to other paradigms that have been in vogue at different historical times.

We turn our attention to the ways in which the conventional and the constructivist paradigms deal with the three questions:

(1) *Ontology.* The ontological question is answered by adherents of the conventional paradigm by asserting that there exists an objective reality, "out there," which goes on about its busines irrespective of the interest that an inquirer may have in it: a *realist* ontology. In answer to the age-old party question, "If a tree falls in a woods when there is no one there to hear it, does it make a noise?" the answer is, "Of course!" The task of science is to discover nature "as it really is," and "as it really works," including its driving mechanisms. An earlier version of realist ontology, often called *naive* realism, held not only that reality existed but that disciplined inquiry could eventually converge onto it. This version has been almost universally rejected in favor of another, often called *critical* realism (see, for example, Cook & Campbell, 1979), recently updated as critical multiplism (Cook, 1985). This view holds that it is impossible to discover reality except within some particular, usually disciplinary, perspective. Nevertheless, even the critical realist view does at bottom rest on a belief in a substantial reality; its view is like the blind men discovering the elephant, for there really *is* an elephant.

This reality is not just an inert mass of "stuff," however. Things go on in that real world, and the *way* in which they go on is determined entirely by certain natural laws (the root belief of which is often called *determinism*). It is because of the existence of such driving laws that science can hope to fulfill its prime directive—to predict and to control. For if there is no order in nature there is no hope that personkind can manage or exploit nature in its own interest.

Many of these underlying laws take the form of cause-effect relationships. Prediction can, after all, be accomplished on purely statistical—correlational—bases. But control requires that natural phenomena be managed—be *made* to act in desired ways. For that to be possible it is necessary for nature itself to be arranged in if-then relationships. It is the discovery of causal laws that represents the bottom line for scientists. Knowing the causes of motion ultimately enables us to send rockets to the moon, knowing the cause of cancer ultimately will enable us to cure it, knowing the causes of the Cold War will ultimately enable us to defrost it, and so on.

The ontological question is answered by adherents of the constructivist paradigm by asserting that there exist multiple, socially constructed realities ungoverned by natural laws, causal or otherwise: a *relativist* ontology. These constructions are devised by individuals as they attempt to make sense of their experiences, which, it should be recalled, are always *interactive* in nature. Phenomena are defined depending on the kind and amount of prior knowledge and the level of sophistication that the constructor brings to the task. Constructions can be and usually are shared, ranging all the way from constructions about subatomic particles to those about cultural mores. That does not make them any more *real* but simply more *commonly assented to.*

It may well be the case, the constructivist might admit, that among things included in a construction are some lawlike attributions. But there is a world of difference between believing that there is some law that one has "discovered" in nature versus believing that it may be useful for a variety of purposes to think in lawlike terms. Thus it may have utility to imagine that one can cause the lights to go on by flipping the switch, but that is not equivalent to saying that "the cause of the light going on is the switch being flipped," as though that statement asserted something fundamental about nature. If there is no objective reality then there are no natural laws, and cause-effect attributions are simply that—mental imputations.

Given these two very different ontological forumations, it is not surprising that what is taken to constitute truth should also differ. Conventionally, truth is any assertion, whether about entitites or their relationships, that is *isomorphic,* that is, that stands in a one-to-one relationship to objective reality. The ultimate test of the validity of any inquiry findings is that they should describe reality *exactly.*[3] On the other hand, "truth" (and note the use of quotation marks to indicate the problematic nature of the term in this case) is defined in the constructivist paradigm simply as that most informed and sophisticated construction on which there is consensus among individuals most competent (not necessarily most powerful) to form such a construction. It is dubious that the constructivist paradigm requires a term like *truth,* which has a final or ultimate ring to it. Multiple constructions that meet the "most informed and sophisticated" criterion *can* exist side by side, a state of affairs well illustrated by the continuing differences of opinion among vanguard thinkers in every field, whether it be economics or physics. Certainly any construction is continuously open to alteration, however it may be treated at some point in time regarding its "truth." As we have already noted, the moral imperative laid upon adherents of the naturalistic paradigm is that they continuously seek out challenging constructions with which to confront their own. Finally, the development of ever more informed and sophisticated constructions should not be understood to mean that they are "truer" constructions; they are simply more informed and sophisticated. They may become harder and harder to challenge, but they can be overthrown in an instant should some really disruptive insight come to light.

(2) *Epistemology.* How the epistemological question is dealt with depends, in the first instance, on how the ontological question has already been answered. For example, if you assert that there exists an objective reality that goes on about its business despite any interest that an inquirer may have in it, it seems entirely appropriate to require that the inquirer should maintain an objective distance while studying it. Subjectivity would inevitably lead to distortion; the inquirer would not see nature "as it really is" or "as it really works" but only through the dark glasses of some bias or prejudice. On the other hand, if you assert that reality consists of a series of mental constructions, objectivity does not make sense; only interactivity can lead to a construction or its subsequent reconstruction. Taking either a realist or a relativist posture with respect to ontology places constraints on the ways in which the epistemological question can be answered.

The epistemological question is answered by adherents of the conventional paradigm by asserting, first, that it is possible to maintain an objective, "exteriorized" posture, a dualism, with respect to the phenomenon being studied, and, second, that it is possible to exclude, as part of this dualism, the values held by the inquirer or any other individual, including clients or sponsors of investigations or (need we say it?) stakeholders. It is this posture that provides a warrant for asserting that scientific data must be absolutely accepted, for if they were properly obtained, they are free of any possible taint of subjectivity, bias, or disjunctive values. Inquiry can, in short, be both objective and value-free.

The epistemological question is answered by adherents of the constructivist paradigm by asserting that it is impossible to separate the inquirer from the inquired into. It is precisely their interaction that creates the data that will emerge from the inquiry. Since this is so, the constructivist position effectively eliminates the ontology–epistemology distinction. For if what-there-is-that-can-be-known does not exist independently but only in connection with an inquiry process (which need not be formalized, of course), then it is not possible to ask the questions, "What is there that can be known?" and "What is the relationship of the knower and the known?" independently.

Furthermore, an inevitable element in the inquiry mix is the values of the inquirer and a whole variety of other persons in and around the inquiry. Inquirers are human, and cannot escape their humanness. That is, they cannot by an act of will set aside their own subjectivity, nor can they stand outside the arena of humanness created by the other persons involved. The values of the inquirer (and of those who influence him or her, especially funders, sponsors, and professional peers) inevitably enter the inquiry in connection with the whole series of decisions involved in designing, mounting, and monitoring. The values of involved individuals, especially those from whom information is solicited (whom we much prefer to call *respondents* rather than *subjects*) also exert influence, not only if they are given some modicum of control over the inquiry, but also because inquiries always take place in value contexts. Values are reflected in the theory that may undergird the inquiry (for example, a theory of reading), in the constructions that the inquirer and others bring to the inquiry, and in the inquiry paradigm itself. Morever, all of these values may be disjunctive—for example, there may be a value conflict between the theory undergirding an inquiry and the paradigm that guides it (a situation we shall later refer to as value dissonance). For all these reasons, say the constructivists, values cannot be ignored; their very influential role in all inquiry must be acknowledged.

(3) *Methodology.* Just as the response to the epistemological question depends on the prior response given to the ontological question, so the response to the methodological question in turn depends on the other two. Having assumed a realist ontology and an objectivist epistemology, it would make sense to adopt a methodology that might include covert

observation and misleading instructions to subjects in order to eliminate reactivity and make "real" behaviors apparent, for example. On the other hand, having assumed a relativist ontology and an interactive epistemology, the use of covert or misleading techniques would be exactly counterproductive; one could not hope to ascertain or to influence constructions by hiding the nature of the desired response from the respondents.

The methodological question is answered by adherents of the conventional paradigm by asserting that inquiry must be mounted in ways that strip the context of possible contaminating influences (confounding variables) so that "the way things really are" and "the way things really work" can emerge—an *interventionist* methodology. Structuring the inquiry so as to be able to discover (or test presumptions about) causal mechanisms is especially important. The ultimate pragmatic criterion of the methodology is that it must lead to successively better means for predicting and controlling phenomena. The key process is *explaining*: making clear the cause or reason for something. In order to reach unequivocal conclusions about causes or reasons, inquiries must be *controlled*. Either physical or statistical controls may be instituted, but both require intervention to accomplish.

The methodological question is answered by adherents of the constructivist paradigm by asserting that the inquiry must be carried out in a way that will expose the constructions of the variety of concerned parties, open each to critique in the terms of other constructions, and provide the opportunity for revised or entirely new constructions to emerge—a hermeneutic methodology. The ultimate pragmatic criterion for this methodology is that it leads to successively better *understanding*, that is, to *making sense* of the interaction in which one usually is engaged with others. In order to carry out such an inquiry, a process must be instituted that first iterates the variety of constructions (the sense-makings) that already exist, then analyzes those constructions to make their elements plain and communicable to others, solicits critiques for each construction from the holders of others, reiterates the constructions in light of new information or new levels of sophistication that may have been introduced, reanalyzes, and so on to consensus—or as close to consensus as one can manage. The process is *hermeneutic* in that it is aimed toward developing improved (joint) constructions, a meaning closely associated with the more traditional use of the term to denote the process of evolving successively more sophisticated interpretations of historical or sacred writings. It is dialectic in that it involves the juxtaposition of conflicting ideas, forcing reconsideration of previous positions.

These then are the basic beliefs undergirding the conventional and constructivist paradigms, stated in very truncated form. It is surely the case that the belief system of the conventional paradigm will sound much more "right" to those reared in Western culture (although constructivism may sound more familiar to the oriental reader, especially with a Buddhist background; see Zukav, 1979). Nevertheless, we plead for a suspension of disbelief, recalling our opening discussion of Euclidean geometry. We ask for a reservation of judgment until we have had the opportunity to demonstrate what a shift to the constructivist paradigm might mean, regardless of the apparent absurdity of its basic belief system.

Before proceeding to that task, however, it will be useful to consider very briefly what evidence can be introduced in favor of the proposition that the conventional paradigm should be rejected and to explore the "theorems" that can be deduced from these two belief systems. We undertake these tasks in the next two sections.

What Evidence Exists That Calls the Conventional Paradigm into Question?

It is utterly impossible to summarize in a few pages the welter of challenges that have come to the basic belief system undergirding conventional inquiry. We devoted most of six chapters in our earlier book, *Naturalistic Inquiry* (1985), to this task, and we urge the interested reader to consult that source. However, we will make a few observations here. The reader should not be deluded into believing that the shortness of our treatment is in direct proportion to the paucity of available evidence, for that is not the case. The evidence is, in our opinion, overwhelming, but that statement, like the basic beliefs themselves, lies beyond proof.

Ontology. The belief in a substantial universe operating according to fixed laws, like a great clockwork, permeated the thinking of virtually every scientist into the twentieth century. It seemed that science would soon converge on complete knowledge of the universe so that there would be nothing left for scientists to explore.[4] And then physics moved into the atomic age.

At first it was thought that the atom would, like everything else, be found to consist of discrete parts, which, once understood, could be synthesized into a model of what the atom looked like (that would be isomorphic to reality). But efforts at modeling were soon abandoned. The postulated subatomic structure consisting of protons, electrons, and neutrons turned out to be a vast oversimplification. New, smaller particles were discovered: positrons, neutrinos, and others. The latest count of different kinds of particles of which we, as laypersons, are aware stands at well over 100, and there seems to be little reason to suppose that the end is in sight. The apparently very substantial structure of matter that we sense at the macroscopic level appears on close examination to consist of ever smaller bits. Each time that science has been able to increase the power of its microscope, metaphorically speaking, that substantial reality becomes more and more insubstantial. Is what we take to be reality a mere illusion? Is it, as some have recently suggested, only a hologram constructed by our brains in response to some energy fields of which we are utterly unaware? Thoughts such as these have shaken the faith of scientists in the substantiality of matter and hence in everything we take to be real.

There were other problems. Physicists had been interested in the phenomenon of light for centuries, but it was not until 1803 that the "definitive" experiment was done showing light to be a wave. That conclusion was commonly accepted unitl 1905, when Einstein published a paper on the so-called photoelectric effect (as manifested, for example, in the variety of photoelectric cells that today turn on lamps, open doors, and perform other magic functions). Einstein's work suggested that light was composed of particles—they have since come to be called *photons* or *quanta* of light. If we accept *that* formulation, what are we to make of the definitive interpretation of light as a wave? The question, "What is light *really?*" suddenly becames a burning issue.

The view now is that light is not really anything, that light manifests itself in ways that depend entirely on the kind of apparatus we set up to detect it. The double-slit experiment that led to labeling light as a "wave" will always lead to wavelike results, *because that is the question we ask*. Photoelectric experiments will similarly always lead to particlelike results.

By 1926 a naive realist ontology was suffering its death throes. Reality seemed to disappear as one looked deeper and deeper into it, and it seemed to be the case that reality took on different forms depending on what questions were asked, and how. The assertion by Werner Heisenberg in 1927 of his Indeterminacy Principle added fuel to the fire. It stated, in effect, that the act of experimentation itself will determine the observed state of the phenomenon being studied, and that the decision to carry out an experiment in a certain way, while making certain observations possible, will invitably make certain others impossible.

Finally, it began to be apparent that the investigator was the key to all of this confusion. Not only did he or she limit, constrain, and direct the findings that could emerge by the particular acts of investigation that were chosen, he or she could be thought of as *creating* the "realities" that were observed. John Wheeler, a particle physicist first at Princeton and later Director of the Particle Laboratory at the University of Texas, asked:

> May the universe in some strange sense be "brought into being" by the participation of those who participate? . . . The vital act is the act of participation. "Participator" is the incontrovertible new concept given by quantum mechanics. It strikes down the term "observer" of classical theory, the man who stands safely behind the thick glass wall and watches what goes on without taking part. It can't be done, quantum mechanics notes. (cited in Zukav, 1979, p. 29)

The same John Wheeler provides an interesting metaphor to help us understand how findings can be "brought into being" by participation. He describes a game of "Twenty Questions" in which he was involved:

> Then my turn came, fourth to be sent from the room so that Lothar Nordheim's other fifteen after-dinner guests could consult in secret and agree on a difficult word. I was locked out unbelievably long. On finally being readmitted, I found a smile on everyone's face, sign of a joke or a plot. I nevertheless started on my attempt to find the word. "Is it animal?" "No." "Is it mineral?" "Yes." "Is it green?" "No." "Is it white?" "Yes." These answers came quickly. Then the questions began

to take longer in the answering. It was strange. All I wanted from my friends was a simple yes or no. Yet the one queried would think and think, yes or no, no or yes, before responding. Finally I felt I was getting hot on the trail, that the word might be "cloud." I knew I was allowed only one chance at the final word. I ventured it. "Is it cloud?" "Yes," came the reply, and everyone burst out laughing. They explained to me there had been no word in the room. They had agreed not to agree on a word. Each one questioned could answer as he pleased—with the one requirement that he should have a word in mind compatible with his own response and all that had gone before. Otherwise, if I challenged, he lost. The surprise version of the game was therefore as difficult for my colleagues as it was for me.

What is the symbolism of the story? The world, we once believed, exists "out there" independent of any act of observation. The electron in the atom we once considered to have at each moment a definite position and a definite momentum. I, entering, thought the room contained a definite word. In actuality the word was developed step by step through the questions I raised, as the information about the electron is brought into being by the experiment that the observer chooses to make; that is, by the kind of registering equipment that he puts into place. Had I asked different questions or the same questions in a different order I would have ended up with a different story as the experimenter would have ended up with a different story for the doings of the electron.... The comparison between the world of quantum observations and the surprise version of the game of twenty questions misses much but it makes the central point. In the game, no word is a word until that word is promoted to reality by the choice of questions asked and answers given. In the real world of quantum physics, *no elementary phenomenon is a phenomenon until it is a recorded phenomenon.* (cited in Davies & Brown, 1986, pp. 23-24)

Or as Jocko Conlan, a famous National League umpire, once put it when asked the difference between a ball and a strike, "They ain't nuttin' until I calls 'em!"

That the constructivist should counter the presumption of an objective reality with one of multiple, socially constructed realities is thus not so bizarre as may at first appear. Clearly the issue of what reality is, is very much up for grabs even in areas like physics in which we would suppose such questions to have been settled long ago. Instead, it is at the forefront of unresolved questions. And if that is the case in the "hard" sciences, how much more must it be true for the "soft"? Can terms like *organization, school, personality, academia, patient care, safetynet, curriculum, task, neurosis*, and the like, stand for anything "real," or are they more fruitfully viewed as constructions that can and should change with time?

The observation made by Lily Tomlin as part of her one-woman show, *The Search for Signs of Intelligent Life in the Universe* (Wagner, 1986), while uttered in jest, makes remarkably good sense to us:

> What is reality anyway? Nothin' but a collective hunch. I made some studies, and reality is the leading cause of stress amongst those in touch with it. I can take it in small doses, but as a life style I found it too confining. Now since I put reality on the back-burner, my days are jam-packed and fun-filled. (p. 18; used by permission of Harper & Row, Publishers, Inc.)

If the existence of an objective reality is as dubious as would seem to be the case, then the proposition that there exist natural laws, including those representing causal mechanisms, is also in serious trouble. And the available evidence bears out that contention.

It is the search for laws that has led scientists to place so much emphasis on being able to generalize from data. Without generalization the findings resulting from any given study would have meaning only in the particular situation and time in which they were found. Obviously purely local data cannot contribute to the development of a systematic body of knowledge that has widespread applicability. The ability to predict and control is lost.

But is it meaningful to search for generalizations? Perhaps it might be in a universe that is completely deterministic and that operates out of a single and consistent set of rules, that is, that could be thought of in reductionistic terms. But Gödel (Hofstadter, 1979) has shown mathematically that it is impossible to account for all phenomena from a single frame of reference, that is, from a single set of rules. One can have consistency or one can have singularity, but not both. Further, the concepts of reductionism and determinism are repugant to and inconsistent with our experience. To imagine that all human activity is completely determined by one human universal set of relationships simply does not square with our own practical insights. While we may not be prepared to accept the optimistic dictum that we are masters of our fates and captains of our souls, we are by no means prepared to accept its pessimistic alternative either.

There are other problems with the concept of generalization as well. We have already seen that generalizations have no meaning in relation to particulars: the nomothetic/idiographic dilemma. The gynecologist cannot order a hysterectomy simply because, in many cases, the symptoms presented by a patient happen to be linked to cervical cancer. But that seems to be only a practical objection; surely, it might be said, the gynecologist is led to look for cervical cancer in this particular patient because of the generalization that can be formed on the basis of statistics from other patients. But generalizations of that sort, if they are even properly called by that name, are a far cry from the kind of time- and context-free assertions that begin to approximate natural laws.

The question of whether there can be time- and context-free generalizations has been dealt with by Lee Cronbach in his 1975 presidential address to the American Psychological Association. In that classic paper Cronbach utilizes the metaphor of the radioactive substance continuously decaying and exhibiting a characteristic half-life:

> Generalizations decay. At one time a conclusion describes the existing situation well, at a later time it accounts for rather little variance, and ultimately it is valid *only as history.* The half-life of an empirical proposition may be great or small. The more open the system, the shorter the half-life of relations within it are likely to be.
>
> Propositions describing atoms and electrons have a long half-life, and the physical theorist can regard the processes of the world as steady. Rarely is a social or behavioral phenomenon *isolated enough* to have this steady state property. Hence the explanation we live by will perhaps always remain partial, and distant from real events . . . and rather short-lived. The atheoretical regularities of the actuary are even more time bound. An actuarial table describing human affairs *changes from science into history* before it can be set in type. (pp. 122-123; emphases added)

Cronbach's notion that all science eventually becomes history demolishes the proposition that generalizations are time-free. His comment about the need for isolation to ensure steady-state properties serves a similar function for the proposition of context-freedom. Generalizations inevitably decay over time, and they inevitably have contextual dependencies. They are clearly mental imputations and cannot be taken to represent unalterable aspects of nature itself.

But what about causality? Can we not rescue that extremely useful concept from the discard heap? Alas, the answer here also seems to be negative. As one might expect, there have been and continue to exist many attempts to reformulate the concept in more meaningful terms. For example, Travers (1980) avers that the primitive notion of causality has been replaced:

> Discussions of causal relationships in research are pre-Newtonian. ... Modern scientists do not use the concept of cause, except during chatty moments. Current psychological literature does not use the concept of cause, and substitutes have been offered. One substitute is the idea of *functional relationships*. At least that term manages to avoid the difficulties that Newton encountered. It simply implies that variables are related in a necessary and invariant way. Thus the radii of orbits of the planets, their periodicities, and their masses are related *functionally*. Only a pre-Newtonian would say that the gravitational pull of the sun *causes* the planets to stay in orbit. (Travers, Robert M.W., "Letter to Editor," *Educational Researcher*, 1980, p. 32; emphases in original; used by permission)

But preoccupation with the concept of causality continues, and there currently exist many formulations offered by persons who believe the concept to be useful and who wish to rescue it from its problems. The pre-Newtonian billiard-ball notion of causality referred to by Travers is indeed given scant attention, but other formulations—known by such names as the *deductive-nomological* (statements of causality are made by stating universal laws and necessary initial conditions; then showing that the initial conditions were met in some way); the *essentialist* (causes are those conditions necessary and sufficient to produce their effects); the *activity* (causal relationships can be inferred from human activity); the *counterfactual* (causes are demonstrated by showing that if they are absent the effect cannot occur); and the *probabilistic* (causes are statistically relevant factors)—abound. Yet all these models have been severely critiqued (the specifics depending on the particular model). But there is one criticism that applies to all these models that has special relevance for our argument here. As we assert in *Naturalistic Inquiry* (1985, p. 143), it has been impossible to divest the concept of causality—for those who wish to maintain it—of influences depending on "human experience, judgment, and insight." Among the examples one can cite to illustrate this point are these:

- Correlation does not imply causality, that is, recurrent regularity does not itself support a causal presumption unless and until some human supplies a logical reason to account for the connection.
- Human judgment is required to determine when a condition is necessary and sufficient to be taken as a cause and to know that no other causes are present that might account for the presumed effect.
- Human judgment is required to judge when a law is applicable and when and if the initial specified conditions are present and adequate to support a causal imputation.
- Causal imputations are usually made with a specific human purpose in mind. For example, the environmental biologist might say that the cause of malaria is the mosquito, because what he or she does is to spray swamplands to eliminate mosquito breeding grounds; while a hematologist might say that the cause of malaria is the introduction of plasmodia into the bloodstream because dealing with blood problems is what he or she does. The question of the "real" cause of malaria is meaningless.
- As Cook and Campbell (1979, p. 30) suggest, "The concept of causality is closely linked to intentions and purposes. Most causal inferences are about attributes of the world that are particularly relevant to an active, intrusive, willful organism."

All of this leads us to reject the traditional concept of causality and to replace it with a different human construction, that of "mutual simultaneous shaping." This construction recognizes (Lincoln & Guba, 1985) that:

- All elements in a situation are in mutual and continual interaction.

- Each element is activated in its own way by virtue of the particular configuration of all other elements—potential shapers—that is assumed at that time and in that place.
- Judgments about which of the potential shapers may most plausibly be implicated in explaining and/or managing whatever it is that the investigator wishes to explain or manage is a matter both of the circumstances that exist *and* of the investigator's purpose; the investigator asks him- or herself, "What is most plausible to invoke given that purpose?"
- The peculiar web or pattern of circumstances that characterizes a given situation may never occur in just that way again, so that explanations and management actions are in a real sense unique and cannot be understood as implying either predictability or control.
- Explanations are at best "here-and-now" accounts that represent a "photographic slice of life" of a dynamic process that, in the next instant, might present a very different aspect.

We believe that this formulation of mutual simultaneous shaping—itself, it should be noted, a matter of imputation or part of a mental construction—is a useful counterpart to the idea of multiple, socially constructed realities. Together these two ideas represent a response to the basic ontological question that is both more informed and sophisticated than the conventional response.

Epistemology. The idea that an observer ought to stand at a respectful distance from the phenomenon being studied is at least as old as Aristotle (Lincoln & Guba, 1985). Aristotle's contention was that only a *passive* observer could see nature as it really was; an active observer would distort nature and produce findings inconsistent with the natural state of things.

Positivism did away with the idea of a passive observer because of the need to control possible sources of contamination. It is necessary for the observer to intervene to the extent necessary to establish controls, but then, as Wheeler so aptly put it, the observer became "the man who stands safely behind the thick glass wall and watches what goes on without taking part" (cited in Zukav, 1979, p. 29). There are at least three countervailing points, however (Lincoln & Guba, 1985):

(1) *The phenomenon of reactivity.* It may be possible to overlook reactivity in physical or even biological experiments, but as soon as

inquiry is extended to include human behavior, that phenomenon can no longer be disregarded. Human respondents are *not* inert, passive objects. They are capable of a variety of meaning-ascribing and interpretative actions, and those possibilities are certainly not held in abeyance simple because the people are labeled "subjects" in an inquiry.

One of the advantages of so-called true experimental designs, to use the terminology introduced by Campbell & Stanley (1963), is that they prevent subject *reactivity* from influencing the outcomes of a study. But true experimental designs are almost impossible to mount in the "real" world; it was just for this reason that Campbell and Stanley were moved to propose *quasi-experimental* designs that *were* manageable in such a context. But quasi-designs are imperfect; they are subject to a variety of "threats" to their internal validity, not the least of which is human reactivity. Campbell and Stanley thus devote a great deal of attention to the question of how to "guard" against this threat, admitting that a complete defense is impossible and leaving the results of such quasi-studies forever open to challenge. This state of affairs represents one way in which the outcomes of a study are *in principle* indeterminate.

(2) *The phenomenon of indeterminacy.* We have already encountered Heisenberg's Indeterminacy Principle. That this principle should also apply to social and human inquiry is hardly surprising. Heisenberg argues that the particular experimental apparatus (reflecting the questions to be asked) that is set up by the investigator may lead to some observations but absolutely militate against others. In similar fashion, the scientist who approaches human "subjects" with a particular set of questions or hypotheses may set the stage for certain observations but may thereby be prevented from pursuing others. The main dynamics of a situation may be utterly missed. This is one of the major objections raised by Glaser and Strauss (1967) to the use of a priori (often, in their field of sociology, "Grand") theory. Application of that theory may lead to interesting results but may not necessarily "fit" and "work" in that situation. Designing a study to focus on one set of variables or concepts precludes (in positivist terms) pursuing others.

(3) *The phenomenon of interactivity.* Outcomes are not only indeterminate; they are *shaped during the course of the inquiry* by the interaction of the investigator and the object of inquiry. We are indebted to the

twenty question game metaphor of John Wheeler to let us understand
how that happens. As he suggests, there is a strong possibility that "the
world is brought into being by the participation of those who participate"
(cited in Zukav, 1979, p. 29). When the object of inquiry is itself a human
being or group of human beings, the number of "participators" is
increased and so is the range of created (and often unanticipated)
outcomes. The in-principle indeterminacy of outcomes is once again
illustrated.

Now this state of affairs is hardly surprising. We have noted that
theories and facts are not independent (Hesse, 1980); investigators "find"
facts that are consistent with the theories that they bring to bear. Human
inquiry is inherently dialectical, reflecting conflicts and contradictions in
constructions. Meaningful human inquiry is impossible without the full
understanding and cooperation of respondents. Insofar as the human
investigator is him- or herself often the major instrument, interaction is
required to allow the full potentialities of that instrument to emerge.
And, finally, inquiry is always shaped by human values.

This last point seems to us to be especially important. Despite the
claim of positivists to the contrary, it is not possible to separate values
from inquiry, especially in the case of human inquiry. The idea that facts
relate to the "real" world (what is) while values relate to some sort of
conjured-up "desirable" world (what ought to be) is simply not tenable.
Consider the following:

(1) We have already noted the impossibility of maintaining separate
theoretical and observational languages. Theoretical languages necessarily involve values because no theory is all encompassing (nor can it be,
according to Gödel's Theorem; Hofstadter, 1979). Choices must be made,
and when choices are involved, values come into play at the choice points.

(2) The history of science is replete with examples of the interplay of
science and values. We refer the reader to *Naturalistic Inquiry* for several
classic examples: the conflict between Galilean astronomy and biblical
ascriptions; the influence of British/French politics on the dissemination
and acceptance of Lavosier's oxygen theory in the eighteenth century;
the *ad hominem* attacks on one another by Darwinian and Lamarckian
evolution theorists while presumably mounting scientific arguments over
the merits of their positions; the particular interpretation of certain

experimental data made by North American psychologists which seemed to their British counterparts to reflect political and cultural biases rather than scientific judgments.

(3) There is a growing body of literature, written in the main by individuals who do *not* see themselves outside the pale of the conventional paradigm, that rejects the idea of a value-free science, notably Bahm (1971), Homans (1978), Kelman (1968), Krathwohl (1980), Morgan and Smircich (1980), and Scriven (1971).

(4) The belief in a value-free science has led to a number of very undesirable consequences (Schwandt, 1980), including:

- *The ritual of method:* Truth becomes defined as the result of an appropriate inquiry methodology, namely, the experiment conducted in a value-free context.

- *Restriction on range of admissable knowledge:* Only those facts accessible to the approved value-free method can count as knowledge.

- *Misdefinition of coherence:* Value-free inquiries are said to display coherence because of their putative imperviousness to any values that might "bias" them. But it is likely that coherence results from nothing more than stability (reliability).

- *Moral inversion:* The fact that value claims *precede* the selection of designs, instruments, and so on (point 3 above) is obfuscated; values are seen as coming into play only during the interpretative phase of a study.

- *False imputation of normative force:* The claim of value-freedom is seen as a license to the investigator to tease out the normative implications of findings while legitimizing them as "facts."

- *Forcing political decisions into a technical mode:* Scientific findings are said to have a special claim on decision makers precisely because they are free from value implications; persons engaging in political decision making are especially pressed to be "rational" in giving scientific data top priority.

- *Inappropriate legitimation:* Putatively value-free facts must be taken at face value; they represent the way "things really are" rather than the way "we would like them to be."

- *Obscuring of balance:* Perspectives that do not accord precisely with the scientific "facts" are dismissed as irrelevant; they are unfairly said to represent mere bias.

These are arguments against the claim of value-freedom, but there is more to be said than just to argue. It is possible to demonstrate that values *do* impinge on inquiry, so that the safest and most intelligent course is to admit that fact and use it to one's advantage. Values enter into inquiry because of hte *personal* choices made by the investigator (often in concert with the values of the funder, the sponsor, or other powerful stakeholding figure). They enter via the *theory* that the investigator elects to bring to bear, which itself represents a value choice from among other possible theories. They enter because of the *paradigm* used to guide the inquiry— and if by this time the reader is unaware or disbelieves that paradigms do reflect different values, he or she has somehow missed a major point of this book. They enter because all inquiry on humans or involving humans is carried out in some *local value context.* Anyone evaluating biology textbooks for use in a religiously conservative state had better be aware of that fact, for example. And finally, values play a role in that the values emanating from any two or more of these other sources may be *resonant or dissonant.* The case in which the theoretical values and paradigm values are dissonant is especially interesting; the reader is referred to *Naturalistic Inquiry* for a discussion of this problem.

If values can be seen as a possible source of contamination in a study of physical or biological objects, they must be viewed as inevitable accompaniments to human inquiry. They cannot be regarded, however, simply as distractors or nuisances that interfere with the efficient conduct of the inquiry, eating up time and resources to control. Instead, values must be accorded a central place in human study because they come closer to the core of humanness than most other characteristics of people. Values provide the basis for ascribing meaning and reaching understanding; an interpretive, constructivist paradigm cannot do without them.

Methodology. The previous discussion of ontology and epistemology was intended to provide the rationale for switching to the constructivist paradigm in the conduct of human inquiry. The methodology of the constructivist paradigm flows from the basic beliefs expressed in its ontological and epistemological positions, as is the case for the conventional paradigm as well. However, the methodology of the paradigm is far more important to us as inquiry practitioners than its philosophic roots. Accordingly, we will not deal with this subject here, but reserve a full discussion for Chapter 6, in which the methodology is developed, and Chapter 7, in which it is specifically applied to fourth generation evaluation. The impatient reader can skip ahead to those chapters, or, alternatively, review the chapter on methodology in *Naturalistic Inquiry* (Lincoln & Guba, 1985) (while being forewarned that much of that chapter is now outdated).

Some Theorems

We had a twofold purpose in mind in introducing the metaphor of Euclidean geometry at the beginning of this chapter. First, we wanted to make the point that, while the basic beliefs of constructivism might sound bizarre to anyone heavily socialized to the scientific paradigm (as everyone in our culture has been), that fact alone ought not be sufficient warrant to reject constructivism without giving it a fair hearing. Second, we had in mind to extend the metaphor by proposing certain parallel and contrasting theorems derivable from the basic axioms that further illustrate the great gap between these belief systems, and suggesting the implications that ensue from following each. We will take up a discussion of such theorems now.

We must again stress that our use of the term *theorem* is different from that of Euclidean geometry. The latter theorems have all been shown, by a formal deductive process, to be logically derivable from, and dependent on, the axioms. The theorems we propose here have not undergone such a rigorous test; we hope, however, that they will appear to be consistent with their respective paradigms on their face. The reader obviously has the right to take exception to that claim.

We shall first propose a number of theorems that apply, in our judgment, to all forms of inquiry,[5] of which evaluation is surely one. But, in addition, we shall propose some theorems which we believe have relevance for evaluation in particular.

Theorems Applying to All Forms of Inquiry

(1) Inquiry problematic.
 Conventional: Scientific inquiry *is not* problematic; it is the naturally sanctioned way to determine the definitive and enduring truth about states of affairs.

Constructivist:	Constructivist inquiry *is* problematic; it is the humanly devised way to entertain constructions about states of affairs that are subject to continuous refinement, revision, and, if necessary, replacement.
Comment:	This theorem follows directly from the basic ontological assumption of an objective reality, on the one hand, and of socially constructed realities, on the other.

(2) Nature of Truth.

Conventional:	The truth of any proposition (its factual quality) can be determined by testing it empirically in the natural world. Any proposition that has withstood such a test is true; such truth is absolute.
Constructivist:	The "truth" of any proposition (its credibility) can be determined by submitting it semiotically to the judgment of a group of informed and sophisticated holders of what may be different constructions. Any proposition that has achieved consensus through such a test is regarded as "true" until reconstructed in the light of more information or increased sophistication; any "truth" is relative.
Comment:	Both forms of this theorem follow logically from the separate ontological propositions. Tests are carried out empirically, that is, by experience or experiment, on the one hand, but semiotically, that is, via signs and symbols, usually language, that permit sharing of a construction among multiple parties, on the other. Scientific truth represents things as they really are; constructivist "truth" represents tentative agreements or consensus among qualified persons who find the proposition credible.

(3) Limits of truth.

Conventional:	A proposition that has not been tested empirically cannot be known to be true. Likewise, a proposition incapable of empirical test can never be confirmed to be true.
Constructivist:	A proposition is neither tested nor untested. It can only be known to be "true" (credible) in relation to and in terms of informed and sophisticated constructions.
Comment:	This theorem follows from Theorem 2 above.

(4) Measurability.

Conventional:	Whatever exists exists in some measurable amount. If it cannot be measured it does not exist.
Constructivist:	Constructions exist only in the minds of constructors and typically cannot be divided into measurable entities. If

something can be measured, the measurement *may fit* into some construction but it is likely, at best, to play a supportive role.

Comment: The conventional form of this theorem undergirds all measurement theory. It is ofen used as a rationalization for asserting that data must be quantified to be meaningful. The constructivist form admits a much wider range of information, *including quantitative,* but does not assign quantitative information the same central position.

(5) Independence of facts and theories.

Conventional: Facts are aspects of the natural world that do not depend on the theories that happen to guide any given inquiry. Observational and theoretical languages are independent.

Constructivist: "Facts" are always theory-laden, that is, they have no independent meaning except within some theoretical framework. There can be no separate observational and theoretical languages.

Comment: The constructivist's claim that there can be no separate observational and theoretical languages follows from the presumption that realities are mental constructions. Thus their elements ("facts") and their organizational structure cannot be independent. The conventionalist's claim rests on a realist ontology. The maintenance of the fact/value distinction is crucial to the conventional argument, however, since Theorem 2 above has no meaning without it.

(6) Independence of facts and values.

Conventional: Facts and values are independent. Facts can be uncovered and arrayed independently of the values that may later be brought to bear to interpret or give meaning to them. There are separate factual and valuational languages, the former describing "isness" and the latter "oughtness".

Constructivist: "Facts" and "values" are interdependent. "Facts" have no meaning except within some value framework; they are value-laden. There can be no separate observational and valuational languages.

Comment: The claim for independence of facts and values rests, for the conventionalist, on the assertion of an objective epistemology. It is, the constructivist avers, an absurd claim in view of the assertion of an interactive epistemology.

(7) Causation.

Conventional: Every observed action (effect) has a cause, and every cause has an effect.

Constructivist: Any observed action is the instantaneous resolution of a large number of mutual, simultaneous shapers, each of which is constantly shaping, and being shaped by, all other shapers.

Comment: The conventional version of this theorem follows from the ontological presumption that nature is driven by certain immutable laws. The metaphor is one of a great machine in which everything is linked; the action of any part inevitably induces an appropriate counteraction (effect) in some other part(s). The constructivist version argues from the base of continuous reconstruction; anything that happens provides new information or provides a press for increased sophistication. But such reconstruction does not occur in simple linear pathways.

(8) Root causes.

Conventional: It is always possible, *in principle,* to determine the root cause of any observed action (although that may prove to be virtually intractable in practice).

Constructivist: One or several mutual simultaneous shapers may be singled out *arbitrarily* for some specific purpose.

Comment: If the metaphor for nature is that of a great machine, then it is possible to follow linkages back and forth to discover that linkage which has produced or resulted in the action in which the inquirer is interested. The constructivist avers that such singling out, itself a mental imputation, is arbitrary, meaningful only for given, limited purposes. So for example, a new curriculum (an evaluand) may be taken to be the dominant shaper of learning by a curriculum developer, while a school ethnographer may instead single out the school's peer culture for that honor.

(9) Successful inquiry.

Conventional: The determination of root causes is the basis for scientific prediction and control. The success of a science can be judged on whether it displays ever-increasing ability to predict and control its phenomena (the ultimate pragmatic criterion for scientific inquiry, Hesse, 1980).

Constructivist: The positing of a shaper or shapers as key in some action provides a basis for purposively simplifying an otherwise very complex field. The success of constructivist inquiry can be judged on whether it displays ever-increasing understanding of its phenomena (the ultimate constructivist criterion for naturalistic inquiry).

Comment: The ability to isolate and identify root causes makes it possible for the conventional scientist to view increasing prediction and control as the most useful criterion for judging the success of inquiry efforts across an area or discipline. On the other hand, the constructivist cannot define such a key role for what are at best only simplifying decisions. However, in some context, if simplification leads to better understanding, it is useful.

(10) The genesis of problems.

Conventional: Phenomena, including problems, scientifically identified are real and have widespread significance, that is, they will be noted in many contexts, and they are generalizable.

Constructivist: Phenomena, including problems, exist only within some construction(s) and have no meaning except in that context in which they are identified and described.

Comment: If science is the way to discover how things really are and the way things really work, then the products of science, including problems, have reality. And if problems exist, they must have a cause, and if they have a cause, that cause can be responded to. The constructivist rejects such a line of reasoning, arguing that if problems are embedded in constructions, it is the construction that must receive attention.

(11) Applicability of problem solutions.

Conventional: Scientifically devised problem solutions have widespread applicability.

Constructivist: Problem solutions devised through reconstruction have local applicability only.

Comment: Both of these positions depend on the respective beliefs regarding generalizability (the existence of universal truths).

(12) Stability of problem solutions.

Conventional: Problem solutions are stable; when these solutions are introduced into specific contexts they will maintain their characteristics over time.

Constructivist: Problem solutions change; when these solutions are introduced into specific contexts they will be at least as much affected (changed) by those contexts as they are likely to affect them.

Comment: This theorem follows from Theorems 7 and 11, above. The conventionalist sees solutions as scientifically designed and developed to be responsive to certain problems; once they are put into place they will continue to deliver whatever curative, restorative or ameliorative power they have. The constructivist realizes that the processes of reconstruction go on continuously, so that any constructed solution is likely to be itself radically changed over time, with its putative curative, restorative, or ameliorative power also altered, redirected, eliminated, or even reversed.

(13) The change process.

Conventional: Change is a process that must be stimulated by outside forces. The natural state of affairs is at best to maintain the status quo and at worst to disintegrate to the lowest organizational/energy level possible (entropy). Change is a process that must be managed.

Constructivist: Change is a continuously ongoing process that requires neither outside stimulation nor direction, even though at times such intervention may be useful. Outside management may often impede change rather than promote it.

Comment: The mechanistic model of the universe persuades the conventionalist that humans, like machines, can run only if there is some outside source of energy continuously provided. Left to their own devices humans will always take the path of least resistance. The constructivist argues that the actions people take depend in the last analysis on the constructions they hold. If there is to be outside stimulation it is most usefully applied in the form of information/sophistication that leads to reconstruction.

(14) Implementing the change process.

Conventional: Change is a linear process that moves through stages from research (basic inquiry) through development (applied inquiry) through diffusion to adoption. Each stage looks to the preceding one for its inputs and provides output to the following stage.

Constructivist: Change is a nonlinear process that involves the infusion of new information and increased sophistication in its use into the constructions of involved human constructors. The infusion received from constructivist inquiry is but one kind that will be and probably should be taken into account.

Comment: The conventionalist appropriately organizes the change process into stages that begin with the "discovery" of scientific information (which might include the needs of target audiences). The information is then put through a cycle of development to produce whatever the scientific information indicates is needed. That developed product is then disseminated (creating awareness in target audiences and making the product available for adoption), and, finally, adopted. The constructivist focuses not on scientifically justified products but on changed constructions, noting that not all information that enters into constructions can or should be information gleaned from some kind of disciplined inquiry.

Theorems Applying More Specifically to Evaluation

(15) Nature of evaluation.

Conventional: Evaluation is a form of scientific inquiry and hence has all the attributes of that genre.

Constructivist: Evaluation is a form of constructivist inquiry and hence has all the attributes of that genre.

Comment: This theorem simply states that all of the theorems developed above also apply to evaluation, in either paradigm.

(16) Values and evaluation.

Conventional: Evaluation produces data untainted by values. Values are intrusive to the evaluation process and distort scientific data by, for example, biasing them.

Constructivist: Evaluation produces reconstructions in which "facts" and "values" are inextricably linked. Valuing is an intrinsic part of the evaluation process, providing the basis for attributed meaning.

Comment: This theorem is an application of Theorem 6 above to evaluation.

(17) Accountability.

Conventional: Accountability can always be assigned because it is determinable via the relevant cause-effect chain.

Constructivist: Accountability is a characteristic of a conglomerate of mutual and simultaneous shapers, no one of which nor one subset of which can be uniquely singled out for praise or blame.

Comment: This theorem is a consequence of the theorems on cause/effect (or mutual simultaneous shapers) outlined above. It is a theorem of great consequence for evaluators, who are often called upon to determine what went wrong and why and, in particular, *who is to blame*. If, as we have suggested, scientific inquiry can be an instrument for maintaining the status quo, particularly, the power of those already in power, the possibly tragic consequences of believing that someone can always be found to bear the accountability burden can more fully be appreciated.

(18) Objectivity of evaluation findings.

Conventional: Evaluators can find a place to stand that will support the objective pursuit of evaluation activities.

Constructivist: Evaluators are subjective partners with stakeholders in the literal creation of evaluation data.

Comment: The conventional form of this theorem is a powerful warrant for evaluators to assume a godlike posture with respect to their findings. They become simple messengers for the messages that nature chooses to send, and thereby their findings are set above challenge. The posture taken by the constructivist is much more humbling, and makes the evaluator an *accountable partner* in the evaluation process.

(19) Function of evaluators.

Conventional: Evaluators are the communication channels through which literally true data are passed to the audience of evaluation reports.

Constructivist: Evaluators are orchestrators of a negotiation process that aims to culminate in consensus on better informed and more sophisticated constructions.

Comment: This theorem is the complement to Theorem 18 above.

(20) Legitimacy of evaluation findings.

Conventional: Scientific evaluation data have special legitimacy and special status that confer on them priority over all other considerations.

Constructivist: Constructivist evaluation data have neither special status nor legitimation; they represent simply another con-

| | struction to be taken into account in the move toward consensus. |
| Comment: | For the conventionalist, evaluation data, representing as they do "how things really are" and "how things really work," provide no "wriggle room"; they must be accepted as the dicta of nature. The naturalist, primarily concerned with reconstruction, does not view evaluation data (information collected in response to claims, concerns, and issues) as having any special power; instead, they are simply items of information to be fed into the negotiation process. |

These, then, are the theorems that we suggest explicitly or implicitly guide conventional and constructivist inquiry and evaluation. We urge the reader not to pass over them lightly; they are basic to an understanding of most of the observations we make in the rest of this book. No doubt there are other theorems, for both paradigms, that we have overlooked. And perhaps our formulation of these theorems deserves challenge. We would be pleased to have additions, shortcomings, or misstatements called to our attention.

A Final Caveat

Our experience in presenting the constructivist paradigm to a variety of audiences over the past ten or more years leads us to realize that a number of confusions exist about the distinctions we make. Moreover, we are often thought to be intransigent in our insistence that the two paradigms are *not* accommodatable, at least, in the present state of the dialectic between adherents of the two camps (and we use this military term advisedly). It may be appropriate at this point to posit and argue against a number of positions often proposed to us:

(1) *The "friendly confines" syndrome.* One of us (Guba) grew up in Chicago and was a great fan of the National League Cubs baseball team. In his younger days he would listen to Cubs games on the radio. Those that were "away" were often "reconstructed" by the announcer from ticker tape information, but those "at home" were "called live," and on those occasions, the announcer would often comment on how good it

was for the Cubs to be "back in the friendly confines of Wrigley Field." Now at Indiana University, Guba welcomes its basketball team back to the "friendly confines of Assembly Hall."

Everyone prefers to play on the home field. There is a home field advantage, after all, and at home one does not have to live out of a suitcase. If athletic teams could manage it they would play all their games at home. And if an inquiry game is to be played, it is better to play *that* in friendly confines too. This time the friendly confines are found in the conventional paradigm.

If there are problems with the conventional paradigm, why not do something specifically about them? Why throw out the baby with the bath? Surely there is little more at stake than redressing some imbalances that have unfortunately occurred. And so:

(a) In the trade-off between rigor and relevance, we have allowed ourselves to become much too preoccupied with internal validity, and external validity has suffered. But there is a solution for that problem, namely, to carry out inquiry in more natural settings with less overt control.

(b) In the trade-off between precision and richness, we have allowed ourselves to become much too preoccupied with precision and have overlooked the rich store of anecdotal and contextual data that would add depth and meaning to the discussion. But there is a solution for that problem, namely, to carry out inquiry in ways that include more qualitative data.

(c) In the trade-off between elegance and applicability, we have allowed ourselves to become much too preoccupied with a priori theory of scope and intricacy and have overlooked the possibility that the theory does not fit or work very well in local situations. But there is a solution for that problem, namely, to carry out inquiry in ways that allow theory to emerge in grounded form rather than be given ahead of time, at least in all of its details.

(d) In the trade-off between objectivity and subjectivity, we have allowed ourselves to become too preoccupied with objectivity, and have overlooked the inevitable interaction between inquirer and inquired-into, and the influence that interaction may have on the outcomes of inquiry. But there is a solution to that problem, namely, to require the inquirer to "come clean" about predispositions and feelings, and rely on critical tradition (e.g., aggregated knowledge) and the existence of a critical community (e.g., journal editors) to expose (eventually) whatever biases may exist.

(e) In the trade-off between verification and discovery, we have allowed ourselves to overlook the latter (perhaps recognizing it in terms such as "creativity," "insights," or "mental experiments") while stressing the former as the "bread-and-butter" act of science. But there is a solution, namely, to define science as existing on a continuum with discovery at one end and verification at the other. Thus any given inquiry can be located somewhere along the continuum, and each process is given its due.

Now very few persons would argue that making such adjustments would have no utility; on the contrary, they would probably improve conventional inquiry a great deal. We think these adjustments serve as the main distinction between positivism and postpositivism. *But the inquiry remains conventional;* the game, is still played within the friendly confines of positivism, the old paradigm.

(2) *The "muddy boots" syndrome.* Positivists have long recognized that there is more to science than the verificatory processes included in the usual received view—the conventional reconstructed logic. The insights, ideas, intuitions, and the like that lead to systematic inquiry must originate somewhere. And that task, they say, is ideal for the constructivist approach. Discovery processes are needed when an area is being studied about which little is known, where there is little insight into the crucial variables or what theory to bring to bear and the like. It is the task of the constructivist approach to provide these. Once such initial insights have been achieved, it is time to develop rigorous questions and hypotheses that are best tested by the verificatory methods of science.

We refer to this as the "muddy boots" syndrome because of a metaphor we are fond of using. Imagine the constructivist, in high boots, jeans, checkered shirt, and other accoutrements of life in the wild, mucking around trying to unearth things of interest. He or she reaches down, selects this clod, that stone, this artifact, all the while looking for something worth pursuing further. At last he or she finds it! Hands dripping with the mud and slop of the field, the constructivist passes the "find" to the conventionalist, who stands at the edge of the field, safely up on a platform, in white coat, polished shoes, and necktie, wearing long rubber gloves. He takes the object we so enthusiastically hold up, being careful not to let the mud drip on any part of him or her. "Look what we've got," we constructivists chorus! "Yes, well," says the conventionalist, "we'll soon see if you have got it right!"

The point is that the naturalistic paradigm is a full-time competitor, not simply a handmaiden to carry out the less interesting (and unrewarding) parts of the task. Constructivism sees itself as fully competent to carry out both discovery *and* verification; if the conventional paradigm is thought to be deficient on the discovery end, well, that's another problem, isn't it?

(3) *The "horse race" challenge.* It is sometimes proposed that the relative quality of the two paradigms should be determined by carrying out a common study, each in its own way, and then judging the outcomes to see which approach provides the "best" data or most insightful findings. But such a horserace would be singularly unproductive. First, it should be clear from the discussion so far that what constitutes a significant problem is likely to be very different in the two paradigms; if a problem *could* be found that could be attacked in one paradigm, it would likely be trivial in the other paradigm. Second, the inquiry products are also likely to be very different: putative "truths" of nature (the way things really are or really work) in the one case, believed to have enduring value, and consensual constructions in the other case, which the constructors hope to overturn as quickly as possible. The products would clearly be noncomparable. Third, even assuming that comparable products might emerge, the criteria for judging their goodness (see Chapter 8) would also vary; there is a vast difference, for example, in asserting that some datum is isomorphic to reality versus saying that it is credible to some constructors. On all three grounds, then, the proposal of a "horse race" is not likely to prove very useful.

(4) *The "proposal of marriage."* As the history of paradigm revolutions indicates (see, for example, Kuhn, 1970), the first response of advocates of a challenged paradigm is to dismiss the challenge as inconsequential, perhaps proposed by "snake-oil salesmen" intending to lead the profession up the proverbial primrose path. But, when it becomes clear that the

challenger can no longer be ignored, the preferred response is to deny the validity of the challenger's position. When the denials of validity no longer work, a kind of "if you can't lick 'em, join 'em" reaction sets in, but it takes the form of saying, "If you can't lick 'em, persuade 'em to join you!" The approach argues that the differences are "not all that different" and that accommodation is surely possible. Indeed, the five efforts at redressing imbalances discussed just above (more natural settings, more qualitative data, grounded theory, "softened" objectivity, and definition of a discovery-verification continuum) are sometimes said to effect just the kind of accommodation needed. The "muddy boots" delegation of complementary roles is another such effort.

But we feel that such calls to ecumenicism will be useless. If there is ever to be an accommodation, it will not be because one paradigm will finally prevail by the sheer power of its arguments, or because paradigms can play complementary roles, or because one paradigm will turn out to be a special case of the other. It will come about, if ever, because adherents of both paradigms will agree to engage in a hermeneutic dialectic discussion that will result in a new construction with which all can agree, not because the new construction is "truer" than other of its predecessors but because it is better informed and more sophisticated.

It is our earnest interest to work toward that goal.

Notes

1. Readers who have followed our work will note that our treatment of the basic axioms differs rather markedly from that of our 1985 book *Naturalistic Inquiry*. In that work we dealt with five axioms, whereas in the present work we deal with three broad philosophic considerations: the ontological, the epistemological, and the methodological. We feel that our current formulation is an improvement over the earlier one and more easily followed by persons to whom these ideas are very new. The informed reader will see that our present discussion of ontology deals with three of our former five axioms: reality, generalization, and cause-effect, while the discussion of epistemology deals with the remaining two: knower/known interaction and the influence of values. The methodological discussion was not formerly introduced as part of the structure of basic beliefs, but that it should be so introduced now seems most appropriate to us.

2. We are well aware that Euclid took it as part of his task to *prove* the theorems he proposed, that is, to show that they were logically deducible from the basic axioms of the system. We have not undertaken such proof and, indeed, would not wish to guarantee that a

proof would be possible for every theorem we draw out. We hope the reader will agree that our assertions-without-proof are reasonable, and that most probably they could be logically derived if one were pushed to do so. Our logic is more intuitive than Euclid would have allowed.

3. It is ironic that the ultimate test of validity for conventional data can never be carried out. For to determine whether the test of one-to-one correspondence can be met, it is necessary to know the standard, that is, to have prior knowledge of the reality that the inquiry is ostensibly probing. But if one had knowledge of the reality, one would not need to mount an inquiry to find it out. The upshot of this paradox is that no hypothesis or theory can be *proved*, although it can be *falsified*. The necessity of converting all actual hypotheses to *null* hypotheses is one example of this dilemma; rejection of the null hypothesis offers absolutely no evidence in favor of the original hypothesis in which the inquirer is actually interested.

4. The keynote speaker for the 1893 international conference of physicists opined that he was pleased not to be entering the profession as a young physicist at that time, because there was little left to do in the discipline except to extend the known constants of nature by a few decimal points.

5. By "all forms of inquiry" we mean to include research, evaluation, and policy studies, which are not, in our judgment, equivalent. For a fuller discussion of the distinctions that we have drawn, see Lincoln and Guba (1986b).

4 Ethics and Politics: The Twin Failures of Positivist Science

Paradigms are called worldviews not only because they premise an undergirding set of beliefs about the nature of the world and how to inquire into it but also because they have profound implications for how we construe our political affairs, how we adjudge activity to be moral or ethical, and how we provide for justice in social relations. They represent more than a philosophical backdrop—the scenery—against which resonant inquiry methodologies—the scenario—can be constructed and tested. They are ultimately the touchstones of our lives.

So long as conventional positivism was seen to apply primarily to the natural and material sciences, the ethical and political stances given warrant by that paradigm went largely unnoticed, and were, in fact, largely immaterial. But once positivism was asserted to be *the* preferred mode for conducting social and behavioral inquiry (as it has been since

John Stuart Mill first urged such a course about 150 years ago), the ethical and political implications of positivist science became much more apparent—and much more troublesome. When science's claim to be value-free failed to survive close scrutiny, so that the intimate relationship of inquiry and values was exposed, it became apparent that, since not all sets of values could simultaneously be served, *every act of science was also a political act,* one that structured power relationships in a particular way and served to maintain them as the status quo. When science's claim to have warrant to pursue the truth wherever it led was successfully challenged on the ground that not all scientific acts could be construed as ethical (consider the grotesque examples of experimentation on human subjects that have taken place in all the wars of this century, or the now well-documented history of questionable human experimentation in our own country—see, for, example Diener & Crandall, 1978), it became apparent that the positivist belief system opened the door, however slightly, to ethically questionable practices.

It is our intent, in this chapter, to illuminate the various ethical and political issues that arise from different paradigm allegiances. We will, in the following pages, endeavor to outline what we believe to be the more glaring flaws that stem from positivism and to suggest how a change in paradigms can obviate some of the more egregious of these. But the replacement paradigm we espouse is, of course, not free from the possibilities of abuse. Being a human construction itself, constructivism has its own litany of problems, on which we shall also comment. We will argue, however, that constructivism's faults, unlike those of positivism, do not tend to disempower, disenfranchise, or abuse human dignity. We do not pretend to provide "final" answers to any of the questions we raise. We simply do not know enough, and in any event, the issues are of such a nature that they deserve widespread discussion and negotiation. We do, however, treasure the hope that a consideration of these matters will further bolster our case that the constructivist paradigm provides a better "fit" in matters of human inquiry, including especially fourth generation evaluation, than does the positivist paradigm.

A final note before we proceed: Our statements should *not* be construed as a personal attack on practitioners of conventional science. We should *not* be understood to be saying that those conventional

practitioners are malevolent—deliberately dishonest, deceitful, unconcerned about human rights and human dignity, and always willing to
put the interests of science ahead of the interests of their subjects. *Nor* are
we contending that constructivist practitioners can always be counted on
to be models of virtue and propriety. We *are* saying that adherence to one
or the other of these paradigms predisposes an inquirer to certain postures in relation to ethical and political questions, even if those postures
are not always consciously recognized and appreciated. Those predispositions have important consequences, as we shall see.

The Warrant of Positivism

The positivist paradigm provides, we believe, a warrant for certain
abuses. Like sin, those abuses can be placed in either of two categories:
abuses of *commission,* which in the main involve breaches of ethics, and
abuses of *omission,* which in the main work to maintain the political
status quo. Positivism accomplishes these breaches of ethics and political
agency by virtue of its realist ontology and its epistemological claims of
objectivity and value-freedom. Each of these claims deserves extended
attention.

A realist ontology supposes the existence of an external reality that
operates independently of an observer in accordance with immutable
and enduring natural laws, including laws of causal relationships. That is,
a realist ontology presumes that there is some "reality" that is "out there."
It is putatively the business of science and scientists to describe that
reality and to uncover the laws that govern it. The hunt for "ultimate
truth(s)" takes precedence over any other principles.

Nature does not make that pursuit an easy task, however. Any variable
in which one might be interested is invariably masked, mimicked, or
overshadowed by a host of "confounding" or "contaminating" variables,
which must somehow be controlled or at least strictly accounted for.
These confounding, masking, or contaminating variables include those
introduced by the humans involved in a study, *both* researchers and
researched. Whether those human confounding variables are introduced
consciously (for example, by deliberately lying to protect one's self-
interest) or unconsciously (for example, by self-delusions or prejudices),

the inquirer must take steps to eliminate them. In order to accomplish rendering the study as confounding- or contamination-proof as possible (and, therefore, to approximate "reality" ever more closely), it is thought sometimes appropriate, or even necessary, to deceive the "subjects" (humans who are, by that very term, dehumanized and objectified, that is, made into objects), to invade their privacy without their prior knowledge, to place them at physical or psychological risk, or otherwise to exploit them for the researcher's or evaluator's own private and professional ends.

Conventional Safeguards

Of course, most scientists stop well short of the extremes painted in the above statements (although some do not; the case study literature is rife with examples of absolutely inhuman treatment of research subjects, not in some faraway country but in asylums, sanatoriums, and other places in the United States). As professional social scientists we have devised sets of ethical rules of the game that we attempt to enforce through agencies such as institutional review boards and through professional statements on ethical principles from learned societies. It is interesting, however, that we should feel that such statements are needed. Apparently the warrant provided by the realist ontology is sufficiently strong to make whole groups of professionals believe that ethical limits will from time to time be breached, unless we adopt stringent means to enforce them.

In both professional organizations' statements and in federal law, four areas of concern are typically dealt with: guarding subjects from harm, physical or psychological; guarding subjects against deception or, if deception can be "justified," "undoing" the effects of the deception after the study is completed (for instance, by debriefing); guarding the privacy of the subjects and the confidentiality of the data obtained from them; and obtaining fully informed consent (although please note that observing this regulation is occasionally impossible in light of the warrant to deceive when necessary; thus this system itself is internally inconsistent). These principles have been more extensively treated elsewhere, both by conventional researchers (see, for example, Diener & Crandall, 1978) and by those who support a more phenomenologically oriented science of social life (see, for example, Heron, 1981; Lincoln, 1988; Lincoln & Guba, 1989; Smith, 1988). Smith (1988) refers to the intricacies of ethical concerns and federal regulations as the "bureaucratization of research ethics."

We have elsewhere argued (Lincoln & Guba, 1989) that there are serious problems with each of these area of federal protection. For instance, with respect to the legal requirement that subjects be protected from harm, either physical or psychological, we have noted that while this provision protects from such overt abuses as testing LSD, or "acid," on unsuspecting subjects, or infecting inmates of mental hospitals with syphilis in order to study the progression of that disease throughout a lifetime, it does little to ensure protection against more insidious and untrackable forms of harm. Those forms of harm include the loss of dignity, the loss of individual agency and autonomy, and the loss of self-esteem that occur upon discovering that one has been duped and objectified. Harm, we believe, has been construed entirely too narrowly. Current legislation protects only from the more public and egregious abuses. There are other forms of harm to which research subjects, respondents, and participants have been subjected that have done as much damage, or that have the potential to do as much damage, as any physical abuse. Thus "harm" is a concept that needs much more consideration, and that could probably benefit from expanded definition.

Privacy and confidentiality are also primitively defined in conventional regulations on human subjects research. The willingness to code names and to protect individual data recognizes only a part of the problem. There is also the aspect that Sissela Bok (1982) calls "discretion," or the willingness to know and understand what is intrusive, what is too personal (even for science), what violates an individual's right to have some inner space that belongs to no one save her- or himself. As social science has moved toward understanding more and more arcane arenas of human behavior, it has also moved into arenas which Bok describes as intensely personal and has, therefore, become sufficiently intrusive that the privacy regulation is compromised, at least in some studies.

With respect to guarding research or evaluation participants against deception, or, if deception is deemed justifiable, then undoing the effects of such deception by tactics such as debriefing, there are several problems with the current system. First among the problems is, of course, the *warrant to deceive* embodied in the conventional paradigm. The warrant to deceive exists because conventional science's search is for a "higher" order of truth. If "truth" is the quest, then whatever means are necessary to discover or uncover that truth are necessary, justified, legitimate, and correct. This includes deceiving research subjects or respondents in order to achieve "contamination-free" results to inquiries.

The countering device of debriefing does little, however, to undo the harm. It fails to address the subtle but powerful issues of how people feel when they have been duped, it does little to buttress science as a worthwhile social activity, it does little to return to persons their dignity and confidence, and it ultimately undermines the credibility of all social science research (Baumrind, 1979, 1985).

From the perspective of the constructivist paradigm, deception is not only unwarranted, but is in direct conflict with its own aims. For if the aims of constructivist science are to collect and debate the various multiple constructions of stakeholders, how can one collect them if research or evaluation participants are confused or misled regarding what it is evaluators wish to know? If evaluators cannot be clear, direct, and undeceptive regarding their wish to know how stakeholders make sense of their contexts, then stakeholders will be unclear, indirect, and probably misleading regarding how they do engage in sense-making and what their basic values are. Thus deception is not only counter to the ethical posture of a constructivist evaluator, in that it destroys dignity, respect, and agency, but it also is counterproductive to the major goals of a fourth generation evaluation. Deception is worse than useless to a nonconventional evaluator; it is destructive of the effort's ultimate intent.

The fourth legal protection guaranteed to human subjects is that of fully informed consent. Individuals are guaranteed the right to know what the purposes of the research or evaluation might be, to understand the role that they will play in it, and to be able to withdraw, taking their data with them, at any time during the study. But many research and evaluation projects cut corners on these requirements, and, indeed, in graduate courses, students are often told forthrightly to tell respondents to their dissertation research "as little as possible" regarding the aims of the study as our own experience in serving on dissertation committees clearly shows. Early on apprentice researchers are warned that the more respondents know about the research, the less likely they are to participate in the study; therefore, tell them only as much as needed in order to assure their cooperation. Such a posture does little, if anything, to redress the problems created by crossing the informed consent requirement with the problem of allowable deception of research participants. Clearly, a person cannot, in fact, give her or his informed consent if duped regarding the true purposes of the research or evaluation or his or her role in it. Thus federal regulation on the protection of human subjects in social science research is internally inconsistent, and in this instance, the inconsistency is tilted in favor of the researcher or evaluator.

Informed consent cannot be given when participants are misinformed or not informed regarding the purposes of the evaluator or researcher. To deprive individuals of this right essentially robs them not only of their autonomy and control but also of their essential rights to be honored and respected as antonomous human beings. A switch to a new paradigm for evaluation not only mandates that deception be eschewed, it promotes full knowledge of evaluation or research purposes in the interest not only of guaranteeing participants their rights but also of eliciting their cooperation in determining the ends and means the evaluation or research activity will encompass.

The Broader Issues

The problems briefly outlined above are but the camel's nose in the ethical/political tent. Holding to a realist ontology provides a warrant for other abuses as well, which we shall discuss under three broad rubrics: science as a political act, the chimera of accountability, and the posture of neutrality and its implications for control of the scientific establishment.

Science as a political act. Science is in the putative business of "getting the facts" and uncovering the natural laws that connect them (in causal relationships). But we know that facts are theory-laden, that they exist within some value system, and that, therefore, they are themselves embodiments of a value position, however hidden beneath "scientific discourse" terminology and, therefore, unavailable for inspection, discussion, or refutation. Scientists nevertheless typically believe that their fact-finding methodologies are value-free. When this belief takes hold, scientists cannot possibly appreciate the political impact of their own knowledge-production and knowledge-utilization activities. As the feminists have made abundantly clear, this political impact of science thus far has been, cumulatively, a maintenance of the political and social status quo (Bleier, 1986; Ferguson, 1984; Harding & Hintikka, 1983; Langland & Gove, 1981).

It is largely the scientists who have the power to define the problems they will study, and to select the means by which to study them. In evaluations, problem definition and method are often initially in the hands of clients and funders, but still evaluators have great leeway in helping to decide what appropriate questions are, from whom data will be sought, and by what means. Often, evaluation contracts are issued as requests for proposals just as research contracts are; in this way, winning evaluators are often those whose definitions of problems, strategies, and methods exhibit "fit" with the clients' or funder's values.

To take an example, one can define urban blight as a problem to be overcome by razing housing deemed to be irreparable or inadequate, and replacing it with public housing, located (if neighborhood associations will allow it) in a more "desirable" part of the city. It may be argued that the land being cleared is more efficiently, economically, and purposefully used for manufacturing or for a shopping mall. By virtue of that scientific and economic analysis, numbers of families, indeed, whole intact neighborhoods, may be uprooted and relocated (being dispersed in the process). Studies done to "get the facts" in such a case, and to determine whether the goals of the relocation were met, would obviously be very different from studies that began with the view that relocating whole neighborhoods imposes social, economic, and cultural stresses that are intolerable for the people involved. Studies of the economics of *land use* and tax bases, for instance, rarely take into account the plight of persons in the only affordable housing to be found in the city. Relocation might be regarded as a "success," while the circumstances of the relocated families and elderly might be entirely disregarded. Depending on whether you see run-down housing as blight, as an economist or land development company might, or whether you see run-down housing as one factor in an intact neighborhood (where roles, statuses, and informal social relations govern conduct of the residents), as a sociologist might, you might make very different decisions about the best use to which the land beneath the housing is dedicated.

Studies such as the example above, justified on the grounds of their scientific merit, may nevertheless disenfranchise large groups of persons who never had the opportunity to help shape the study, to decide what questions should be asked, or how, or by whom, or of whom. These same studies may disempower groups by failing to recognize their rights or preferences, such as for having run-down, but affordable, housing or by making it even less possible than before to muster their political strength through some integrated and coordinated action. The status quo is maintained, perhaps even enhanced (in the sense that power becomes even more concentrated in the hands of still fewer persons), in the process, precisely because the findings are said to be factual, that is, value-free, and merely descriptive of "the way things really are."

We have noted that the value-free claim of positivism papers over the realization that science, like every human activity, is a *political* act. Science, by asking only certain questions maintains (or reinforces) the status quo; it asks those questions that have been formulated by its own theories, and never takes account of the emic formulations of its "subjects." We would argue that conventional science is as a result a force for disenfranchisement and disempowerment, for maintenance of the status quo.

The chimera of accountability. It is the case that scientific studies, particularly evaluations, are sometimes mounted in an effort to determine who or what is accountable for some undesirable state of affairs (including evaluating why a given program is not achieving its objectives). A realist ontology, with its accompanying "natural law" mandate, suggests that it is possible to examine any situation from the perspective of effectiveness of action, to pinpoint the weak link(s) in the cause-effect chains that exist, and therefore, rightly, to hold that or those weak links accountable for the general program failure.

If schools are producing weak products (read: students who have not mastered basic reading, writing, and critical thinking skills, for example), as assessed by, say, national tests of achievement, it is because some link has broken down. The laws of learning are reasonably well known. One such law, for example, states that learning is proportional to the time spent on the learning task. It is, therefore, possible to examine a classroom, or a school or entire school system, to determine the time-on-task for any given learning outcome that may be desired. If the time-on-task is insufficient (as judged for example against the norms of time-on-task developed for "exemplary" or "excellent" schools), then the cause of failure is clear. Time-on-task is a variable that is within the control of the classroom teacher; insufficient time-on-task can only mean that he or she has failed in curricular and managerial responsibility.

One may look further to discover the "cause" of the teacher's misfeasance. Perhaps, it may be surmised, the failure may be traced to the fact that he or she was inadequately trained in the teacher training institution. Schools of education, it may be shown, do not stress sufficiently the importance of time-on-task. Or perhaps he or she is teaching in an area where he or she holds no certification, but the state licensing requirements allow such placement of teachers. One can take one's choice about where to fix the responsibility.

One thing seems clear: There is no hiding from the terrible swift sword of science. By its methods, one can ferret out the true state of affairs and determine where to place the responsibility. But science, as we have just seen, works to maintain the status quo. The questions to be asked—how, and of whom—are determined not by the teachers or the teacher trainers, but by others in the hierarchy—who often have much to gain and everything to lose if blame is not fixed at some point in the organization remote from their own positions. It should come as no surprise from our foregoing arguments that accountability is almost always fixed at a point in the chain that is politically weak. The Reagan years argument that the homeless are homeless because that is what they desire is precisely this sort of argument. The homeless, having no home addresses, do not often vote, and they are far removed from the pomp and circumstance of the White House and Capitol Hill. Accountability, far from acting as the standard for stewardship of a public trust, more often acts to remove responsibility for blame from those paid most highly to accept it. The pursuit of normal science too often abets this tendency.

The posture of neutrality and its implications for control of the scientific establishment. We have seen that facts are closely related both to the *theory* and to the *value system* that we bring to bear in their determination and interpretation. Complications enough—philosophical and political—are produced by that relationship, even if there is only a single value system at stake to which everyone subscribes. But almost every society extant in 1989 is pluralistically valued. Holders of these different values will think it important to collect quite different facts (or even to take account in a different way of facts that are already gathered) from persons not regularly sought out. Science, by claiming value-freedom, simply substitutes its own values in the process, probably without realization on the part of evaluators or scientists, who—we are willing to assume—operate from positions of integrity; at least, they would vigorously defend their objectivity or freedom from bias. If multiple values, however, mean multiple truths, then science's claim can at best be but one of those truths. Now their claim is one that should certainly be taken seriously, but it is, nevertheless, but *one* claim. And given what we now understand about the leanings of the scientific establishment, it should be taken with a grain of salt. Namenwirth (1986, p. 29) has been quite clear about this presumption of "innocence" in the conventional scientific establishment:

> The scientific mind and the scientific method are thought to ensure the neutrality and objectivity of scientific research, and of the scientist's pronouncements. All scientists need to do is to steer clear of political and social movements that could undermine their objectivity. . . . Yet science has not been neutral. Repeatedly, in the course of history, the pronouncements of scientists have been used to rationalize, justify, and naturalize dominant ideologies and the status quo. Slavery, colonialism, laissez faire capitalism, communism, patriarchy, sexism, and racism have all been supported, at one time or another, by the work of scientists, a pattern that continues unabated into the present. . . . In truth, scientists are no more protected from political and cultural influence than other citizens. By draping their scientific activities in claims of neutrality, detachment, and objectivity, scientists augment the perceived importance of their views, absolve themselves of social responsibility for the applications of their work, and leave their (unconscious) minds wide open to political and cultural assump-

tions. Such hidden influences and biases are particularly insidious in science because the cultural heritage of the practitioners is so uniform as to make these influences very difficult to detect and unlikely to be brought to light or counter-balanced by the work of other scientists with different attitudes. Instead, the biases themselves become part of a stifling science-culture, while scientists firmly believe that as long as they are not *conscious* of any bias or political agenda, they are neutral and objective, when in fact they are only unconscious. (emphasis in original)

Bleier (1986, p. 7) makes it startlingly clear what in the "cultural heritage of the practitioners" is so "uniform": "With women concentrated in low-paid work within science, the *research faculty in both the United States and Britain is overwhelmingly male, white, and middle-class* (emphases added)," a situation that has led to "excessive reliance on conceptual paradigms related to social preoccupations of this class of males" (Namenwirth, 1986, p. 36).

Feminists, critical theorists, and other nonorthodox researchers have been quite critical and quite convincing in their analyses of who controls the research establishment in the United States. When we argue that power has historically resided in the hands of evaluators and their client-funders, we are not arguing from a position of either ignorance or pique. In fact, we are arguing from simple demographics, and those demographics reflect a concentration of power and decision making that ill suits and ill serves a pluralistic and literate society.

Some Counterarguments

Scientists offer two arguments in justification for their position on the matter of power and control of the evaluation process. First, they argue, there is a need for control. Philosophically, the argument may be rendered thus: Nature cannot be expected to provide the "right" answers unless the researcher's or evaluator's questions are put to her in just the "right" way. Never mind that the "right" questions are dictated by the form of discourse that science has adopted to shield itself from accusations of political partisanship, a method "generally viewed as the protector against rampant subjectivities and the guarantor of the objectivity and validity of scientific knowledge" (Bleier, 1986, p. 3). Both the form of discourse and the particular method conventional science employs embody values, which in turn "affect what observations scientist make and...what questions they ask. . . . They affect the assumptions scientists make: what language they use to pose questions; what they see and *fail to see*; how they interpret their data; what they hope, want, need and believe to be true" (Bleier, 1986, p. 3, emphasis added). Nevertheless, they argue, the inquirer cannot relinquish control of a study lest confounding variables creep in. The need to maintain what is euphemistically called "technical adequacy" supersedes all other considerations. To reverse John Tukey, it seems better to get a precise answer to the wrong question than a fuzzy answer to the right question.

In the case of evaluation, for example, input may be sought from stakeholders, but if that input threatens the evaluation's technical adequacy, as judged by conventional standards, it is disregarded. So the RFP published by the National Institute of Education (NIE, 1978) for the evaluation of Project Push/Excel noted that the evaluation was to be conducted in the stakeholder mode, but was careful to add that this approach implied "no technical compromises which will satisfy consumers but [lack] methodological rigor and clarity" (p. 8). The Reverend Jesse Jackson and others who supported this project could not have been very pleased by this elevation of rigor over relevance, as seen from their perspective. Similarly, Stake (1986, p. 145) notes, in relation to the evaluation of the Cities-in-Schools project much favored by then President Carter, that the Technical Review Panel

> did not see the stakeholder approach as requiring a substantial departure from the pursuits of quantitative [read: conventional] social science. Stakeholder evaluation was little discussed, and when discussed it was treated unenthusiastically—a constraint, perhaps a challenge, certainly not an opportunity. It was interpreted primarily as a basis for adding to the list of measureable variables. Without diminishing his advocacy of a stakeholder approach, Gold [Norman Gold, NIE's program spokesman and monitor] assured the panel at its first meeting that the AIR study was to be a "fundamentally sound piece of research."

It is very clear as one follows the history of the project outlined in Stake's excellent review that the stakeholders themselves did not feel very well served by this approach. Variables that may be confounding must either be controlled (an effort usually constrained by both limited resources and inadequate knowledge) or randomized. Randomization combats, among other sources of confounding with human subjects, indifference, corruption, irascibility, and untidiness. Randomization is "fair." For example, research or evaluation participants randomly assigned to experimental and control groups have a fair chance of receiving some treatment from which they might profit!

A second counterargument that scientists often cite is the priority of verification as a goal for "scientific" studies (whether research, policy analysis, or evaluation). While inquiry has both discovery and verification aspects, science proper deals only with verification: the testing of hypotheses and the falsification of rival hypotheses. The realm of discovery is often relegated to the role of "creative imaginings," and, therefore, is uncontrolled and uncontrollable and hence nonscience. It is imperative that the researcher or evaluator have thought through, in explicit detail, the hypotheses to be tested and/or the questions that must be answered. The understandings or explanations proffered by research subjects (or respondents) about their states of affairs (or states of mind) are irrelevant. Emic formulations are worse than useless to a conventional scientist, who remains convinced that his or her own questions are the only right and proper questions that need to be asked. It is only the inquirer's etic formulations that are at issue and not the subjects' emic formulations. Rigorous studies must take steps to exclude those local constructions as biasing, subjective, ill informed, unsystematic, and unscientific.

A third counterargument sometimes offered rests on the claim that the goal of science must be to predict and control. Differences between oriental and occidental views have often been noted to revolve on the question of whether one simply accepts nature and lives in harmony with it as best one can, or whether one fights to exploit the laws and treasures of nature to one's own advantage. Oriental beliefs often rest on the idea of karma, a sort of quiet acceptance of things that will happen because they will happen. We are the complete victims of a world that plays with us as a cat with a mouse. Occidental beliefs, on the other hand, often rest on the belief that one can take nature by the throat, as it were, and by discovering her immutable (real) laws, predict and control matters to our advantage. We have a means to exploit nature. In occidental culture, there is a long and hallowed tradition of striving for domination over nature, a tendency that some have thought analogous to rape, plunder, male domination, and despoilation (Easlea, 1986; Merchant, 1980; Rose, 1986).

But note that this posture is still mainly reactive, that is, we cannot change the laws (once we presumably know them), but we can react to them in ways that turn their force away from us to a large extent. In short, we can exert a form of control over our destinies.

Constructivism provides for a *proactive* posture; we can *re-create* our context, our situatedness. We are no longer victims (as we are in science even if we are partly in control) but are shapers of our destinies. The idea of free will comes back into play. We create the realities we live in; we write the scenarios by which we play out our roles.

Such posturings have led practitioners of the scientific paradigm to take on the trappings of an arcane and special priesthood. Rather like the Lowells of Boston, who were spoken to only by the Cabots and who themselves spoke only to God, scientists have assumed the role of inter-mediaries, as it were, between humankind and nature. It is easy to ignore the subjects of research, who, to quote Robert Boruch's extemporaneous comment made during his plenary address at the 1986 annual meeting of the American Education Association, "don't know a fact from a bag of popcorn" (1986). When the scientist returns from a sojourn in the temple of nature with certain findings that may be objectionable to some, his or her plea is usually: "Don't kill the messenger; I am after all simply telling you how it is. Blame nature, not me, if you don't like the findings or the outcomes." Such claims are simultaneously arrogant, self-serving, and irresponsible, because they trumpet the superior wisdom of the inquirer while allowing him or her to hide behind the realist claim of simply "telling it like it is." As Namenwirth (1986, pp. 35-36) argues,

Science is a powerful tool for good as well as evil, for emancipation as well as for exploitation. . . . Residing, as we do, inside a universe filled with enigmas, many of which lend themselves to research approaches congenial to our personal styles, many with applications beneficial to segments of society that are due for some benefits, how do we justify working on research whose applications threaten to be deeply destructive of natural resources, of human life, of the dignity and self-respect of a racial or ethnic or gender group?...[And some of] the more tradition-bound scientists [will surely] moan: "Heaven help us! That would be the end of legitimate science. Harness science to social or political purposes and it will be totally destroyed."...[But] as scientists and as human beings, we are obliged to make responsible choices about what we do in our work. We must be knowledgeable about how our research is likely to be applied, and do what we can to prevent dangerous, detrimental applications while promoting beneficial ones. ...We must cope responsibly with the by-products of our research designs;...[and] finally, scientists must accept some responsibility for the ways in which their research is communicated to the public.... Science reports need not forever mislead, frighten, and alienate the nonscientist, or *disadvantage the underprivileged, or simply serve to confirm in the minds of many "that their social prejudices are scientific facts after all."* (emphases added)

Risks of the Constructivist Paradigm

While the constructivist paradigm avoids many of these problems, there is no doubt that in some ways constructivist inquiry poses greater ethical risks than does conventional scientific inquiry. We have tried to anticipate some of these risks (Lincoln & Guba, 1989) and will briefly recapitulate them here. The first risk we comprehended was that of face-to-face contact. Undistanced as constructivist responsive evaluation or research is, it provides for intensive and often tenuous and fragile relationships, which are subject, as are all intense and intimate relationships, to violation of trust, to shading the truth, to misunderstandings regarding the purposes or relationships with other respondents on site.

A second risk posed by constructivist, responsive, and particularly fourth generation evaluation is the difficulty of maintaining privacy and confidentiality. The heavy reliance on natural language, direct quotations, and continuous hermeneutic feedback loops on participants' constructions means that often, persons and/or positions and/or role incumbents will become apparent. The hermeneutic circle (about which we will talk later on), with its constant input of constructions and reconstructions often will make it easy for one participant readily to identify another.

We should not be surprised by this state of affairs. Settings are remarkably stable, and over time, persons who are members of the setting come to know each other's positions on various issues and concerns rather well. This may be unavoidable, even though the evaluator or inquirer makes every effort to protect identities. As Skrtic, Guba, and Knowlton (1985, p. 111) noted:

> such protection [privacy, confidentiality, and anonymity] must be difficult to extend and impossible to guarantee. Even if all the names and places and dates are changed "to protect the innocent," it is quite likely that other locals will be able to pinpoint the agencies and parties involved. And that breach of confidence may have the most serious consequences of all, for it is these other locals who may be in positions of authority or influence with respect to the research participants and thus may have the most powerful sanctions to apply.

But there are ways in which stakeholders and research particpants can protect themselves and their identities. For instance, when the case study is finally written up, each stakeholder can and does retain the right either to correct erroneous information or to have removed direct quotations that he or she feels may be too obviously attributable to him or her. We should note here that in no research or evaluation project we have ever worked on or conducted has any participant or stakeholder asked to have a direct quotation removed from the final case study—even though it has become clear that others in the setting can identify its "voice." Few of our graduate students ever have to remove quotations from their dissertations, either, in the member check process. There does appear to be a predisposition in favor of fairness in presentation of multiple realities from stakeholders that operates to lower their concern with strict privacy and confidentiality. That speaks strongly to us with respect to the relative weights research or evaluation participants place on fairness, openness, and involvement in the inquiry process relative to strict privacy and confidentiality concerns or legalistic rights.

This is not to say that the federal laws on privacy and confidentiality are useless or outmoded in constructivist inquiry. Quite the opposite. But this discussion does center on the special risks from the emergent-paradigm form of inquiry, and its open and democratic nature as opposed to the closed-system and hierarchical format for most conventional inquiries and evaluations.

A third risk we believe can be part of the hermeneutic and dialectic form of inquiry is that of violation of trust. This form of inquiry is built on an almost axiomatic assumption of intense and nonmanipulative trust between researchers or evaluators and their research participants and stakeholders. Sometimes, monumental amounts of work (interviewing, observation, and flowing around and through a hermeneutic circle) must be accomplished in a very short time. Because trust is normally built between individuals only over a long period of time, this means that evaluators must sometimes work within constraints that do not normally apply to, say, the cultural anthropologist, who is often in a setting for years at a time. But inquirers must elicit maximum cooperation from all of those with whom they work if the work is to be successful and to possess integrity.

Because some evaluation efforts require short time frames (relatively speaking), achieving trust, building rapport, and engaging in negotiation from positions of mutual power are sometimes difficult to achieve. Such projects

> demand [just] such efforts in small segments of time [however] and hence produce intra- and inter-psychic efforts on the part of researchers and researched alike. . . . [Evaluators] cannot, in short time frames, afford the casual contacts which permit trust to build over time and participants cannot afford to be misled about the intents and purposes of the research. The normal constraints of doing fieldwork [hermeneutic dialectic evaluation] relying on the human instrument become attenuated if time frames are collapsed, hence the need for powerful self-awareness before entering the field. (Lincoln & Guba, 1989)

The need for open negotiations presents a fourth risk to this form of inquiry. Because conventional inquirers are not required by law or axiomatic premises to engage in open negotiations with their participants, and in fact, may be permitted under some circumstances to deceive their subjects, open negotiation is not an issue for those operating under the scientific paradigm. Exactly the opposite is the case for the fourth generation evaluator. Deception is expressly forbidden, both because of ethical constraints and because it is counteraxiomatic and counterproductive. Thus negotiation—of concerns, issues, claims, and constructions—is mandatory. Ethical constraints within this paradigm suggest that such negotiations ought to be carried out with great attention to egalitarian concerns and with attention to requirements of human dignity, self-esteem, and self-agency. How is such openness achieved, particularly in short time periods? We cannot give a wholly satisfying answer to that. We can merely offer this advice: Evaluators operating in this paradigm need to be extremely conscious of their own motives and need to spend some time each day examining and reflecting on their interactions with persons to discover whether they have been as honest and straightforward as humanly possible and whether there have been occasions where respondents or stakeholders were misled or led to believe things that were not true. Social scientists have long been in the largely unconscious habit of justifying what they do in the name of science or truth; overcoming that frame of mind with intense self-scrutiny is a habit that will need great cultivation.

The fifth risk that we have identified is that inherent in the framing of case studies. Case studies in whatever paradigm have always represented an inclusion/exclusion, or selection, problem for their authors. Typically, fieldwork (whether scientific or constructivist) has generated more data than could be profitably included in a single case or monograph. The inquirer has always had to choose what the purposes of the case were to be, and to draw on data that could illuminate those choices.

But the risk inhering in fourth generation evaluation is much more convoluted. The inquirer or evaluator is *not* the single determiner of what the problem is (or, in the case of an evaluation effort, what the salient claims, concerns, and issues might be). The evaluator is only one of many important participants, each of whom, acting individually or in stakeholding groups, may nominate concerns and issues felt to be salient. Presentation of those multiple constructions is a responsibility for the case study drafter, who must deal with the presentation of multiple social realities, with the reconstruction of those constructions, with deciding how to make the case for each construction, and with deciding about what data can or may be marshaled to support, defend, or render uncredible any given construction.

In the process of engaging in hermeneutic and dialectic inquiry, of course, many participants will come to more sophisticated and informed constructions (or reconstructions) than they held before, and many points of agreement will be found between constructions, which were not earlier thought possible. But in any reasonably honest effort, points of disagreement and value conflict will still remain. They will become a part of the agenda for negotiation (about which we will speak more later). As such, they will need to be displayed in such a way as to have the evidence for and against different positions presented sharply and cleanly. And this need is what creates the inclusion and exclusion, or selection, problems, in the main. Since the evaluator's role is to collect evidence on each of the points of the agenda for negotiation, how does she or he determine what shall be included and what excluded? How does one make a determination that some items are essential for re-creating a stakeholding group's construction and others are not?

The inclusion/exclusion problem, and the larger issue of how one frames a case study, is part of the *craft* of evaluation. As with any craft, the knowledge of how one goes about it with skill, balance, and a sense of the artistic is the same as for any craftsperson: practice. The more case studies one helps frame, and the larger input one seeks about whether or not one "got it right," the better one gets to be at it. In this sense, evaluation craft integrity is parallel to artistic integrity: One can be judged to have rendered a product of excellence and beauty and "goodness" (Lincoln & Guba, 1988) if the product demonstrates integrity, originality, passion, commitment, and balance. And like artistic renderings, there is no simple set of rules for saying whether a given product is better than some other product. There is, for example, no *intrinsic* reason for stating that a silver teapot crafted by Paul Revere is "better" than a teapot crafted by a Sheffield silversmith of equal reputation. Both hold tea, and both exist as artistic statements in and of themselves. But if you are a museum curator searching for a signed Revere teapot to complete a collection, then the Sheffield may be beautiful but fails to serve the purpose.

The same is true for evaluation case studies. The question to ask is, beyond the goodness criteria, simply this: Does a given case study serve the needs of the various audiences (all of them) who have some stake in its use? Thus case studies can take multiple forms, and the problem of selection, inclusion or exclusion can only be resolved on the basis of what is needed and appropriate *in this setting, in this place, in this time, and for these stakeholding audiences.*

Redeeming Features of Constructivism

The foregoing problems are those ethical and political ones we believe to be special to fourth generation evaluation. There may be others, but we believe these are sufficiently compelling enough to keep potential practitioners concerned. On the other hand, the basic ontological and epistemological positions of the naturalistic paradigm militate against many of the difficulties noted earlier in this chapter.

For one, the warrant of a search for ultimate, abiding truth is removed. Social reality is not objectively "out there," but exists only as a series of mental and social constructions derived via social interaction. Rather than looking for an external reality the naturalist looks for internal realities—the sense-making and belief structures that order human existence and that exist only inside individuals. It is the holders of those realities—the subjects, as the positivist would call them, or the respondents, participants, and/or stakeholders, as the constructivist would refer to them—who provide whatever warrant exists. The warrant is thus no more powerful or pervasive than are the persons who hold the constructions and who have the role of gatekeeper in social and educational contexts.

Second, the use of deception, sometimes considered justifiable in positivism in order to control human variables that might be confounding, is actually counterproductive for the constructivist. If the purpose of inquiry is to uncover realities as they are constructed by the persons involved, then to deceive the respondents about the purpose (or any other aspect) of the inquiry is to stimulate them to report on matters irrelevant to what is at hand (or worse, to deceive the inquirer in turn, even if only to "give the researcher what he or she wants," a well-known effect in conventional studies). Only holders of constructions can tell us what they are, and if we ask them to perform some other task, we are certain to get misleading or erroneous information.

Third, both the need for control and the primacy of verification procedures disappear as parameters of inquiry within the naturalistic paradigm. The situation can be appreciated from a study of Figure 4.1, "A Typology of Inquiry Based on the Dimensions of Construction and Control."

As we have noted, control of an inquiry is thought to be an essential condition by positivists, for the sake of eliminating (or at least randomizing) possible confounding variables (the *exogenous* column of Figure 4.1). But there are at least two other alternatives: to hand over control to the respondents, as might be the case in an action study in which respondents make all important decisions while the inquirer serves only as a "consultant" (the *endogenous* column of Figrue 4.1), or to share control *collaboratively,* as is typically the case in so-called participatory or experiential studies (see Reason & Rowan, 1981, or Reason, 1988), or for "democratic evaluation" (see Elliot, 1986; Hustler, Cassidy & Cuff, 1986; or Payne & Cuff, 1982) such as that developed at CARE at the University of East Anglia by Barry Macdonald and his colleagues (the *collaborative* column of Figure 4.1).

The primacy of verification procedures is eliminated since there is nothing to verify. The object of a naturalistic inquiry is to identify and describe various *emic* constructions and place those constructions in touch—with the intent of evolving a more informed and sophisticated construction than any single one of the emic constructions *or,* the researcher's or evaluator's *etic* construction, represents. The outcome is a *joint,* or collaborative, construction (or, more appropriately, a reconstruction of formerly held constructions).

This analysis suggests that whereas positivism must, by its own principles, operate in the upper left hand cell of Figure 4.1 (the etic/exogenous cell), constructivism is inclined to operate in the lower right-hand cell (the joint/collaborative cell).

The effect of operating in the joint/collaborative cell should be noted in relation to the ethical and political problems with which this chapter has been concerned. First, the constructivist position is *empowering* to all

Figure 4.1. A Typology of Inquiry Based on the Dimensions of
Construction and Control

The Reality Dimension: Construction	The Political Dimension: Control		
	1 — Exogenous	2 — Endogenous	3 — Collaborative
A — Etic	Positivism		
B — Emic			
C — Joint			Constructivism

of the parties involved in the inquiry. Far from maintaining the status quo, and assimilating and interpreting information within the value framework of those in power, the constructivist *shares* power. The constructions of all are solicited *and* honored; that is, there is a genuine effort to connect them and to evolve from them a construction that is consensually derived and that is more informed and sophisticated than any of the individual constructions were prior to the initiation of the study or evaluation.

Second, the constructivist position is *educative* for all of the parties concerned. All have the opportunity to confront and develop criticisms of their own constructions as well as the constructions of others. Each stakeholder has more information than formerly and is in a better position to appreciate, comprehend, and determine how to use that information. From the foregoing, it is also clear that accountability can no longer be assigned on the basis of "natural law" or "hard data." Accountability is something that all share as they form constructions and make action decisions based on those constructions.

Finally, it is clear that the naturalistic approach does not seek justification of anyone's present position but rather seeks *connection* between the positions as a means to move to higher intellectual, moral, and ethical ground.

Another note is in order here. We are well aware what a move to the kind of evaluation we propose might mean for evaluators, especially those who live with outside funding. While some would argue that qualitative (phenomenological, constructivist) approaches are as readily accepted as more conventional experimental and quantitative approaches, serious researchers attempting to work in this paradigm know otherwise. Reinharz and Rowles (1988), researchers who have and do utilize phenomenological approaches to their work, have summarized the situation as clearly and distinctly as we might ever do:

> It is certainly not our intention to polarize and exacerbate mistrust between the two research styles [qualitative and quantitative]. However, in our view, these myths [regarding the objectivity of the conventional view and the subjectivity of the phenomenological, the secondary role of qualitative data to quantitative, the preliminary quality of qualitative studies as opposed to the verificationist quality of quantitative, and so on] are fed by differences in power. Since quantification is associated with a reified view of science, which is dominant in the ethos of Western culture,... quantifiers have the upper hand in a kind of power struggle in universities and research centers. Some have argued that this epistemological struggle ultimately rests on the fact that science has become gendered; i.e., numbers are defined as hard data, which are equated with reason and masculinity; language is defined as soft data, which are equated with emotion and femininity....
>
> When, as is frequently the case, power resides in the hands of those engaged in quantitative research, people wishing to engage in qualitative scholarship may be denied publication opportunities, research funding, or jobs. By excluding qualitative research, quantitative researchers *limit competing viewpoints. As a result, the quantitative paradigm is reinforced, reproduced in succeeding generations of researchers, and further institutionalized. Researchers who use qualitative methods become obliged to present extraordinary justification for their choice.... They may also be forced to work within a milieu in which their research is viewed as inferior or peripheral to the core scientific enterprise.* (1988, p. 14, emphases added)[1]

We are not unmindful of the problems. But we have a commitment to defend the right of any inquirer or evaluator who wishes at least to experiment for him- or herself with what we are proposing.

Note

1. From Shulamit Reinharz and G.D. Rowles, editors, *Qualitative Gerontology*, copyright 1988 by Springer Publishing Company, New York 10012; used by permission.

5 Constructions and Reconstructions of Realities

The major task of the constructivist investigator is to tease out the constructions that various actors in a setting hold and, so far as possible, to bring them into conjunction—a joining—with one another and with whatever other information can be brought to bear on the issues involved. As Joe David Bellamy suggests in his introduction to Tom Wolfe's (1982) *The Purple Decades*, that is not an easy task:

> How can a non-fiction writer pretend to know exactly what a person is thinking or feeling at any given moment? He *asks them.* If a reporter bases his reconstruction of the subjective side of life of the character on the most scrupulous reporting..., he can get close to the truth of the inner life.... His approach is to cultivate the habit of staying with potential subjects for days, weeks, or months as a time, taking notes, interviewing, watching and waiting for something dramatic and

revealing to happen. *Only through the most persistent and searching methods* of reporting . . . can the journalist's entree in point-of-view, the subjective life, inner voices, the creation of scenes and dialogue, and so on, be justified. (p. ix, emphases added) (Excerpt from "Introduction" by Joe David Bellamy from *The Purple Decades* by Tom Wolfe. Introduction copyright ©1982 by Farrar, Straus and Giroux Inc. Reprinted by permission of Farrar, Straus and Giroux.)

Now constructions are, quite literally, *created realities.* They do not exist outside of the persons who create and hold them; they are not part of some "objective" world that exists apart from their constructors. They consist of certain available information configured into some integrated, systematic, "sense-making" formulation whose character depends on the level of information and sophistication (in the sense of ability to appreciate/understand/apply the information) of the constructors.

Constructions come about through the interaction of a constructor with information, contexts, settings, situations, and other constructors (not all of whom may agree), using a process that is rooted in the previous experience, belief systems, values, fears, prejudices, hopes, disappointments, and achievements of the constructor. To fall back on the terminology of the philosophy of science, constructions come about by virtue of the interaction of the knower with the already known and the still-knowable or to-be-known.

Of course, malconstructions are possible. For example, constructions may be incomplete, simplistic, uninformed, internally inconsistent, or derived by an inadequate methodology. But constructions can be properly judged only by criteria appropriate to the paradigm out of which the constructor operates (we shall talk more about criteria for goodness in a later chapter). So, for instance, a religious construction can only be judged adequate or inadequate utilizing the particular theological paradigm from which it is derived. A legal construction can only be judged adequate within its own historical roots and tradition; for example, judgments rendered under Napoleonic codes may be different from those rendered in the same case under a system derived from British constitutional history, but the case can only be judged to have been adequately or inadequately tried depending on whether the crime was committed in France or Great Britain. The French system of jurisprudence might bring about a different judgment than a British court might render, but we cannot judge a French legal opinion or verdict in terms of a British legal model. All constructions must be treated as meaningful, unless evidence to the contrary can be adduced.

There are as many constructions as there are constructors. That is the case not only because the several constructors are likely to differ in their available information and their ability to handle that information, but also because of the problem of underdetermination: The same information is subject to many equally plausible interpretations. An example may serve to make the point clearer.

Let us suppose that a "new math" type curriculum is undergoing an evaluation. Emphasis in this course is on binary number systems. It seems clear to everyone that the children are learning this new system very well, as evidenced not only by their examination scores but also because they propose and carry out highly imaginative projects that depend on base-2 arithmetic. A high level of enthusiasm is also apparent; for example, the children challenge one another with number "puzzles" on the playground, and they enter into "new math" contests eagerly. Parents find their children challenging them at home as well, even when they do not mean to, chattering on about those new ideas that are so foreign to their parents' background and knowledge. Requests for help with homework leave the parents utterly dumbfounded.

The children's teachers and the school administrators, observing all these matters, are highly pleased. They believe the children are getting a kind of education that will challenge their minds, reinterest them in school, and prepare them well for the future. After all, aren't computers and space exploration, to take two prominent ongoing developments, dependent on this kind of mathematics? Parents, on the other hand, are less pleased. They sense an alienation from their children, which they blame on the new curriculum. Unable to help their children with their homework, they come to feel inadequate and helpless. Further, they wonder whether the assessment about preparing for the future is right. So far as they can tell, their children cannot yet balance a checkbook or make a sensible estimate of what the supermarket checker ought to be charging for a basketful of items.

Both school personnel and parents have essentially the same "facts" at their disposal. Yet their constructions (the way they "make sense" of the "facts") are remarkably different, illustrating the point that the *same* "facts" can be interpreted in very *different* ways. Moreover, there is no a priori way to settle the question of "who is right." Indeed, we assert that it is a nonsense question.

A construction once formed is likely to maintain itself. What counts as information or evidence within that construction is in part determined by the construction itself. Freudian evidence, for example, is not likely to influence the construction of the behavior modification practitioner of therapy because it falls outside the pale of what behavior modification theory encompasses. In the same way, conventional scientists have some difficulty dealing with feminist research (as one example) because the nature of the knowledge presented falls outside forms of discourse that are considered appropriate for traditional science (Belenky, Clinchy, Goldberger, & Tarule, 1986).

Constructions are thus self-sustaining and self-renewing. Constructions, like other forms of knowing such as theories, are able to "wall off" contravening evidence, by their very nature. The problem of inducing change is thus not a matter simply of raising consciousness or introducing new rational considerations (in fact, *rational* considerations are usually the last ones that will change a construction) but a matter of coming to grips with the problematic nature of constructions. If constructions are regarded as true, the possibility of considering a competitor construction is virtually nonexistent. The same, of course, is true with a formal scientific theory: If this one is true, then the competitor will win ascendence only when the contravening evidence becomes so powerful and contradictory, and when the competitor theory "explains so much more," that the competitor cannot be ignored.

Constructions are challenged whenever new information and/or an increase in sophistication to deal with information become available. There are four possible conditions, as displayed in Table 5.1:

(1) *Condition 1: Stability.* In Condition 1 new information is introduced that is consistent with the existing construction (the information was probably sought to answer some question or to test some hypothesis raised by the existing construction) and that does not require any change

Figure 5.1. Four Conditions of Challenge

Increase in Level of Sophistication	New Information Consistent with Existing Information?	
	Consistent	Inconsistent
None	Condition 1: Stability	Condition 2: Information disjunction
Some	Condition 3: Sophistication disjunction	Condition 4: Information and sophistication disjunction

in the constructor's level of sophistication to deal with it. This is the common condition of "normal" science as that term is used by Thomas Kuhn (1970). The existing construction is expanded to include the new knowledge, and we say that our knowledge is growing, that is, that we are able to aggregate the new knowledge with the old in a meaningful way. Another brick, so to speak, is placed in the growing edifice of our knowledge. There is no resistence to the addition of such knowledge; stability is the hallmark of Condition 1.

(2) *Condition 2: Information Disjunction.* In Condition 2 new information is introduced that is inconsistent with the existing construction, that is, that could not be predicted from that construction or be accommodated by it, but that does not require any change in the constructor's level of sophistication to deal with it. For example, the well-known Hawthorne experiments (Roethlisberger & Dixon, 1939), designed to answer certain questions about worker efficiency that were generated by the prevailing scientific management construction, produced certain irreconcilable information that implied that human characteristics were as important as situational ones in efficiency considerations. A usual first response to Condition 2 is to regard the new information as in error (produced by a methodological lapse?), but when the information is replicated several times, a change in the prevailing construction is forced. So in the Hawthorne case a new variable, morale, was conceptualized and introduced into the construction in order to accommodate the

previously irreconcilable data. This response is consistent with the conventional claim that science is self-correcting: A construction (theory) that is "in error" will soon be corrected as more information is uncovered. Condition 2 is not nearly so common as Condition 1 and results in a somewhat more reluctant adjustment. Change is slower than under Condition 1, and some resistance is met (although this resistance may be healthy in that it militates against a "bandwagon" effect).

(3) *Condition 3: Sophistication disjunction.* In Condition 3 new information is introduced that is consistent with the existing construction but that requires an altered level of sophistication to enable the constructor to appreciate/understand/apply it. So, for example, the very precise observations of the planets made by Tycho Brahe (1546-1601) did not lead to the rejection of earlier observational data but only to their refinement. But the availability of these refined data made it clear that earlier theories of planetary motion were no longer tenable. Building on Brahe's data, Johannes Kepler (1571-1630) was able to show that the planets moved in their orbits in such a way as to sweep out equal areas in equal periods of time, speeding up or slowing down as they moved in their elliptical paths around the sun. Such a very sophisticated demonstration would not have been suggested by, let alone demonstrated from, the earlier data. This Condition 3 state of affairs may prove challenging and puzzling to constructors and force them to reconsider their constructions, usually with positive outcomes. Typically, however, the change does not require a paradigm shift: the basic belief system is untouched. Change under this condition, while not easy, is usually accomplished without major disruptions. Constructors need not make wrenching shifts in their interpretations.

(4) *Condition 4: Information and sophistication disjunction.* In Condition 4 some new information is introduced that requires not only a substantive adjustment, as in Condition 2, but also an increase in the constructor's level of sophistication in order to appreciate/understand/ apply it. For example, neuroses were initially classifed as "mental illnesses" to fit the prevailing medical model in which virtually all clinical practitioners had been trained. Freud's cases not only introduced new information about the etiology and course of neuroses and what might be done to contribute to their "cure," but also required a radical

change in the practitioner's sophistication in order to appreciate/understand/use that information. Far from being viewed solely as symptoms of illnesses, neuroses could now be understood as fulfilling some need for their victims—concrete adjustments to otherwise intolerable situations. The major problem with neuroses is not that they occur (for they could be seen, initially at least, as helpful responses) but that they are carried over to other situations in which they are *not* appropriate (a case, we cannot resist adding, of being stuck in a construction that is retained unremittingly even when it is no longer responsive to changed circumstances).

Condition 4 places a great deal of stress on holders of an existing construction. It requires a wrenching readjustment that may be beyond the ability of some constructors to make: they will stoutly resist any change. The extreme case is encountered when the sophistication disjunction is of such an order as to require a shift in the basic belief system—the paradigm—that undergirds the old construction. In such a case we are dealing with what Kuhn (1970) calls a period of "extraordinary" science, a veritable scientific revolution. Most practitioners of science find themselves in a state of bewilderment and confusion, conceptually immobilized so long as they are unable to gain the perspective needed to facilitate a paradigm shift. Change is then very slow and painful indeed.

The ease with which a construction may be changed thus depends on which of the four conditions outlined above is encountered. If the holders of a given construction are to change, it is essential that they be exposed to new information and/or given the opportunity to grow to whatever level of sophistication may be needed to appreciate or understand or use that information. Obviously the constructor's values must be open to change as part of that process.

Constructions are not usually held lightly, and this is particularly so if the constructions involve some deep value commitment. Typically, their holders are persuaded of their "truth" and their utility. What is needed to effect change is an open negotiation during which all available constructions, *including that etic construction which the inquirer/evaluator brings to the inquiry,* must be open to challenge—and to the possibility of being discarded as not useful, unsophisticated, or ill informed. All constructions must be afforded an opportunity for input and must be taken seriously, that is, the input must be honored.

The Hermeneutic Dialectic Process

We shall use the term *hermeneutic dialectic* to describe the process that meets the conditions we have just outlined. It is *hermeneutic* because it is interpretive in character, and *dialectic* because it represents a comparison and contrast of divergent views with a view to achieving a higher-level synthesis of them all, in the Hegelian sense. Nevertheless, the major purpose of this process is not to justify one's own construction or to attack the weaknesses of the constructions offered by others, but to *form a connection* between them that allows their mutual exploration by all parties. The aim of this process is to reach a consensus when that is possible; when it is not possible, the process at the very least exposes and clarifies the several different views and allows the building of an agenda for negotiation (about which more will be said later).

If the process is successful, or, to the extent that it is, all parties (including the inquirer) are likely to have reconstructed the constructions with which they began. This is so even when consensus is not achieved. All parties are thus simultaneously *educated* (because they achieve new levels of information and sophistication) and *empowered* (because their initial constructions are given full consideration and because each individual has an opportunity to provide a critique, to correct, to amend, or to extend all the other parties' constructions).

Conditions for a Successful Hermeneutic Dialectic Process

A *productive* hermeneutic dialectic negotiation thus requires that certain conditions be met if it is to be successful as a process. These conditions include the following:

(1) A commitment from all parties to work from a *position of integrity*. There will be no deliberate attempt to lie, deceive, mislead, hide, or otherwise offer misconstructions. (Misconstructions can, of course, be offered un-

knowingly or unwittingly.) We are aware (all too aware!) of the old adage: Age and treachery will more often than not compensate for youth and skill. But this process is predicated on the belief that participants who understand its benefits will be moved to act with integrity. When that does not occur, it will be the place of the inquirer and other participants in the process to cry "foul," and to attempt to right the process. As we shall see, deliberate attempts to miscarry the process are quite likely to be detected— much more so than in the case of the conventional paradigm.

(2) *Minimal competence* on the part of all parties to *communicate*. Holders of different constructions must be able to offer their own constructions, and to offer criticisms of the constructions of others, meaningfully. Specifically excluded from the class of competent constructors are the following persons:

(a) Children (a matter of relative age). So, for instance, teenagers might well be able to offer constructions of their lives in high schools, or of their home lives, or of their part-time employment. But very young children lack the sophistication to be able to participate meaningfully in such a process—although, please note, the process comes close to what many experts believe reflects the best of child-rearing practices.

(b) The mentally handicapped (a matter of relative severity of handicap).

(c) Psychotics or other self-deluded personalities. (Note: Constructions are self-delusional when they arise not from an interaction but solely from within the constructor's own mind.)

(3) A willingness on the part of all parties *to share power*.

(4) A willingness on the part of all parties *to change* if they find the negotiations persuasive. Those who are "true believers" in some construction, or who fear "revisionists," de facto cannot carry out a meaningful negotiation.

(5) A willingness on the part of all parties to *reconsider their value positions* as appropriate. This condition shares the same caveats as the preceding item.

(6) A willingness on the part of all parties to *make the commitments of time and energy* that may be required in the process (a by no means insignificant amount of either).

These are conditions that we believe to be minimal. That is, all of them are required, and so are necessary, but we do not yet know whether they are a sufficient set. These conditions are derived from our own experience in the field; others must continue to test whether they constitute all the conditions that must be met.

How Does One Carry Out Such a Process?

There are several ways in which to carry out a hermeneutic dialectic negotiation. We prefer the process captured in Figure 5.1, which represents one of what will be a number of stakeholder circles. As a first step, an initial respondent, R_1, is selected by the inquirer for any convenient or salient reason. The reason could be nomination by a gatekeeper, the respondent's elite or specialized position within the setting, or any other good or compelling reason (probably not to include random sampling). This respondent is engaged in an open-ended interview to determine an initial and emic construction of whatever is being investigated or evaluated—the focus of the inquiry. The respondent is asked to describe the focus as she or he constructs it, to describe it and comment on it in personal terms. In evaluations, these comments might include observations about claims, concerns, and issues, and observations about what is liked and disliked about the evaluand (the entity being evaluated).

Second, the respondent is asked to nominate another respondent, R_2, who is as much different in her or his construction from R_1 as R_1 is able to identify. This is often done quite handily by simply asking, "There must be someone in this context who feels very different from the way that you do. Would you be willing to give me that person's name?"

The central themes, concepts, ideas, values, concerns, and issues proposed by respondent R_1. are analyzed by the inquirer into an initial formulation of R_1's construction, designated as C_1 in Figure 5.1. The data analysis process, the constant comparative method, is thoroughly described in our earlier book, *Naturalistic Inquiry* (1985). Note that data analysis follows closely on the heels of data collection, and is completed for R_1 before R_2 is approached (if at all possible). If the issues at hand are of great importance, for instance, politically sensitive, it may be useful to check the completed analysis with R_1 to be sure the inquirer "has it right." In addition, of course, the inquirer carries out a member check at the end of the open-ended interview (see Chapter 8).

Next, R_2 is interviewed and allowed the same freedom of expression as was the first respondent, R_1. When, however, R_2 has volunteered as much

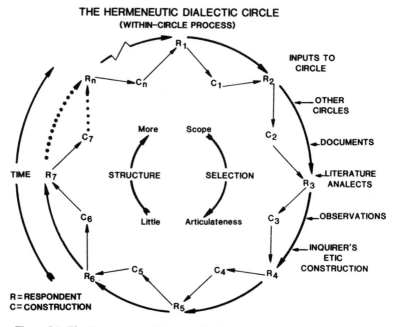

Figure 5.1 The Hermeneutic Dialectic Circle

as it appears that he or she will, the themes from the R_1 analysis are introduced, and R_2 is invited to comment on those themes. As a result, the interview with R_2 produces information not only about R_2, but also a critique of R_1's inputs and construction.

The inquirer solicits a nomination for R_3, and completes a second analysis resulting in the formulation of C_2, a now more informed and sophisticated construction based on the *two* sources R_1 and R_2. This is the beginning of the ultimate joint construction sought.

The process is repeated with new respondents being added until the information being received either becomes redundant or falls into two or more constructions that remain at odds in some way (typically, because the values that undergird the different constructions are in conflict).

As the process proceeds, the basis on which successive respondents are selected varies. Initially the effort is to identify new respondents who can add something to the emerging construction(s) that enlarge its scope. The object of this portion of the evaluation is to maximize the *range* of information collected, and to assure that as many stakeholding groups and persons as can possibly be identified have an opportunity to contribute their own constructions.

As the several constructions begin to take shape, however, certain elements will seem to be more salient than others (and will probably first appear this way to the inquirer). This salience will emerge as a result of increased mention by respondents and participants, for example, because of the vehemence with which stakeholding groups discuss an issue, because of funders' interests, or for any other reason that seems important in the context. The identification of high-salience issues is in part an interaction process between inquirer and participants and depends on an intense study of analyzed constructions and reconstructions. The process of selection of salient issues thus gradually changes the aim of sampling from securing respondents who can add the widest range of information to respondents who can be *articulate* about the emerging salient themes that the inquirer believes have been identified.

Similarly, the degree of structure of the interviews also changes. Initially the interviews are very unstructured, with the inquirer soliciting the respondent's emic construction in the respondent's own terms. As the emerging construction or constructions (because there may be two or more that are in conflict) become clearer, however, the inquirer is able to ask more and more pointed questions.

When the circle of respondents has been completed, it may be useful to "make the circle" a second time. Earlier respondents will have had relatively little opportunity to react to the constructions of others and should be given this opportunity. The circle may be "spiraled" by making it a second time with a set of respondents similar to those in the first circle, as an alternative. In either approach the educative and empowerment criteria we have earlier mentioned (that will be described in more detail in Chapter 8) are well served.

The information and sophistication available to the respondents participating in a circle need not be limited to what they (and the inquirer) bring to it. It is possible to introduce other inputs as opportunity and need arise. For instance, there are constructions that may be emerging from *other stakeholder circles* that may be introduced. In the case of an investigation centered in a school district, for example, a circle of classroom teachers may receive inputs from circles of parents or from circles of administrators, students, taxpayers within the district, or others such as curriculum specialists.

Documents may be searched for yet other constructions or for information relevant to the emerging constructions. *Analects,* that is, selections from the relevant literature may be introduced. Such analects may either confirm one or more constructions or may directly contradict them (having been produced by processes other than hermeneutic and/or dialectic inquiries). *Observational data* relevant to the emerging constructions, for instance, that test them in practice, may be introduced. Observations may be undertaken because of insights generated during the interviews, or observational data may be introduced into the interviews for comment. Observations and interviews can thus feed upon one another.

Finally, the inquirer's *own etic (outsider) construction* may be introduced for critique. Please note that this highly subjective and, therefore, positivistically repugnant action violates no principles of constructivism so long as all respondents have the opportunity to criticize the inquirer's formulations as they must do with their own. Indeed, the inquirer's own formulations have no particular privilege save that he or she is quite possibly the only person who has moved extensively between participants, stakeholders, and respondents and, therefore, has the benefit of having heard a more complete set of constructions than anyone else in the setting is likely to have heard. Thus that particular construction is likely to be one of the most informed and sophisticated, at least toward the end of the process. This does not procure for the evaluator more power, merely a greater ability to facilitate the negotiation process that must occur.

One caveat is necessary in relation to introducing materials into a circle that may appear to come from authoritative sources and hence not be subject to challenge. Documentary data, literature analects, or the inquirer's own construction may seem, to respondents, to be beyond reproach. One is reminded of the naive question that journalists love to bandy about, "If it isn't true, they couldn't print it, could they?" And, of course, the inquirer him- or herself may be seen as an "expert" whose judgment cannot be called into question. We recommend, therefore, that such external materials be introduced in a way that does not reveal their source. Instead of saying, for example, "Census bureau documents show..." or "The literature on learning shows that..." or "It is my own opinion, based on years of research, that...," one might simply introduce any proposition by saying, "Some people believe that..." or "It is sometimes said that..." and invite comment. The solicitation ought to indicate the problematic nature of the proposition, as viewed by the inquirer: "Does that seem to fit in here?" or "Does that make sense to you given the situation here?" or "Would that work here?" or some such comment.

Circles need not, of course, be made up only of similar individuals, that is, persons who fill similar roles, are the same sex or the same age, or who resemble one another on some other factor thought to be important in this setting, in this time. Circles can consist of persons who are widely different from one another. But the probability that the minimal conditions for a successful hermeneutic dialectic encounter will be met (discussed earlier in this chapter) is lessened, because such circles are likely to contain persons of, for instance, widely varying power within the context.

The general process outlined in Figure 5.1 is basic to all of naturalistic inquiry, whether research, evaluation, or policy analyses. We expand on these ideas in Chapter 6, and apply them specifically to the case of evaluation in Chapter 7.

We have in this chapter skirted the issue of how one can judge the goodness of a hermeneutic dialectic process and its outcome, although we have hinted at criteria such as educativeness and empowerment. A full treatment of this important topic is undertaken in Chapter 8.

6 *Paradigms and Methodologies*

Defenders of the positivist paradigm have mounted a variety of arguments against the proposition that alternative paradigms, and particularly the constructivist paradigm, need be taken seriously. Early on, they dismissed the alternatives as, variously, too subjective, too unreliable, and/or insufficiently generalizable—in short, too "soft." But it was soon noticed that the criteria brought to bear in making these judgments were grounded in the self-same assumptions that undergird the conventional paradigm (Morgan, 1983; also see Chapter 8). Thus the fairness and appropriateness of applying them to alternative paradigms were called into question.

The counterargument then shifted to the assertion that paradigms are distinguishable *only* at the level of methods, that is, as mere collections of different inquiry tools and techniques. Thus, as Schwandt (1984, p. 194) put it, the conventional paradigm is often seen as a collage of experimental, quasi-experimental, and survey research in which data are gathered by means of standardized sociometric and psychometric instruments and analyzed via statistical procedures. The alternative model is similarly reduced to a different assembly of ethnographic/anthropological fieldwork techniques including case-study designs, unstructured interviews, and non-mathematical data analysis techniques. Conceiving of models in this way, one reduces the issue of paradigmatic conflict to the problem of allegiance to different collections of methods.

As Schwandt suggests, the fatal flaw in this argument is that it begs the question of paradigm differences, missing the real challenge of the alternative that presents a rival ontological and epistemological posture.

A third and more recent counterargument is to assert that while there may be quite meaningful differences at the ontological and epistemological levels, these differences *do not matter* in the day to day conduct of inquiry *because methods and paradigms are independent*. At the level of practice, inquirers find it impossible to choose between the two (or more) paradigms; instead they *blend* them as the problem or situation requires. So for example, Miles and Huberman (1984b, p. 20) assert:

> It is getting harder to find *any* methodologists solidly encamped in one epistemology or the other. More and more "quantitative" methodologists, operating from a logical positivist stance, are using naturalistic and phenomenological approaches to complement tests, surveys, and structured interviews. On the other side, an increasing number of ethnographers and qualitative researchers are using predesigned conceptual frameworks and prestructured instrumentation, especially when dealing with more than one institution or community.

Similarly, Cook and Reichardt (1979, p. 19) suggest that "evaluators should feel free to change their paradigmatic stance as the need arises." Patton (1982, p. 190) feels that an evalutor can make "mind shifts back and forth between paradigms" even within a single, particular investigation. Finally, Miles and Huberman (1984a) counsel their readers simply to ignore the paradigm conflict:

> We contend that researchers should pursue their work, be open to an ecumenical blend of epistemologies and procedures, and leave the

grand debate to those who care most about it. (Miles, Matthew B., Huberman, A. Michael, "Drawing Valid Meaning from Qualitative Data: Toward a Shared Craft," *Educational Researcher*, 1984, p. 20; used by permission)

Leaving aside the know-nothing character of this piece of advice, we intend to dispute this position by arguing that it confuses *methods with methodologies*, that is, tools and techniques with overall guiding strategies. To take a homely example, it may not be possible to tell whether an individual holding a hammer is a carpenter, an electrician, or a plumber, but the person holding the hammer knows, and that intention will lead to the hammer being used in very different ways. Similarly, while it may not be possible to label an individual a positivist simply because he or she is using a survey instrument, or a constructivist simply because he or she is conducting an interview, those persons know (or should know) from which paradigm they operate, and that knowledge has significant consequences for the ways in which those tools are used. The point of this chapter is to document just what the differences in methodologies between paradigms are, and to illustrate how those differences affect the "day-to-day" conduct of inquiry. In the next chapter we shall explicitly apply this constructivist methodology to the case of evaluation.

Naturalistic [Constructivist] Evaluation of the First and Second Kinds[1]

Before we undertake to explicate the paradigm differences in methodology, it is instructive to consider what effect the confusion between methodologies has had upon the practice of evaluation labeled *naturalistic* (which we now prefer to call *constructivist*). In a recent volume titled *Naturalistic Evaluation* edited by David D. Williams (1986), the variety of definitions offered by the several chapter authors is bewildering. Williams himself seems to equate *naturalistic evaluation* with *qualitative evaluation*:

the qualitative perspective, defensibly obtained, can radically improve many evaluation efforts. More and more evaluators have begun to explore the naturalistic approach to see if and how it may be applied in a variety of settings. Some have attempted evaluations that are exclusively naturalistic (including no quantitative methods) while others have combined naturalistic components (such as participant observation and repeated informal interviews) with more traditional tests, questionnaires, and structured interviews to create mixed-method designs. (p. 1)

In another chapter David Fetterman believes that the term *naturalistic evaluation* cannot be understood as a "monolithic entity" but as a "generic term for many different kinds of qualitative appraisals," in which the "tools and designs used . . . are very similar" (p. 23). Mary Lee Smith in yet another chapter, having averred that the term *qualitative* is *broader* than the term *naturalistic,* defines the qualitative approach as involving

the long-term and first-hand study of a case by the investigator for the purpose of understanding and describing human action in the context of that case. Field methods are used to collect data, including direct observation of action in its natural context, clinical interviews to elicit the multiple meanings of participants in that case, and the collection of documents. A qualitative approach leads to reports primarily in the form of words, pictures, and displays rather than formal models or statistical findings. (p. 38)

Smith's introduction of the terms *natural context* and *multiple meanings of participants* surely adds dimensions missing in the other formulations, and suggests a break from conventional thinking about inquiry. Nevertheless, the emphasis remains on methods rather than paradigms.

Only Sari Knopp Biklen and Robert Bogdan, in this volume, propose a definition that makes the distinctions implied by paradigm differences plain and unmistakable:

Naturalistic methods can be used in two ways. First, and less forcefully, they can be used as techniques in a study that has not been framed from a naturalistic perspective. . . .

Second, the evaluator conceptualizes the study around what we call "thinking naturalistically." That is, the evaluator approaches reality as a multilayered, interactive, shared social experience that can be studied by first learning what participants consider important. In this case, the first days in the field are spent learning how participants think about and conceptualize issues. (p. 95)

Thus Biklen and Bogdan identify two quite distinct modes of working with naturalistic approaches: as a collection of tools and techniques—the methods level—or as a wholly different way of viewing the world—the paradigm level. We shall refer to these two levels as "naturalistic evaluation of the first kind" and "naturalistic evaluation of the second kind," respectively. Nevertheless, Biklen and Bogdan further assert, these two distinct approaches "share some common threads when they are applied to naturalistic evaluation." These common threads include collecting descriptive data in the natural setting, with the evaluator serving as the inquiry instrument; focusing on "educational issues as they are perceived and experienced by people" (p. 95); and utilizing an inductive process that focuses and narrows as the evaluation proceeds.

Thus, even when naturalistic methods are used simply as techniques, they nevertheless have many properties that are also typical of the approach in which the evaluator *thinks* naturalistically. Thus it is not surprising that there exists widespread confusion about whether the term *naturalistic* denotes technique or paradigm, although many more people adhere to the former than to the latter viewpoint. It is possible to use naturalistic techniques, alone or as a part of a multimethods study, without stirring from the limits of the positivist paradigm, from what we have already called its "friendly confines." Thinking naturalistically, however, requires a paradigm shift of revolutionary proportions that, once made, inevitably changes both the meaning and the practice of evaluation in similarly revolutionary ways.

The reader may not find it amiss if we divert from our main argument for a moment to point out that naturalistic evaluation of the first kind has achieved fairly widespread prominence. In a recent analysis one of us (Guba, 1987) noted the following types of applications:

(1) *Exploration.* Naturalistic approaches may be used to explore areas that are initially impossible to conceptualize and so lay the basis for a more rigorous investigation later. The parallel in research is often called the *discovery/verification* distinction on which we have already com-

mented. An interesting example of exploration is found in that subset of
stakeholder-oriented evaluations that utilize qualitative methods to elicit
audience inputs about the issues or questions that the evaluation should
pursue, but that are otherwise conducted conventionally. The evaluation
of Push/Excel (NIE, 1978) is an instance.

(2) *Description.* Naturalistic approaches can be used in the service of
description, first, by providing "rich" contextual information within
which the more rigorous quantitative findings can be interpreted, and,
second, by providing a means for the ongoing monitoring of the processes
involved in implementing some evaluand. The series of five case studies
conducted by Skrtic, Guba, and Knowlton (1985) assessing services provided to handicapped youngsters by rural cooperatives illustrates the first
application; the study of a preschool art classroom by Swann (1986)
illustrates the second.

(3) *Illustration.* Naturalistic approaches can be used to illustrate or
exemplify what has been uncovered at a more general level through
more conventional evaluation approaches. The U.S. General Accounting
Office study (U.S. GAO, 1982) of the effects of block grants on housing
provides an illustration. The case cited in the referenced report, Dallas,
was one of a series of four that were carried out. These case studies were
"not intended to comprehensively evaluate program effectiveness" but to
"provide insight on the kind and extent of housing activity under the
Community Block Grant Program."

(4) *Realization.* Naturalistic approaches can be used to help audiences realize—in the sense of "make real"—both the particulars of a case
and the construction of those particulars entertained by each of the
several audiences. Cases are said to provide depth or realism, anecdotal
materials, or vicarious experience. Some of the best examples of this use
of naturalistic evaluation are found in the contributions of various
students of Elliot Eisner, such as the excerpts reprinted in *The Educational Imagination* (Eisner, 1979). One begins with this gripping paragraph: "This classroom is almost a caricature of society. The curriculum
is served up like Big Macs. Reading, math, language, even physical
education and affective education are all precooked, prepackaged, artifi-
cally flavored" (p. 229). The report on a critical care neonatal unit offered
by Bogdan, Brown, and Foster (1984) is another compelling instance.

(5) *Testing.* Naturalistic approaches can be used, however unlikely it may seem, to test hypotheses or to answer questions that the investigator specifically targets ahead of time. The study by Pierce (1981) investigating whether government bureaucracy is capable of implementing laws in ways consistent with the intent of legislators, and the study of Roncek and Weinberger (1981) to test the hypothesis that certain federal funds available to support public housing were used in ways that concentrated such housing in less desirable portions of the city, are cases in point.

It should be noted that these five types are rarely found alone; they are usually intermingled, particularly in side-by-side approaches intended to exploit their putative complementarity (e.g., M. L. Smith, 1986), or in so-called multimethod or mixed-method studies. A variety of applications of the latter type appear. Often two approaches (typically) are used in alternating fashion to facilitate the emergence of the evaluation or inquiry design (Sieber, 1973); observation, for example, generates questions that may be followed up in interviews, while the interview may generate the need for certain types of observations, and so on. In other cases, multimethod or mixed-method designs have been used for purposes of triangulation (Denzin, 1978; Smith & Kleine, 1986); to offset obtrusiveness, by inserting an unobtrusive qualitative technique to augment and illuminate data collected by more conventional but also more reactive means (Williams, 1986); or to facilitate integration, capitalizing on the putative synergistic effects of multimethods (Smith & Kleine, 1986).

The readers should note that *none* of these applications, whether used singly or in combination, requires the evaluator to move away from the basic belief system of positivism. They are all instances of *naturalistic evaluation of the first kind.* It is not our purpose to dwell on these applications; our intent is to move to a consideration of *naturalistic evaluation of the second kind,* which *does* require a paradigm shift. Fourth generation evaluation, as we have earlier described it, surely falls into this latter category.

It is time, then, to consider in detail what is implied by the phrases *the methodology of conventional inquiry* and the *methodology of constructivist inquiry.* We move to this task in the next two sections.

The Methodology of Conventional Inquiry

Rendering the complexities of the inquiry process, whether conventional or constructivist, into a flowchart or series of steps inevitably results in an oversimplification. Such an approach cannot hope to capture the creativity and the infinite adaptability that most inquirers of whatever ilk bring to their tasks. Yet, in the interest of making certain distinctions that we feel to be crucial, we attempt such an analysis here. The critical question, it seems to us, is not whether our analysis captures all the nuances and intricacies of a methodology but whether it captures its essential features. We leave it to the reader to decide how well we accomplish that goal.

At the outset it is also important to distinguish between inquiries that are intended to add knowledge or understanding in some significant way and those intended to assess some state of affairs. Many polls, surveys, needs assessments, questionnaire studies, and the like are of the latter sort, and represent inquiries that might be carried out *within either paradigm* so long as they are mounted and interpreted in ways consistent with the paradigm's basic belief system.

So, for example, the inquirer who interprets a needs assessment, say, as representing "real" needs is likely to be operating within the positivist paradigm, whereas an inquirer who regards such responses as representing the momentary constructions of the people involved is more likely to be operating from the constructivist paradigm. To see the difference, the first inquirer might proceed, having completed the inquiry and determined what the needs are, to propose (invent, develop, engineer) some response to them. The second inquirer might, at the same point, take those findings to represent an opening construction of a state of affairs that can be negotiated and renegotiated so long as that exercise seems fruitful. What may be done in relation to those constructed needs is decided by all those relevant parties whose initial constructions are represented in the assessment, utilizing the hermeneutic dialectic described in Chapter 5.

The difference extends beyond the particular meaning that will be ascribed to the findings of a poll, survey, needs assessment, or questionnaire study, however—it is also characterized by a difference in how the instrument would be constructed in the first place. The conventional inquirer is likely to have devised the questions asked on the basis of some a priori theory or position. Thus the respondents can only confirm or reject the inquirer's etic formulation. Such an etic view, even if confirmed by the respondents (i.e., they see it as having applicability in their situations), may nevertheless miss what is most important to the respondents. They cannot register those other elements, however, because the structure of the instrument neither elicits nor provides a means for registering them. The constructivist inquirer, on the other hand, when using such a broadside instrument, would first *ground* that instrument in the emic view(s) of the respondents.

Despite these quite important differences in the ways that such instrumentation would be developed and used within the paradigms, it is probably most useful to consider these instruments as *congeries of methods* rather than as distinct methodologies. In this chapter our emphasis will be on the latter, and specifically, with the general strategy supported by a paradigm for inquiring in ways that make substantial contributions to knowledge and understanding.

With these *caveats* clearly in mind, we may proceed with a discussion of conventional methodology.

The broad outlines of conventional methodology are sketched in Figure 6.1. We note, first, the distinction between the contexts of *discovery* and *verification*, which is basic to this paradigm. Discovery in conventional terms is best thought of as the *precursor* to inquiry, the phase from which theory—or at least hypotheses and questions—emerge. It is the most creative part of the process, but, by a quirk peculiar to positivism, is relegated to a place outside the inquiry process itself. It is the place in which the "theoretical language" is formulated, which will later be tested through observation (hence the crucial importance of keeping theoretical and observational languages separate, as noted in Chapter 3). Inquiry may be thought of, in these terms, as the *empirical* part of science; it will *verify or justify* the assertions or propositions that emerge from discovery.

Now discovery is a mysterious, creative process. The theory (or hypotheses or questions) may arise from the theorizer's tacit ("gut-level") knowledge, the gleanings from which may be characterized as "hunches"

THE METHODOLOGY OF CONVENTIONAL INQUIRY
DOMAIN OF DISCOVERY (NON–SCIENCE)

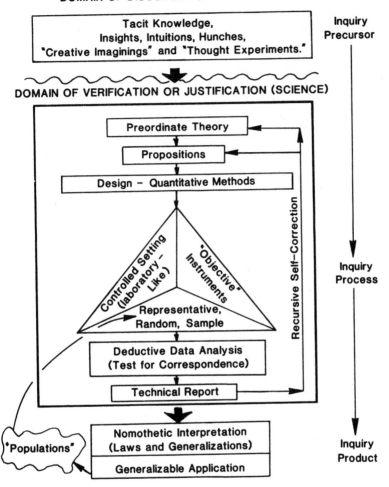

Figure 6.1 The Methodology of Conventional Inqiry

or "intuitions," or, in more professionally acceptable language, as "insights." Discovery can be untrammeled, leading to "creative imaginings," or disciplined, as in the well-known case of Einstein's "gedanken-experimente" (thought or mental experiments). It may even be very rigorously formulated, as, for example, in the equations of mathematical or theoretical physics. In all events, what is to be inquired into is conceptualized *outside* the realm of *empirical* science—the realm of verification, or as it is sometimes called, of justification (this despite the fact that theories can never be proved or verified; at best they can be falsified). Of course, it is possible that the theory has arisen from earlier scientific work—probably most propositions tested by inquiry are of this sort. But that does not obviate the fact that first origins are invariably found elsewhere than in the realm of empirical science.

It is worth noting that among the various proposals for an accommodation between the conventional and naturalistic paradigms is one that assigns constructivist inquiry to the discovery domain and conventional inquiry to the domain of verification, as we have already observed in Chapter 3 (see the "muddy boots syndrome"). This proposal misses the point that *both* discovery and verification are essential to the pursuit of conventional inquiry. The placement of discovery *outside* the central scientific process is occasioned more by the positivists' need to maintain the separation of theoretical and observational languages than by an intent to denigrate discovery. At the same time, discovery and verification are, within the constructivist paradigm, *inseparable, synergistic* processes that are carried out in such close relationship as to make Catholic marriage look like rampant free love. The possibility of accommodation on such a basis seems doomed from the start.

Within the domain of verification—empirical science—the conventional paradigm demands certain steps. First, we observe that the theory emerging from discovery may give rise, by deduction, to a large number of hypotheses or questions, depending on its seminality (or, the hypotheses or questions may be a direct product of the discovery process, say, in areas in which too little information exists to permit a full-scale theory to emerge). Some selection must be made for the inquiry at hand, based on such (value) criteria as inquirer interest, presumed heuristic utility, the possibility of performing "critical" tests, available instrumentation, possibility of support, and the like.

A design that will test the hypotheses or answer the question is developed next. It is crucial to note that in this step the inquirer deals entirely with *propositional,* as opposed to *tacit,* language. The hypotheses or questions to be dealt with in the design must be stateable in language form if a rigorous and objective design is to be developed. They cannot be ill formed, only partially understood, or imperfectly intuited. The requirements of an objectivist, dualist epistemology demand that the inquirer be *detachable* from those statements in order to be able to provide a neutral empirical test. Whatever cannot be precisely stated at the outset is forever banned from the inquiry (unless the inquirer determines to abandon *that* inquiry and start anew as new insights emerge—a procedure neither encouraged nor abetted by current funding and review processes).

Because hypotheses and/or questions *are* stated in propositional form from the outset of the inquiry, it is usually possible to translate them into some precise operational definition, with each variable (construct, factor, or whatever) specified in some measurable or assessable way. Such statements are, moreover, easily further translated into quantitative form, so that the design is converted into a *statistical* design. Selection of a particular design from among several options is made on such criteria as relative power (loosely, the ability to discriminate with the smallest number of cases) and the inquirer's ability to manage the mandated conditions of the inquiry (e.g., maintain control, eliminate confounding, select subjects randomly, and the like), in such a way that the assumptions underlying the statistical techniques will be met.

The ease with which this transformation from raw theory or hypotheses/questions to operational definitions to quantitative instruments to statistical design may be accomplished is a major advantage of positivism. The collection and processing of quantified data yield improved rigor, increase ability to predict and to control (through precise formulation of predictive equations to which causal meaning may be assigned), and make possible the application of an impressive array of mathematical and statistical tools. However, it should *not* be inferred from this observation, or from the flowchart, that *only* quantitative data are admissible within the conventional paradigm. Qualitative data are not only admissible but may at times prove to be equally useful, or at least complementary. But it is also the case that quantitative data are preferred for the advantages that they confer (when the world is constructed from a positivist view). An empirical assessment of positivist studies would no doubt yield a high correlation with the use of quantitative methods.

Once the design is developed, the positivist inquirer is ready to implement it. A trio of specifications is involved at this point, which must be adhered to closely if the study is to be meaningful in positivist terms—hence their incorporation in Figure 6-1 into a stable triangle.

First, the inquiry must be carried out under controlled conditions. If the goal is to discover "how things really are" and "how things really work," it is absolutely necessary to establish controls to avoid being misled or confused by confounding factors. If one wishes to know the laws that determine the speed with which an object falls, it is necessary to conduct the inquiry in ways that rule out the possibility of confounding by, say, the surface that an object presents to the air. In the "real" world, feathers and cannonballs do not fall at the same rate; if one wishes to demonstrate that the laws of nature nevertheless act on such dissimilar objects in the same way, the study must be carried out in a vacuum. Now the laboratory represents the epitome of control (indeed, it was the necessity for maintaining control that led inquirers to establish laboratories in the first place); thus it is little wonder that positivists opt for a laboratory setting whenever they can. True experimental designs (Campbell & Stanley, 1963) virtually require a laboratory, but when one is forced to work in a more lifelike setting, quasi-experimental designs may be used productively (Campbell & Stanley, 1963). We may note in passing that while laboratorylike settings may improve the *internal* validity of an inquiry, they are also an Achilles heel. From the point of view of *external* validity, results from a laboratory can, in the final analysis, be reasonably generalized only to another laboratory. Thus, within the positivist paradigm, internal and external validity stand in a trade-off relationship: every effort to increase one inevitably results in a decrease in the other. It is mainly because of a realization of this fact of life that positivists, seeking to remedy some of the problems of conventional research, have been willing to consider conducting inquiry in more "natural" settings, thereby somewhat redressing the imbalance between internal and external validity.

A second specification is that the instrumentation used in the inquiry must be certifiably objective, that is, beyond manipulation or misdirected interpretation by inquirer, sponsor, funder, subjects, or anyone else. The instruments must be of a sort that put questions directly to nature and have the capability of recording nature's direct answer. Paper-and-pencil and brass instruments represent the ideal, especially if they have been independently standardized and normed. The intent is to interpolate a layer of objectivity between investigator and investigated that prevents any untoward interaction between them. Obviously the objectivity of the instrumentation is severely threatened, perhaps compromised, if the instrument *is* the investigator (as in the case of an open-ended interview or free observation), for then subjectivity may be rampant. The messages sent back by nature in response to our inquiry must be received without distortion if we are to be assured that they represent the way things "really are" and "really work."

A third and final specification is that the inquiry be conducted utilizing a representative or at least a random sample. There are two reasons for this specification. First, it is the intent of the positivist to produce generalizable findings; thus the question arises, "Generalizable to whom?" Normally, there exists some population (which may be arbitrarily established by definition, such as the population of elementary school children in the New England area) to whom the findings are expected to apply. Most often, this population is too large to permit including all its elements in the study, for fiscal and logistical reasons or because the population cannot be enumerated. Thus it becomes impera-tive that a sample be drawn that is in some way representative of that population, so that findings on the part can be inductively applied to the whole. Representativeness can be accomplished only if the investigator possesses or can acquire the information needed, such as the IQ scores of the members of the population if a sample demonstrably representative on IQ is to be selected. In the absence of such information (which is often the case), the inquirer falls back on a *simple* random sample, which also permits generalization to occur, but with less power than if the sample had been representative (i.e., the number of cases must be larger to reach the same levels of confidence). Generalization cannot be legitimately accomplished unless a representative or at least random sample has been drawn.

A second reason for requiring a representative or at least random sample is to protect the internal validity of the study. Studies frequently compare different treatments or interventions, one of which is almost always a control (no treatment). Now if subjects are not assigned randomly to those several groups, the possibility arises that one or more of the groups may be biased in some way. For example, a learning experiment would be severely compromised if it turned out that the higher-IQ subjects happened to be assigned to Treatment A and the lower-IQ subjects to Treatment B. Thus subjects must not only be randomly selected (for the sake of external validity or generalizability) but also randomly assigned (for the sake of internal validity).

When these three specifications—controlled setting, objective instrumentation, and randomly selected and assigned sample—have been met, the inquirer is ready to carry out the steps previously stipulated in the design. These steps may include collection of preexperimental data, administering and monitoring the treatments, collecting postexperimental data, and so on. While only a naive inquirer would expect no deviations from the original plan, deviations that do occur (and they *will* occur) will be regarded as sources of error and, therefore, to be avoided or suppressed. They will, at the very least, require remedial adjustments (with a concomitant increase in resource expenditure and a likely increase in the size of the "error term" in subsequent statistical tests) and, at worst, may confound the information sought or further enlarge the error term to a point at which the "real" effect becomes undetectable and the only recourse is to abort the study. Throughout this process the inquirer is expected to keep "hands off," for any intervention will be constructed as a possible point of error or as an introduction of unwanted subjectivity. The data that result from this process are those that were projected in the original design (indeed, some inquirers seem to feel that a design is not adequate unless and until it specifies in "dummy tables" the nature of the data to be filled in).

When the inquiry has been completed through the data collection step, data analysis may begin (and, typically, not before, lest the inquirer be tempted to "redesign" the analytic procedures to take advantage of interesting tendencies in the data in opportunistic ways). The analysis is carried out in terms of the procedures and tests—usually statistical— prescribed in the design statement. Essentially these tests are intended to determine the degree of correspondence of the findings with the "real" world, which is the ultimate test imaginable within the bounds of the realist ontology to which positivism adheres. In practice, the hypotheses are not subjected to verification but to *falsification*: It is the *null* hypothesis that is accepted or rejected; rejection of the null hypothesis does not compel acceptance of any particular alternative hypothesis. Indeed, it is over this point that the conventional paradigm suffers one of its major embarrassments. If the test of validity of an inquiry is that its findings should be isomorphic with reality (i.e., tell us the way "things really are" and "really work"), nothing would be more peruasive than to demonstrate that correspondence directly. But to be able to do that implies that one has certain knowledge of just what that reality *is*, and if one already knew that, there would be no point to doing a study to find it out. Hence the test is not made (for it cannot be made) by using the real world as criterion but rather by employing a statistical model that is based on an assumption exactly counter to that of positivism: that reality is a series of chance happenings, random and unrelated. To assert, as the result of a statistical test, that the "null hypothesis" is rejected is simply to assert that the proposition of randomness is not tenable, but it does not assert that, therefore, reality must have thus-and-thus form.

That difficulty aside, if it has been possible as part of the design to specify "dummy tables," these are now filled in; otherwise, appropriate tables are constructed. Conclusions relevant to the hypotheses and their generative theory are drawn. But note that the investigator is not compelled by the force of the data to a particular conclusion; rather, an *interpretation* is involved. Such interpretations imply values. It should not surprise us, therefore, to discover that no matter how closely a study adheres to scientific principles in its execution, science does not and cannot dictate the interpretations to be drawn.

Finally, in completing the *process* steps involved in conventional inquiry, the inquirer will develop a technical report. This report is expected to set out the problem or other focus of the inquiry clearly, to demonstrate its connections with what is already known (usually by reviewing relevant literature), to explicate and defend the methodology employed, to display the data, and to set out the interpretations and conclusions reached by the investigator. But we cannot lose sight of the fact that this entire study was done in relation to certain theoretical formulations, hypotheses, or questions that were posed at the outset. The question then arises, "Do the conclusions and interpretations support or falsify these original propositions?" *If* the original propositions are supported, then those propositions are assimilated into the field of knowledge and may be used to generate the next questions or the next steps. But if they are *not* supported, then the propositions need to be adjusted or restated in light of the findings, and new studies mounted. This step is the much-vaunted self-correcting loop putatively build into scientific inquiry: Even though original premises may be wrong, perhaps wildly wrong, the iteration and reiteration of such interlocking studies will eventually lead us to converge on the way "things really are" and "really work." The same or similar studies are recycled, or related studies are done ("more research is needed") until a stable base of evidence has been built up that supports the (refined) theory.

It should be evident that this recursive self-correcting process that assures the eventual validity of the theory is an *internal* one; it seeks only those data that may confirm or repudiate the formulated theory, but it is essentially *closed* to new data that might suggest that an entirely different theory is appropriate. New data that challenge "established" theory tend to be regarded as anomalies. When a sufficient number of anomalies collect, a Kuhnian paradigm crisis arises, which is resolved with the adoption of a new theory or paradigm.

When there has been a sufficient number of iterations so that the theory and its implications may be considered to be established, its propositions may be regarded as applicable—generalizable—to the population from which the sample(s) were drawn. If the sample(s) themselves are sufficiently large and diverse, the generalizations produced by this group of studies may be regarded as virtual natural laws—nomothetic statements that have widespread applicability. Thus the inquiry product is at the least improved theory and perhaps a whole new set of nomothetic interpretations, which have meaning within that population represented in the sample(s). The aim of predicting and controlling those populations becomes achievable.

The Methodology of Constructivist Inquiry

Before we undertake to describe the methodology of constructivist inquiry, it may be useful to note several caveats. First, we may recall our earlier warning that any rendering of a complex methodology is bound to be simplistic. If that were true of the flowchart depicting conventional inquiry, it is doubly or triply true of a flowchart depicting constructivist inquiry. The idea of devising a flowchart that captures an essentially nonlinear process seems far-fetched and unlikely to produce satisfactory results. So the reader will note, on consulting Figure 6.2, that there are portions of the chart *not* joined by lines or arrows, parts that just seem to "float" in space. Further, the lines that *do* appear, while as bold and black as any, have a much more tenuous quality, as we shall see. Finally, at least a portion of the chart—the hermeneutic dialectic circle—cannot be adequately represented in two dimensions. One can more appropriately think of that circle as a sphere, extending out of the paper front and back, so that the motions within it can occur in three-dimensional form. And even that representation would be incomplete. The nature of constructivist methodology cannot be inferred adequately from a two-dimensional chart; probably only practicing that methodology will permit accomplishment of that end.

Second, we want to be clear that Figure 6.2 is not developed simply in reaction to Figure 6.1 and its representation of conventional methodology. Rather, it may be deduced from the basic belief system of constructivism itself. It is doubtful that someone beginning with those basic beliefs—axioms and theorems—and ignorant of positivism as an inquiry mode, would have devised a methodology substantially different. That is to say, the methodology of constructivism is not simply a reaction to positivism but represents a strong position generated from its own assumptions—a proactive posture.

With these thoughts firmly in mind, we may begin. Attention is directed to Figure 6.2, which sets out the methodology in a manner that parallels Figure 6.1. This methodology also has a set of specifications—a quartet this time—which must be adhered to closely if the study is to be

THE METHODOLOGY OF CONSTRUCTIVIST INQUIRY

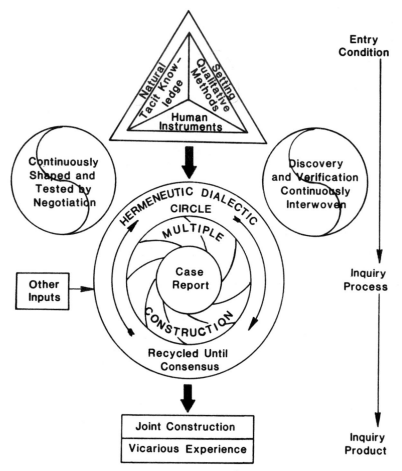

Figure 6.2 The Methodology of Constructivist Inquiry

meaningful in constructivist terms. These too are incorporated into a stable triangle, represented in Figure 6.2 as a set of *entry conditions*. If these conditions cannot be met, there is no point in undertaking the inquiry, at least not one to be graced with the name of constructivist.

First, there is a requirement that the study be pursued in a natural setting—a consequence of the relativist ontology that undergirds constructivism. If multiple realities are assumed, and they are dependent on the time and context of the constructors who hold them, it is essential that the study be carried out in the same time/context frame that the inquirer seeks to understand. If some other frame is used, for example, a laboratory, the findings (understandings) will not be relevant. Contexts give life to and are given life by the constructions that are held by the people in them.

Second, constructivists are unwilling to assume that they know enough about the time/context frame a priori to know what questions to ask. That is, it is not possible to pursue someone else's emic construction with a set of predetermined questions based solely on the inquirer's etic construction. If constructivists *did* know, it would, of course, be possible to identify appropriately framed instruments. But constructivists typically enter the frame as learners, not claiming to know preordinately what is salient. Another way to say this is that, whereas positivists begin an inquiry *knowing* (in principle) what they don't know, constructivists typically face the prospect of not knowing what it is they don't know.

What is needed under these circumstances is a highly adaptable instrument that can enter a context without prior programming, but that can, after a short period, begin to discern what *is* salient (in the emic views of the respondents) and then focus on *that*. Hofstadter (1979) has elegantly made the case that the *perfection* of an instrument is a trade-off with its *adaptability*—the more perfect an instrument is, the less adaptable (e.g., IQ tests measure *only* IQ, and probably very well, but they cannot reattune themselves to discover what may be situationally more important characteristics of the resident humans). The human being, however imperfect, is nevertheless virtually infinitely adaptable, meeting all of the specifications we have just outlined. The human is the instrument of choice for the constructivist, and, it should be stressed, the *only possible* choice during the early stages of an inquiry. Objections that humans are subjective, biased, or unreliable are irrelevant, for there is no other option.

Third, given that the human instrument is to be employed, the question of which methods to use is easily answered: those that come most readily to hand for a human. Such methods are, clearly, qualitative methods. Humans collect information best, and most easily, through the direct employment of their senses: talking to people, observing their activities, reading their documents, assessing the unobtrusive signs they leave behind, responding to their non-verbal cues, and the like. It is for this reason that qualitative methods are preferred, and *not* because these methods are the basis for defining the constructivist paradigm (as they are often taken to be; consider again the case of naturalistic evaluation of the first kind). Moreover, there is nothing in this formulation that militates *against* the use of quantitative methods; the constructivist is obviously free to use such methods without prejudice when it is appropriate to do so (for example, using a questionnaire, poll, survey, or other assessment device to gather information from a broad spectrum of individuals once the need and utility of that information has been established by grounding it in the emic views of local respondents).

Finally, the constructivist insists on the right to incorporate and use *tacit knowledge* (Polanyi, 1966). Tacit knowledge is all that we know *minus* all we can say—the latter (all we can say) is propositional knowledge, which we noted earlier, represents the limits of what can be studied within the conventional paradigm. In that paradigm, it is the requirement of the methodology that verification—the real work of science—deal with the testing of *propositions*. But the constructivist moves into a situation without prior propositional formulations in mind; indeed, it is a premise that the constructivist will initially have very little idea of what is salient and, therefore, ought to be examined. How can he or she go about sensing out what to examine? The constructivist's answer to that question is to bring one's tacit knowledge to bear. Of course, it is unlikely—indeed, impossible—for the constructivist (or anyone else) to enter a situation with a *tabula rasa;* the fact that the investigator selects this particular problem or focus to investigate implies that a great deal is already known or understood, and those constructions can be laid on the table early on. But it is the emic material that remains opaque to the investigator's propositional formulations; if the investigator is to be prohibited from using tacit knowledge as he or she attempts to pry open this oyster of unknowns, the possibility of constructivist inquiry would be severely constrained, if not eliminated altogether.

There is nothing mysterious or mystical about tacit knowledge. We all know more than we can say. An expert automobile mechanic may know little of the thermodynamic principles on which an engine is based, but very often by "listening" to it can determine what needs to be repaired. The same is true of the experienced cardiologist listening to the heart sounds of a patient. Most of the readers of this book are likely to be educationists. Most of them can walk into a school building that they have never seen before, and, after spending a bit of time there, even without talking to anyone, can answer questions like, "Is the principal of this school authoritarian?" or "Are the children in this school happy?" or "Is the science curriculum up to date?" How do all of these people—the mechanic, the cardiologist, the educationist—come to their conclusions? Ask them and they probably won't be able to tell you. But you can rely on their judgment, for it will more often than not be right. It is precisely this same tacit understanding of a situation that serves the constructivist in the beginning stages of an inquiry, and it is exactly this tacit knowledge that is ruled irrelevant by the positivist on the grounds of its subjectivity.

These four specifications—entry conditions—are the basics on which the constructivist must insist if the constructivist inquiry is to have any hope of success. Time/context frames determine and are determined by constructions; hence, carry out the study in its normal, natural setting. The inability to specify what is salient requires an adaptable instrument, which, while not pre-programmed, can nevertheless ferret out what should be examined more closely. The use of a human instrument suggests that the methods employed should be primarily those that are congenial to humans—qualitative methods. Finally, to serve the end of adaptation (and, as we shall see, of an emergent design), the human instrument must have the privilege of drawing on his or her tacit knowledge, without which the inquiry will quickly bog down.

When these specifications are met, it is possible to mount a constructivist inquiry. The process used in this next phase of stage is the hermeneutic dialectic, which has already been briefly described in Chapter 5 (see Figure 5.1). It would be remiss not to review and enlarge upon the salient strategic considerations that underlie that approach, however. Four continuously interacting elements are involved, cycling and recycling until consensus (or nonconsensus) emerges.

First, respondents who will enter into the hermeneutic process must be selected. But such sampling is not carried out for the sake of drawing a group that is representative of some population to which the findings are to be generalized. Nor is the sample selected in ways that satisfy statistical requirements of randomness. The sample is selected to serve a different purpose, hence the term "purposive sampling" is used to describe the process. Patton (1980) has described six different types of purposive samples (that is, serving some other purpose than representativeness and randomness): sampling extreme or deviant cases, sampling typical cases, maximum variation sampling, sampling critical cases, sampling politically important or sensitive cases, and convenience sampling. For the constructivist, maximum variation sampling that provides the *broadest scope of information* (the broadest base for achieving local understanding) is the sampling mode of choice. Such samples display two characteristics. First, the sample is selected *serially,* that is, no sample element is chosen until after data collection from the preceding element has already been largely accomplished. Second, the sample is selected *contingently,* both in the sense that each succeeding element is chosen to be as different as possible from preceding elements and in the sense that elements are chosen in ways that best serve the particular needs of the inquiry at that moment. Early on, for example, we may need respondents who can provide constructions different from those we've heard before. Later in the process, however, as certain elements become identified that appear salient in that time/context frame, we may wish to select respondents who can be particularly informative and articulate about those items.

The second element in the hermeneutic circle has to do with the continuous interplay of data collection and analysis that occurs as the inquiry proceeds. As a constructivist interviews a first respondent, or makes a first observation, or reads a first document, he or she endeavors to uncover items of information that appear, on their face, to be relevant to the study's focus (in the case of evaluation, the evaluand). Only broad-ranging questions are asked of these sources, so that the respondent (or document) can offer up testimony in its own terms. In effect, the inquirer says, "Tell me the questions I ought to be asking and then answer them for me." General responses of this sort are analyzed as soon as they are obtained, so that they become part of the agenda in all subsequent data collection. During a second interview, for example, the investigator may say, after having elicited an open-ended response as before, "I've been talking to some other people and they've mentioned some things that we haven't talked about. I wonder if you would mind reacting to those." And so on.

The third element in the hermeneutic circle has to do with grounding the findings that emerge in the constructions of the respondents themselves. As data collection proceeds, analysis proceeds at the same pace, generating ever-more complex and stable agendas to guide subsequent data collection. Over time, and especially as successive respondents are asked to comment on and critique the constructions already developed, a *joint* construction begins to emerge about which consensus can begin to form (or with which selected subgroups can agree to disagree, thus forming a consensus of their own). This joint construction differs from the individual constructions originally offered by respondents, and certainly from the construction entertained by the investigator at the beginning of the study. But is is *grounded* in all those constructions, derived from them via the hermeneutic dialectic process. It is the most informed and sophisticated construction that it is possible to develop in this context, at this time, with these respondents.

This joint, grounded construction must meet certain criteria. First, it must *fit* and it must *work* (Glaser & Strauss, 1967). It is judged to *fit* when the categories and terms of the construction account for data and information that the construction putatively encompasses. It is judged to *work* when it provides a level of understanding that is acceptable and credible to the respondents (or some subset of them) and to the inquirer. It must, additionally, have *relevance* (Glaser, 1978), that is, it must deal with those constructs, core problems, and processes that have emerged in the situation (rather than, for example, those that are predicted by a grand theory but appear at best to be of secondary or tertiary importance here). Finally, and perhaps most important, it must exhibit *modifiability* (Glaser, 1978), that is, the construction must be open to continuous change to accommodate new information that emerges or new levels of sophistication to which it is possible to rise.

The final element in the hermeneutic circle is that of emergent design. Initially, given that the inquirer does not know what he or she does not know, it is impossible to be very specific about anything. But as the design proceeds, the constructivist seeks continuously to refine and extend the design—to help it unfold. As each sample element is selected, each datum recorded, and each element of the joint construction devised, the design itself can become more focused. As the constructivist inquirer becomes better acquainted with what is salient, the sample becomes more directed, the data analysis more structured, the construction more definitive. Thus the constructivist cycles and recycles the hermeneutic circle, sometimes retracing steps or leaping across intervening stages, until there is consensus.

Whereas the conventional paradigm focuses on the criterion of correspondence (between findings and reality), the constructivist focuses instead on consensus. If there exist multiple realities (constructions), and as many of those as there are actual or potential respondents, there is probably little hope that a final overall consensus can ever be achieved. But one can hope for the development of one or more constructions, each of which is internally consistent, with which respondents can form allegiances—which seem (feel, sound, smell) "right" to them. If consensus can be reached, it should not be assumed that there is no need for further inquiry; new information or new levels of sophistication may soon signal the need for a further reconstruction. If consensus cannot be achieved, the process will at least make clear what the points of difference are, about which further negotiation is required.

The final product of the multiple iterations of the hermeneutic dialectic circle is a case report. A case report is very unlike the technical reports we are accustomed to seeing in positivist inquiries. It is not a depiction of a "true" or "real" state of affairs. It does not provide a series of generalizations that might be applied in other settings that can be presumed to be drawn from the same population of settings. It is definitively not the investigator's own construction; it does not culminate in judgments, conclusions, or recommendations except insofar as these are concurred on by relevant respondents.

Instead, the case report is the *joint construction* that emerges as a result of the hermeneutic dialectic process. Throughout this process, as we saw in Chapter 5, the constructions of a variety of individuals—deliberately chosen so as to uncover widely variable viewpoints—are elicited, challenged, and exposed to new information and new, more sophisticated ways of interpretation, until some level of consensus is reached (although there may be more than one focus for consensus).

The case report helps the reader come to a realization (in the sense of making real) not only of the states of affairs that are believed by constructors to exist but also of the underlying motives, feelings, and rationales leading to those beliefs. The case report is characterized by a thick description that not only clarifies the all-important context but that makes it possible for the reader vicariously to experience it.

The gaining of *vicarious experience* is crucial for a number of reasons. First, the basic mechanism for learning in humans is experience. While psychologists may not understand the process of learning by experience very well, there is no doubt that such a process does go on. While vicarious experience is not equivalent to actual experience, it does provide many of the same opportunities to learn. It is via this process that even idiographic (non-generalizable) knowledge can be applied in a second setting. Further, vicarious experience is an excellent way to introduce a reader to new information and new levels of sophistication that can, with a little effort and assuming only good intention on the part of the reader, lead to a reconstruction, perhaps even a radical one, of the reader's original construction. The case report is thus a major vehicle for the dissemination, application, and (individual) aggregation of knowledge.

Little is known about the process of case report writing, and little advice can be found that helps a case report writer in the actual writing process. Zeller (1987) has proposed that a useful model for case writing is to be found in the New Journalism, particularly as that craft has been practiced by Tom Wolfe. She provides a variety of examples showing how passages may be constructed, and how they might differ depending on which of the common New Journalism techniques are applied in a given situation.

Finally, the case report cannot be complete without an appendix that describes in detail the methodology followed and makes it possible to judge the extent to which goodness criteria (see Chapter 8) have been met. An example of such an appendix may be found in Skrtic, Guba, and Knowlton (1985).

We are left with two additional considerations in Figure 6.2: the two curiously divided circles that are "off" the direct flow but that nevertheless impinge on it. These circles are the oriental symbol for the "yin-yang" relationship. *Yin* is the feminine aspect and *yang*, the masculine; they are in continuous interaction. (The original oriental version contains a dark point at the "fattest" part of each, to symbolize the fact that each contains within it the "seed" of the other.) Yin and yang mirror one another; some functions may be shared, but each has some complementary functions as well as other functions that require the presence of the other to be carried out. The two halves are thus mystically intertwined; to separate them invalidates both. It is this image of mutual support and operational complementarity that we wish to invoke here.

The left-hand yin-yang circle in Figure 6.2 portrays the fact that the processes and outcomes of constructivist inquiry are continuously shaped (the strong sense of collaboration) and tested (the weak sense) through negotiation between inquirer and respondents. The entry conditions must be agreed to by both. The sampling is carried out with a heavy reliance on a nomination technique, in which respondents already involved nominate others who might provide either supportive or divergent constructions. Each new sample element is expected to react to information already gleaned from other sources—dialectically. As data are analyzed, a process that must, in this spirit of collaboration, involve inputs from the respondents, the resulting analysis is tested via other yet-to-be-tapped sources. The joint construction that emerges must reflect the emic (insider) view as well as the etic (outsider) perspective. Judgments of that joint construction's fit, work, relevance, and modifiability must be made by inquirer and respondents jointly. Thus design, emergent theory, and "findings" will all represent a unique combination of inquirer and respondent values and judgments—truly collaborative, truly yin-yang interactive.

The right-hand yin-yang circle of Figure 6.2 protrays the fact that, in the constructivist paradigm, discovery and verification are also continuously interactive processes. Indeed, were if not for the fact that the issue of their separation is raised by the conventional paradigm, the constructivist would probably be unaware of any need to make such a distinction. For as soon as any item of information is identified, however provisionally, as salient in the local situation, say, through an interview, it becomes immediately subject to scrutiny in all subsequent interviews as well as in connection with all other data sources, such as observations or document analysis. Reconstruction begins as such scrutinizing takes place; the design is aimed more specifically in the indicated direction so that additional discoveries related to that item may be facilitated. Discovery and verification are not, however, merely the two sides of the same coin; they are processes so tightly interwoven as to be indistinguishable. Thus, while the positivist would have no difficulty in responding to the question, "Are you in a discovery or a verification phase?" the naturalist would find that question meaningless.

A Final Note

Methodology is best understood as the overall strategy for resolving the complete set of choices or options available to the inquirer. Far from being merely a matter of making selections among methods, methodology involves the researcher utterly—from unconscious worldview to enactment of that worldview via the inquiry process.

Thus the methodology of the constructivist is very different from that of the conventional inquirer. The latter is linear and closed. By contrast the former is iterative, interactive, hermeneutic, at times intuitive, and most certainly open. That it is the more difficult methodology to enact may be taken as axiomatic. Far from being the "easy way out" that "undisciplined, lazy, ignorant, or incompetent" inquirers might choose, in contrast to the more rigorous, disciplined, and demanding conventional approach, it makes demands of its own so heavy that anxiety and fatigue are the constructivist's most constant companions. It is a different path, one perhaps strewn with boulders, but one that leads to an extravagent and hitherto virtually unappreciated rose garden.

Note

1. The contents of this section draw heavily on the paper "Naturalistic Evaluation," a plenary address to the 1986 annual meeting of the American Evaluation Association, which was subsequently published (Guba, 1987). We have retained the older term *naturalistic* in this section in order to remain consistent with this paper's usage.

7 *The Methodology of Fourth Generation Evaluation*

Fourth generation evaluation is a marriage of responsive focusing—using the claims, concerns, and issues of stakeholders as the organizing elements—and constructivist methodology—aiming to develop judgmental consensus among stakeholders who earlier held different, perhaps conflicting, emic constructions. We have previously reviewed the reasons for preferring to use stakeholder claims, concerns, and issues (hereafter CC&I) as organizers and the constructivist belief system as the methodological generator. The effort to devise *joint, collaborative,* or *shared* constructions solicits and honors the inputs from the many stakeholders and affords them a measure of control over the nature of the evaluation activity. It is thereby both educative and empowering, while also fulfilling all the usual expectations for doing an evaluation, primarily value judgments. The relativist ontological position of constructivism provides the warrant to consider emic constructions of stakeholders (those held individually prior to the onset of the process) legitimate, rather than regarding them simply as biased perceptions. The claims, concerns, and issues of stakeholders, together with whatever may be substantively implied by them, constitute the "stuff" of which their constructions are made.

In this chapter we seek to provide specific operational guidelines for carrying out the methodology of fourth generation evaluation. Those guidelines are grounded in the principle of the hermeneutic dialectic circle, as outlined in Chapter 5, and in the methodology of naturalistic inquiry, as outlined in Chapter 6. Twelve steps are involved, summarized in Figure 7.1. Although the steps appear to be linear in sequence, it is not the case that such a linear flow either must or should be adhered to rigidly. Rather, the chart indicates progression only in a general way; it is the case that frequent back and forth movement, sometimes involving jumps over multiple steps, is not only possible but desirable. The twelve steps are indicated below:

(1) initiating a contract with the client or sponsor commissioning the evaluation;
(2) organizing the evaluation;
(3) identifying stakeholders;
(4) developing within-stakeholder-group joint (collaborative, shared) constructions via the hermeneutic/dialectic circle process, specifically focusing on claims, concerns, and issues;
(5) testing and enlarging within-group constructions by introducing new or additional information and by enabling group members to achieve higher levels of sophistication in dealing with such information;
(6) sorting out resolved CC&I—those on which consensus has been achieved;
(7) prioritizing unresolved CC&I;
(8) collecting information bearing on unresolved CC&I;
(9) preparing an agenda for negotiation;
(10) carrying out a negotiation;
(11) reporting via the case study—the joint construction as product; and
(12) recycling.

We consider each step in detail below.

THE FLOW OF FOURTH GENERATION EVALUATION

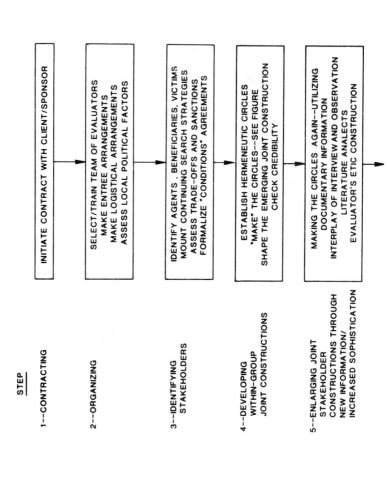

STEP

1--CONTRACTING

INITIATE CONTRACT WITH CLIENT/SPONSOR

2--ORGANIZING

SELECT/TRAIN TEAM OF EVALUATORS
MAKE ENTREE ARRANGEMENTS
MAKE LOGISTICAL ARRANGEMENTS
ASSESS LOCAL POLITICAL FACTORS

3--IDENTIFYING
    STAKEHOLDERS

IDENTIFY AGENTS , BENEFICIARIES, VICTIMS
MOUNT CONTINUING SEARCH STRATEGIES
ASSESS TRADE-OFFS AND SANCTIONS
FORMALIZE "CONDITIONS" AGREEMENTS

4--DEVELOPING
    WITHIN-GROUP
    JOINT CONSTRUCTIONS

ESTABLISH HERMENEUTIC CIRCLES
"MAKE" THE CIRCLES--SEE FIGURE
SHAPE THE EMERGING JOINT CONSTRUCTION
CHECK CREDIBILITY

5--ENLARGING JOINT
    STAKEHOLDER
    CONSTRUCTIONS THROUGH
    NEW INFORMATION/
    INCREASED SOPHISTICATION

MAKING THE CIRCLES AGAIN--UTILIZING
DOCUMENTARY INFORMATION
INTERPLAY OF INTERVIEW AND OBSERVATION
LITERATURE ANALECTS
EVALUATOR'S ETIC CONSTRUCTION

186

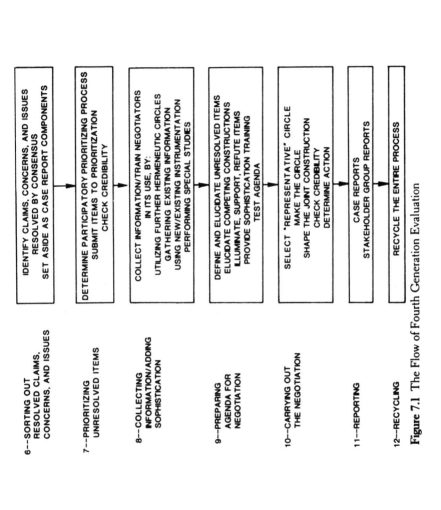

6—SORTING OUT
RESOLVED CLAIMS,
CONCERNS, AND ISSUES

IDENTIFY CLAIMS, CONCERNS, AND ISSUES
RESOLVED BY CONSENSUS
SET ASIDE AS CASE REPORT COMPONENTS

7—PRIORITIZING
UNRESOLVED ITEMS

DETERMINE PARTICIPATORY PRIORITIZING PROCESS
SUBMIT ITEMS TO PRIORITIZATION
CHECK CREDIBILITY

8—COLLECTING
INFORMATION/ADDING
SOPHISTICATION

COLLECT INFORMATION/TRAIN NEGOTIATORS
IN ITS USE, BY:
UTILIZING FURTHER HERMENEUTIC CIRCLES
GATHERING EXISTING INFORMATION
USING NEW/EXISTING INSTRUMENTATION
PERFORMING SPECIAL STUDIES

9—PREPARING
AGENDA FOR
NEGOTIATION

DEFINE AND ELUCIDATE UNRESOLVED ITEMS
ELUCIDATE COMPETING CONSTRUCTIONS
ILLUMINATE, SUPPORT, REFUTE ITEMS
PROVIDE SOPHISTICATION TRAINING
TEST AGENDA

10—CARRYING OUT
THE NEGOTIATION

SELECT "REPRESENTATIVE" CIRCLE
MAKE THE CIRCLE
SHAPE THE JOINT CONSTRUCTION
CHECK CREDIBILITY
DETERMINE ACTION

11—REPORTING

CASE REPORTS
STAKEHOLDER GROUP REPORTS

12—RECYCLING

RECYCLE THE ENTIRE PROCESS

Figure 7.1 The Flow of Fourth Generation Evaluation

187

Initiating a Contract

Evaluations are not undertaken out of whimsy; they are commissioned by some party or parties, typically called *clients* or *sponsors,* who are legally and fiscally in a position to contract for such service. The fact that evaluation results are frequently contestable ought to be sufficient warrant, particularly in today's litigious society, for the prudent evaluator to seek a written contract. If it is, moreover, proposed to practice fourth generation evaluation, it is crucial to take into account the fact that this form of evaluation is neither widely known nor commonly accepted; it is not what one would call "mainstream." A contract should, therefore, be drawn that protects both the client from evaluator misrepresentation or malpractice and the evaluator from client misunderstanding or misexpectation. Such a contract ought to cover at least the following points:

(1) *Identification of the client or sponsor of the evaluation.* Persons involved in an evaluation that purports to be empowering are, at the least, entitled to know who the client or sponsor is, since that position clearly represents a priori power. The names of people, agencies, and organizations must be on the public record so that anyone who cares can be informed about the interests of this client or sponsor. Is it a developer who has some stake in a positive evaluation in order to recoup developmental expenses and open a market? Is it a decision making body such as a school board that has some stake in having its adoption decisions justified? Is it a funding agency such as a foundation or federal or state agency that is concerned about its public image as a prudent investor of the taxpayers' money and a judicious steward of the responsibilities vested in it by law? And so on. The evaluator must be at special pains to determine that the client entering into the contract is the de facto client and not simply an agent for an undisclosed party. The client or sponsor's credentials that provide warrant for entering into a contract must be plain.

(2) *Identification of the evaluand (the entity to be evaluated).* The evaluand is no more "real" than any other mental construction. Even if its nature and character are carefully spelled out in written documents,

the documents do not speak for themselves. Different readers will make different interpretations, build different constructions. Among the constructions is that held by the client or sponsor, which might be called the "official" construction. But in the process of implementation, especially if there are multiple sites, different constructions will gain ascendancy; field observation will disclose variations between implemented version and "official" construction and between varieties of implemented versions. And as if that were not enough, the version implemented at any given site will itself change, over time, as agents (teachers, say) adapt the evaluand to local circumstances; are forced into alterations because of defaults in resource allocations, schedule maintenance, materials availability, and the like; or simply revert to older and perhaps more comfortable patterns of work. Of course, the alert evaluator expects such changes and provides a mechanism for monitoring the changes that do occur. Indeed, since the hermeneutic/dialectic is expected to change constructions, the evaluation process itself contributes to the changes that the monitoring mechanism will detect. Nevertheless, it is important, first, to have in written form the client's initial construction, and, second, to make plain in the contract that changes in the evaluand are expected and will be abetted. The client's initial construction is one benchmark for what is likely to be a series or progression of constructions that emerge, not to preclude changes in the client's construction itself over time.

(3) A *statement of purpose for the evaluation.* In our earlier book, *Effective Evaluation* (Guba & Lincoln, 1981), we showed that the purpose for evaluation could be conceptualized in one of four ways. Imagine a 2×2 table whose dimensions are, respectively, the nature of the judgment to be made, whether merit or worth, and the intent of the evaluation, whether formative or summative. A given evaluation could thus be concerned with formative merit, formative worth, summative merit, or summative worth. Thus

- A *formative merit evaluation* is one concerned with assessing the *intrinsic* value of some evaluand with the intent of *improving* it; so, for example, a proposed new curriculum could be assessed for modernity, integrity, continuity, sequence, and so on, for the sake of discovering ways in which those characteristics might be improved.

- A *formative worth evaluation* is one concerned with assessing the *extrinsic* value of some evaluand with the intent of *improving* it; so, for example, a proposed new curriculum could be assessed for the extent to which desired outcomes are produced in some *actual context of application,* for the sake of discovering ways in which its performance might be improved.
- A *summative merit evaluation* is one concerned with assessing the *intrinsic* value of some evaluand with the intent of determining whether it meets some minimal (or normative or optimal) standard for modernity, integrity, and so on. A positive evaluation results in the evaluand being warranted as meeting its internal design specifications.
- A *summative worth evaluation* is one concerned with assessing the *extrinsic* value of some evaluand for use in some actual context of application. A positive evaluation results in the evaluand being warranted for use in that context.

A formative merit evaluation might be of greatest interest to a development team designing and "building" an evaluand; the audience for the evaluation results is the design team. A formative worth evaluation might be of greatest interest to a group considering whether an existing evaluand might be adapted to some actual context of use and considering the means for doing so. The audience for such an evaluation is the group charged with making the adaptations. A summative merit evaluation might be of greatest interest to the group concerned with making available or marketing the evaluand; the audience is both the marketing agency as well as the group(s) of potential adopters. A summative worth evaluation might be of greatest interest to a group charged with an actual adoption decision; the audience for such an evaluation is the decision makers involved. These types of evaluation are so different, and the audiences served by them so variable, that it is unlikely that any single evaluation could service more than one purpose. In particular, the mixing of formative and summative intents is likely to be disastrous, given that the respondent openness so essential to formative evaluation is conspicuous by its absence in most summative evaluation situations. Constructivist evaluators may work in each arena but are more likely to be interested in formative rather than summative efforts. When summative evaluation is at issue, it is clear to the constructivist that the context of application is always a specific, idiographic one, not a generalized context.

(4) *A statement of agreement from the client or sponsor to adhere to the "Conditions for a Productive Hermeneutic Dialectic"* (see Chapter 5). These conditions include working from a position of integrity; willingness to exclude from negotiations parties unable to communicate clearly and effectively (e.g., children, the mentally handicapped, and psychotics or other self-deluded individuals); willingness to share power; willingness to change in the face of persuasive negotiations; willingness to reconsider value positions as appropriate; and a willingness to make the commitments of time and energy that may be required. In Chapter 5 we made the case that the methodology proposed under the rubric *hermeneutic dialectic* could not be carried out meaningfully except under the conditions noted; it is essential that the client, as a major power figure, agree to them. Of course it may be argued that an unscrupulous client could agree while retaining mental reservations; the possibility of unethical behavior exists within any inquiry paradigm and, when it occurs, it is usually destructive of the inquiry in all cases. This requirement cannot, therefore, be naively managed; the evaluator needs to be constantly on the alert for miscreant behavior. (In fairness, it should be noted that evaluators and other stakeholders are also capable of miscreancy.) But by placing this stipulation in the contract, the client is on notice of the conditions, agrees to them publicly, and provides a basis for action should the conditions be abrogated.

(5) *A statement of intent from the evaluator with respect to stakeholding audiences.* If stakeholder CC&I are to serve as the focus for the evaluation, it is clearly necessary to identify, seek out, and involve all relevant stakeholders. The client must be on notice with respect to the evaluator's intention to do so. Insofar as such groups can be identified before the fact, they may actually be listed in this part of the contract. The client should also be aware of the further intent to continue the search throughout the period of the evaluation, and to involve new groups of stakeholders as they may surface. Such action may mean recycling a part of the evaluation, especially the evolution of joint or shared constructions. Since stakeholding groups almost inevitably have gatekeepers, the evaluator should be empowered in the contract to negotiate terms with such persons in order to secure their active cooperation and assistance. Additional approval from the client to engage in

such activity as new stakeholders are identified should not be required. Finally, this section of the contract should also stipulate that as stakeholders are brought into the evaluation, they too will be required to agree to the "Conditions for a Productive Hermeneutic Dialectic" in order to be actively involved. We may note the same caveats with respect to "hidden agendas" as in the case of the client.

(6) *A brief description of the methodology to be used.* This description may recapitulate the points made in this chapter, as well as some supporting statements based on the materials of Chapters 2, 3, and 5. If this statement appears to be unduly lengthy, or perhaps overly technical for some readers, it may be placed in an appendix. Since not all parties to the evaluation can be assumed to be knowledgeable about the agreed-to methodology, it is essential that it be recorded or referenced at some point in the contract. This statement should make ample reference to the *emergent* nature of the design, lest the approach be judged deficient because a "normal" design document cannot be produced.

(7) *A guarantee of access to records and documents.* It would be an unusual evaluation that did not, or could not, appropriately utilize a wide variety of available documents and records. It is hard to imagine a setting in which an evaluation might occur—a school, say, or halfway house, hospital ward, juvenile detention center, social service agency, and on and on—that did not already have in its files many relevant documents and records: minutes, memos, correspondence, grant proposals, test results, demographic data, and a host of other items. Some such materials are legally protected, while others are open to public scrutiny. Many others, however, fall into the gray area of being neither denied to public scrutiny nor mandatorily open to it. And even in cases in which access is legally guaranteed, there are often impediments that make access difficult if not effectively impossible. The contract should clearly spell out what documents and records will be available, the processes by which they can be accessed, the use that can be made of them, and the procedures to be followed in the event that access becomes blocked. Of course, such stipulations must meet federal and state requirements respecting privacy, national interest, and so on.

(8) *A statement of the evaluator's intent to guarantee confidentiality and anonymity of information sources insofar as that can be legally*

accomplished. The hermeneutic/dialectic process does not flourish in the face of anonymity—it is difficult to imagine how consensus can be reached on important issues if the contenders are blind to one anothers' identity. Joint constructions are best hammered out face-to-face. Nevertheless contingencies will occur in which it is desirable to maintain a respondent's anonymity, or to keep information provided by them in confidence. Respondents ought to be able to feel that their wishes in these matters will be respected. While information may lose its force if the source remains unidentified, it may nevertheless retain some weight even under those circumstances. Thus the evaluator needs to make plain that confidentiality and anonymity will be given high priority. Of course, respondents may waive these rights under conditions of fully informed consent—and appropriate assessment of the risks involved.

But an evaluator does not enjoy special privilege in the way that a clergyman, physician, or attorney does. Evaluators can be required by the courts, for example, to offer up collected data (including interview notes, observations, or other items through which a respondent could easily be identified); to refuse is to be subject to contempt of court and face possible imprisonment (an extreme case, to be sure). In the end, every source—including the client—may be "exposed."

(9) A *description of the reporting mode to be utilized.* As noted in Chapter 6, the case report is the preferred mode for reporting on any constructivist inquiry, including an evaluation. The purposes of the case report include providing thick description, giving vicarious experience, serving as a metaphoric springboard, and challenging constructions in ways that lead to reconstructions. The report is not a series of evaluator conclusions and recommendations but a frame and an impetus for action. Different reports may be needed for different audiences, in part, because their CC&I were initially different, but also because the degree of sophistication they possess and the nature of action best suited to them varies. The evaluator needs to retain the option of negotiating with each stakeholder group to determine the kind of report it needs and wants. But some form of case study seems most appropriate except under very unusual circumstances.

(10) A *listing of technical specifications.* Clients need to know something about each of the following:

- *The agents.* Who will carry out the evaluation activities? What are their credentials, their experience, and their training? Insofar as much of the information is to be collected via the agency of the human instrument, the client has the right to know something about the agents *as instruments,* and about validity, reliability, and the like of any conventional instruments.

- A *tentative schedule.* Because of the nature of emergent design it is not possible to identify milestone events, let alone their timing. Nevertheless it is possible to develop some realistic estimate of events (for example, the events listed in the introductory section of this chapter and treated in detail throughout the chapter) and, from that, to suggest what a time frame might look like.

- A *budget.* The budget is essential for realistic planning, on the part of both the evaluator and the client. Each needs to know something about the resources involved. But the budget cannot be devised, as program budgets usually are, by identifying specific activities and costing those out (mailing out a needs assessment instrument, following up with nonrespondents, analyzing returns, and the like). Since only a gross estimate can be made of events and their timing, it is clearly not possible to generate detailed budget figures. But the task is not so difficult as such an analysis makes it sound. The overall time available for the evaluation is usually given ("we *must* have a report by June 15"). Often the budget available is stipulated ("evaluation funds will be available up to 10 percent of program costs"). The size of an available staff is also often known ("we can free up three persons to work on this full-time for the next six months"). The client needs to be aware that what he or she is bargaining for is what can be turned up using the constructivist approach within the parameters of resources available. Instead of proposing to do an evaluation of *given* scope for X dollars with Y people over Z time, where X, Y, and Z are estimated given the scope of work statement, x, y, and z are given (or stipulated) and the scope of work is whatever it turns out to be given those parameters.

- A *listing of likely "products."* What the constructivist responsive evaluator seeks is a consensus about the evaluand that includes agreement about its characteristics, the processes involved and how they are to be carried out, and difficulties or problems that are constructed to exist, as a guide to needed further action. The evaluator developing the contract statement needs to be creative about the kinds of products that can be expected. What are examples of the kinds of constructions that might be found to exist initially? How might those constructions be altered? How would such reconstructions assist in improving the evaluand? Or lead to a judgment of its worth? How would political action be facilitated? How might personnel be further stimulated? And so on. These statements must be treated as exemplars and not as promises of the actual outcomes. The intent, however, is to provide the client with some sense of what he or she will get.

These stipulations are only suggestive of the elements that might be included in an evaluation contract, although we believe they constitute a desirable minimum. Another aspect that might be considered is an appeal mechanism, to be used if any party to the contract feels the other(s) is (are) not living up to their commitments. There might be an "escape clause," reserving the rights of all parties to withdraw from the contract under certain conditions (for example, nonperformance by the evaluator or the client). If the evaluation is very politically sensitive, fiscally weighty, or simply very large in scope, it may be useful to have the contract drawn by attorneys so that there can be no question about its legal status. But all in all, the purposes of the contract will be well served if, by virtue of having entered into it, all parties are sensitized to their rights and obligations. As we have repeatedly stressed, the hermeneutic dialectic will not work in the absence of trust and integrity (although we ought to note that the same statement could be made for any kind of evaluation). No contract can guarantee those conditions. Entering into the contract does not absolve any of the parties from taking ethical responsibility for their actions. It may, however, serve to illustrate the inappropriateness of bad actions, should that contingency ever arise, as well as protect innocent parties against an accountability they ought not to have to bear alone.

Organizing to Conduct the Evaluation

A number of problems confront the principal evaluator—the person who has negotiated the contract with the client and who will bear chief responsibility for the implementation of the evaluation activity—almost before the ink is dry on the contract. These problems, which must be dealt with before the evaluation has moved very far along, may for convenience be collected into four categories: selecting and training a team of evaluators, gaining entrée and getting established, making logistical preparations, and taking account of local social/political/cultural factors.

(1) *Selecting and training a team of evaluators.* Virtually all evaluations being done nowadays are sizable and require multiple personnel to handle the many functions and activities that may be necessary. But, as we observed in *Effective Evaluation* (Guba & Lincoln, 1981), there are advantages to composing and using a team even if the evaluation is small enough that it could be accomplished by a single person. Teams provide for the multiple roles that evaluation demands; not all persons interview equally well, or are equally adept at striking arrangements with gatekeepers, or are equally skillful at locating and interpreting historical documents. Teams can provide multiple perspectives, as, for example, in the various value patterns that tend to characterize different stakeholding audiences. Teams can make possible the use of multiple strategies: some CC&I can be better dealt with quantitatively than qualitatively, some better with preordinate designs than with emergent designs, and so on. Teams allow for representation from both methodological *and* substantive experts; the dilemma of whether it is better for the evaluator to know more about evaluation than about the discipline area of the evaluand, or vice versa, need not be raised. Obviously a first major task for the principal evaluator (hereafter the PE) is to organize such a team.

There are two contingencies that in many cases necessitate training activities for team members: the fact that, in fourth genertion evaluation, the principal instrument for data collection and analysis is the *human* instrument, and the fact that the methodology utilized rests on a paradigm which may be foreign to some of the team members. The first contingency requires team members to learn about, practice, and hone the skills necessary to act as primary instrument; the second requires resocialization.

From a positivist point of view, the utilization of human instruments inevitably introduces a degree of subjectivity that makes the entire inquiry suspect. In *Effective Evaluation* (1981) we made the case that the human instrument possesses certain properties that make its utilization indispensable in constructivist inquiry. Further, we suggested that the human instrument was at least as capable of successive refinement and improvement as instruments of any other ilk:

> Makers of paper-and-pencil instruments may not intuitively see how the human instrument can be refashioned and refined. And yet they

will readily admit that fine sopranos can, with good training, be transformed into breathtaking coloraturas; that persons who know relatively little about wine or painting or sculpture can, with practice, be turned into connoisseurs; and that other similar kinds of redirection, refashioning, and retraining can produce surprising results. We think the same can happen with human beings as data collection instruments. (Guba & Lincoln, 1981, p. 145)

We suggest that there are two

proven ways of improving the instrument, as attested by the reports of anthropological and social science inquirers who have written on their own training and socialization, for example, Wax (1971) and Reinharz (1979). One way is to throw oneself into as many new situations and environments as possible, the purpose being to gain experience and exposure. The other way is to actually practice, in a clinical or training situation, with an expert qualitative inquirer; that is, to practice doing interviews, to practice observations of various sorts, to practice listening skills, to perform a series of document analyses, and the like, under the guidance and critical eye of a trained [constructivist] inquirer. Videotapes, recordings, analyses of "field notes" of interviews, and other forms of feedback are readily available to provide training in each of these skills areas (and, indeed, these techniques are now regularly used to train other types of clinicians, practitioners, and observers, including social welfare workers, counselors, and physicians who need training in taking medical histories). Each of these feedback techniques can be targeted to one or more fieldworker behaviors and used to hone skills in singly or multiply focused fashion. Instrument improvement is not a recondite science; it is being regularly utilized in the social service professions and can be easily extended to social science inquiry. (p. 146)

Even if the team members for a given evaluation are experienced in the techniques essential to constructivist inquiry, it is probably the case that they will not have employed them in the ways discussed in Chapters 5 and 6 and to be operationally detailed later in this chapter. Some practice in "making" hermeneutic/dialectic circles or in the techniques of continuous data analysis is probably required. Should the PE be fortunate enough to assemble a team that does have such experience, additional training may not be necessary; in most cases such training will be essential.

The second contingency, resocialization, is much more difficult to manage. As we noted in Chapter 2, switching from the positivist to the constructivist paradigm is hampered by lifelong socialization to, and the language embeddedness of, positivism. The PE needs to pay particular attention to this matter because it is unlikely that all team members that it is possible to recruit will be committed constructivists. Reinharz (1981) has provided a four-phase model for retraining as well as a suggested list of resources necessary to mount a retraining program. She, of course, envisions a program of considerable scope and depth; nevertheless her comments and suggestions may be helpful in devising an approach for team members who need some resocialization.

While it is advantageous to carry out evaluations in a team mode, there are certain trade-offs that must not be lost sight of. The presence of multiple human beings on the team opens the possibilities of miscommunication, clashes of different constructions (although a team-internal hermeneutic/dialectic is useful in moving toward a joint construction), overspecialization, breakdowns of coordination, personal rivalries, and other difficulties that typically beset joint human endeavors. The astute PE will be constantly aware of these possibilities and quick to intervene when any of them surfaces.

(2) *Gaining entrée and getting established.* Evaluations are almost always commissioned by a person or persons legally and ethically empowered to do so. At first glance, then, it might be assumed that gaining entrée is no problem given that the evaluation activity has been duly legitimated and endorsed. Local respondents will cooperate because their superiors have committed them to do so.

Such a view would be extremely naive, however. Every respondent is his or her own gatekeeper and decides to what extent to be forthcoming. Every organization has units, departments, levels, or other compartmentalizations, each of which is likely to have one or more formal and informal gatekeepers. Formal gatekeepers have authority and informal gatekeepers have influence, but either has the power to support or hinder an evaluation. More to the point of fourth generation evaluation, many of the stakeholding audiences are not under the authority of the power figures that commission the evaluation; for example, most secondary beneficiaries (e.g., parents, of schoolchildren, spouses of alcoholics or felons, children of geriatric patients), and many victims, stand outside the formal organizational lines. Each of those stakeholding groups—and, often, subgroups within—will have their own gatekeepers. Each gatekeeper requires a separate negotiation (although each successful negotiation makes the next easier). Each gatekeeper will have essentially the same questions (often related to the purposes of the study, the risks to which the particular stakeholder group will be exposed, and the possible payoffs to the group that make participation desirable). Each may require a particular quid pro quo to ensure cooperation. The task may seem unending, since new gatekeepers are likely to be uncovered every day—as new stakeholders are identified, to be sure, but also because each venture onto new "turf" is likely to turn up a new gatekeeper.

A second matter requiring early attention is that of negotiating consent. We do not mean here the consent of the gatekeepers, but consent in the sense of the "fully informed consent" that ethical inquiry requires. The problem of ethics is thorny, and while movement away from the positivist paradigm obviates certain common ethical problems, movement into the constructivist paradigm raises certain others, as we have indicated in Chapter 4. In *Naturalistic Inquiry* (Lincoln & Guba, 1985) we provided a list of items that might be included in a consent form. Under no circumstances does the commission for the evaluation supersede the need to obtain informed consent signatures from all respondents involved in the evaluation, unless respondents have waived that privilege earlier (as, for example, the signing of a general consent form by the patient in a teaching hospital obviates the need to obtain specific releases each time the patient is to become part of a study). And, while many consent forms will be negotiated in the very early stages of an evaluation, the process must continue as new respondents are involved, throughout the period of the evaluation.

An important aspect of gaining entrée and getting established is that of building trust. As we suggested in *Naturalistic Inquiry*, (1985, p. 256) "while no one would argue that the existence of trust will automatically lead to credible data, the inverse seems indubitable. Respondents are much more likely to be both candid and forthcoming if they respect the inquirer and believe in his or her integrity." We go on to say,

The development of trust . . . is something to which the [constructivist] inquirer must attend from the very inception of the inquiry. In a very real sense the ultimate credibility of the outcomes depends upon the extent to which trust has been established. But trust is *biographically specific*, that is, it is a relationship existing between two persons on a one-to-one basis; thus, the constructivist inquirer will have to attend to the development of trust with *each* respondent. Further, the building of trust is a *developmental task*; trust is not something that suddenly appears after certain matters have been accomplished ("a specificable set of procedural operations"), but something to be worked on day to day. Moreover, trust is not established once and for all; it is fragile, and even trust that has been a long time building can be destroyed overnight in the face of an ill-advised action. The question, "What have you done for me lately?" is one that the [constructivist] should keep constantly in mind, for it will certainly be in the forefront of the respondents' thinking. (p. 257; emphases in original)

A third matter to which the PE must attend from the very beginning is that of logistical arrangements. A whole lot more is involved than simply making sure that evaluation team members have transportation, a confirmed schedule of appointments, and notebooks, tapes, and pencils with which to collect data. In *Naturalistic Inquiry,* we discuss five different points at which logistical decisions and arrangements must be made: the project (evaluation) as a whole, the logistics of field excursions prior to going into the field; the logistics of field excursions while in the field, the logistics of activities following field excursions, and the logistics of closure and termination. While the comments in that source are intended for research and policy studies at least as much as evaluation, their applicability in the latter case is clear. The applicability of our final piece of advice in that source is also indubitable: "Things always take much, much longer than they do" (p. 247).

Finally, and at least as crucial as any of the others, is the matter of becoming acquainted with local social, political, and cultural factors. Every evaluation context inevitably has its own unique mix of such factors; knowledge about them is absolutely essential if the evaluation is to be a success. Fourth generation evaluation is focused via the claims, concerns, and issues of stakeholders, and there are no holds barred with respect to what claims, concerns, and issues are eligible for inclusion. The fourth generation evaluator does not preclude certain CC&I because, say, they are political in nature and hence beyond the pale of disciplined inquiry. Value issues are as admissible as putatively factual ones. The question of whether a proposed new curriculum in biology subverts the religious teaching that parents would like their children to believe is as important as whether the curriculum achieves its objectives. Empowering the powerless is as important as honoring the power of those who have it. But the social, political, and cultural norms, mores, practices, and conventions are as much contextually shaped as anything else; they cannot be understood except through intensive involvement with that context.

There are a number of ways in which such social/political/cultural appreciation can be obtained. One way is to practice what is sometimes called "prior ethnography," that is, actually to live in and experience the context for some time as a participant observer without simultaneously engaging in the evaluation activities. Such activities are undertaken *before* the formal evaluation begins and may be thought of as part of the training activity that team members are likely to want to undertake anyway. Another way is to enlist the aid of local informants, that is, persons who are bona fide members of the local groups who are willing to serve as teachers and guides for the evaluators as they become oriented. As we observe in *Naturalistic Inquiry*, however, informants have reasons for being willing to serve in that role, and their reasons are not always in the best interests of the evaluation. Another way is to surface these issues and deal with them within the hermeneutic/dialectic circles. In all events, some portion of the evaluation team's time and effort should be devoted to this matter, and, as much as possible, it should be dealt with early on in the implementation.

Identifying Stakeholders

We have defined *stakeholders* as persons or groups that are put at some risk by the evaluation, that is, persons or groups that hold a stake. In *Effective Evaluation* (Guba & Lincoln, 1981) we identified three groups of stakeholders: *agents*, those persons involved in producing, using, or implementing the evaluand; *beneficiaries*, those persons who profit in some way from the evaluand; and *victims,* those persons who are negatively affected by the evaluand. These types have also been briefly reviewed in Chapter 1. Agents are most easily identified, and the evaluation is almost always commissioned by one or more subgroups within this broad group. Potential beneficiaries can also almost always be identified (they are most likely the "targets" or "markets" for the evaluand or persons closely related to them, such as parents or spouses), but very often beneficiaries not initially contemplated as such ("unintended beneficiaries") turn up. Victims are the most difficult to identify, partly because they are never intended to be victims (at least in an ethical operation), are often unaware that they are victims (for example, because they do not know that resources expended in behalf of the evaluand might have otherwise been used for some purpose more closely allied to their own interests), and sometimes are virtually invisible, perhaps because of their own interest in "maintaining a low profile." Nevertheless, in most cases the major stakeholders can be identified with a minimum of effort at the beginning of an evaluation.

It is likely, however, that, as an evaluation progresses, new stakeholding audiences may emerge. Indeed, it is the duty of the evaluator to make every effort to uncover additional audiences, and, once uncovered, to take their CC&I into account with as much seriousness as those of earlier audiences. Multiple strategies may be pursued in achieving this goal. At the beginning, the client may be solicited for nominations (the fact that stakeholders' CC&I will be used to focus the evaluation will already be clear to the client). Every respondent involved in the study may be asked to review a list of stakeholders identified at that point and to suggest others. Advertisements may be placed in the local media soliciting self-nominations. A special point to pursue is the existence of stakeholder subgroups within larger groups; for example, it may well be the case, with respect to a new curriculum, that some parents feel victimized by it while others feel it is very appropriate indeed.

It may be the case that, in many evaluations, the variety of stakeholders identified may lie beyond the power of available resources to accommodate. Some means must be found to sort out the audiences into *included* and *excluded* categories. It is our position that the only reasonable and ethical criterion that can be used for this sorting purpose is *relative stake.* Obviously some audiences are placed at much greater risk than others. It would hardly seem reasonable, for example, to exclude agent audiences because of their relatively high stake, but excluding third- or fourth-level beneficiaries seems both rationally and ethically justifiable.

Now determining the relative stake of audiences is often difficult. Each audience is likely to rank its own stake higher than it would be ranked by other audiences, especially those whose interests are at cross-purposes with the first. Hence the inclusion or exclusion of audiences cannot be arbitrarily determined by the evaluator or the client, nor can it be turned into a popularity contest. Inclusion or exclusion, like most matters in fourth generation evaluation, must be determined by negotiation, in which each audience that wishes to do so can present its case from a position of equal power. The evaluator's task is to arrange that situation. We shall return to this problem later as we consider how the evaluator can set up the negotiation described in Steps 9 and 10 of Table 7.1.

It is perhaps worth mentioning that certain criteria that *might* normally occur to people to apply are definitively *not* appropriate here. First and foremost is the *relative power* of the stakeholding audience. It is a major goal of fourth generation evaluation to operate in an *em*powering way, not a *dis*empowering one. There can be no question then of resolving the sorting problem by reference to relative power. Second, it may seem reasonable to exclude audiences judged (by whom?) to possess *insufficient knowledge or sophistication* to engage in a meaningful discourse about the evaluand, in terms of either proposing CC&I or participating in the later (Steps 9-10) negotiation. But again, a major goal of fourth generation evaluation is to be educative, to open a discourse leading to possible *re*construction based on added knowledge or sophistication. If audiences are not sufficiently knowledgeable or sophisticated at the start, it is the evaluator's moral obligation to take steps necessary to bring them to whatever minimal level is required for full participation (even if that means providing them with advocates—the root function of attorneys). Finally, it may seem appropriate to exclude some stakeholding audiences on the grounds that their inclusion would threaten the *technical adequacy* of the evaluation, an argument likely to be mounted by the positivist who feels that turning over any control is tantamount to reducing the internal validity of a study, whether evaluation, research, or policy analysis. But the fourth generation evaluator, working from the constructivist belief system, would find that an uncompelling argument indeed.

Finally, when negotiations have been entered into with identified stakeholders (or, more probably, with their gatekeepers), agreements must be formalized. These agreements may in part consist of ratification of the contract that has been drawn with the sponsor—or in renegotiating that contract to accommodate those reasonable demurrers that may have been raised. The fully informed consent form may be approved and actually signed by the gatekeepers (which does not obviate the necessity for getting signatures from respondents within those groups, of course). And the "Conditions for a Productive Hermeneutic Dialectic," already consented to by the client in the formal contract, should be affirmed here as well.

Developing Within-Stakeholder-Group Joint Constructions

This step involves the first full application of the hermeneutic dialectic circle as described in Chapter 5 and displayed in Figure 5.1. Once a given stakeholding audience has been identified, as discussed in the preceding section, it is possible to begin with the circling process.

A first question to arise is simply this: "Who shall be the first respondent in the circle?" that is, the first teacher in the teachers' circle, the first probation officer in the probation officers' circle, and so on. The answer is surprising: It doesn't matter! Whoever might be chosen will have *some* construction to proffer, and some set of CC&I to describe. The purpose of "making the circle" this first time is to uncover as *many different* constructions as possible—the full range of constructions held. It is scope that counts. We are not interested in an average or typical construction; if we were, we might well be concerned that inappropriate sampling might yield some "biased" perspective. Of course, that is a positivist position and of little concern here.

If *scope* is what is important, then *it* needs to be sought for, rather than, say, representativeness or typicalness. The first respondent might as well be the person nominated by the gatekeeper; he or she will, after all, propose a construction in which we are interested. The fact that it may coincide with the gatekeeper's construction is of little moment. But we must be as sure as we can that the *second* respondent is as different as possible from the first. Again, it's surprising, the easiest way to identify that different respondent is to ask the first for a nomination!

Focus for a moment on Respondent 1, a parent in a parent circle, say. That respondent is asked, in a very open-ended way, to tell about his or her knowledge of and experience with the evaluand:

> "I understand your son is in this fifth grade mathematics program that we are looking at. What can you tell me about the program? What's it like for your son? For you?"

And so on.

Later, attention is focused on CC&I.

> "What do you like about the program? Is it doing some good things for your son?"
> "What don't you like about it?"

And finally:

> "Thank you very much for sharing your thoughts with me. All you've told me is interesting and useful, and I am sure will make an important contribution to our effort. But I'll bet that there are other parents who have rather different ideas and feelings about this program. Can you give me the name of a parent who would have a different view from yours?"

After a number of respondents have been interviewed (with data analyses occurring between interviews as described in Chapter 5), numbers of items will begin to emerge that seem to be of special importance or salience to the respondents, particularly, of course, CC&I. At that point the evaluators will be less interested in uncovering yet other constructions (the likelihood that many such still exist undetected is low, in any event) than in getting more specific and detailed information about those that have emerged. Hence the evaluator "making" this first circle will begin to seek out respondents who can be especially articulate on those matters. Again nominations may be useful:

> "From what we've said as well as what I've learned in talking to other people, it appears that many parents feel rather strongly that the new mathematics program may be doing a good job of teaching kids about number systems other than base-10, but not helping them to balance their checkbooks or estimate what they're spending as they heap items on a grocery cart. Who is there around here who feels especially strongly about that, or who may have some experience with that concern?"

Thus, this first circle, in which one seeks to get some sense of how this particular group of stakeholders views the evaluand, and what they believe to be the major CC&I related to it, is sampled by paying attention, first, to the matter of *scope* (exposing the variety of constructions that exist, or, in more technical jargon, sampling for maximum variation), and, later, to the matter of *articulateness*. There is one further consideration that needs to be kept in mind in relation to sampling, and that is the extent to which the persons included in the circle are or will be accepted by the stakeholders as representing their interests. Obviously if a marginal group is chosen their joint construction, regardless of how reasonable or well articulated, is not likely to receive assent from the other members of the group. The object of the game, after all, is not simply to achieve consensus in this group, but also to devise a construction that is acceptable to other, similar stakeholders. There is, of course, no formula that will guarantee acceptance. Nevertheless this kind of representativeness (political, *not* statistical) is important for the evaluator to keep in mind.

Let us return now to the circle of Figure 5.1, and recall that each interview is followed immediately by a data analysis, most likely using the method of constant comparison proposed by Glaser and Strauss (1967), Glaser (1978), and Lincoln and Guba (1985). The purpose of doing an *immediate* analysis is to make the materials from preceding interviews available for commentary in subsequent ones. In the circle, Respondent 2 is not only asked about his or her own constructions, including CC&I, but is also asked to comment on and critique the construction proferred by Respondent 1. Following Respondent 2 a new data analysis incorporates the constructions of *both* Respondents 1 and 2, which Respondent 3 has the opportunity to critique. And so on. What emerges in the process is a more and more inclusive construction, which takes account of the inputs from each and all of the respondents already involved. Of course, there is no guarantee that a joint construction encompassing everyone's input can be attained, but consensus is the goal. When there is no consensus, competing constructions can be carried forward; it is on matters of nonagreement that Step 7 and those following (Figure 7.1) are based.

Two questions are often raised at this point by positivists. First they ask whether it is not the case that this process *changes* the constructions that respondents proffer; we do not assess their own constructions but the constructions they come to as part of the process. And, of course, that is the case, but that is of import only within positivist ontology. Since the naturalist does not agree with the proposition that there exist "real" states of affairs, the observation that the fourth generation process changes constructions is of no import. Second, positivists ask whether the evaluator does not abrogate objectivity when he or she becomes involved in shaping others' constructions. Again that is the case, but objectivity is only meaningful on the assumption of an objectivist epistemology. Indeed, as shall see, the major input from the evaluator does not come at this point but in Step 5 (Figure 7.1) to follow. We shall defend the evaluator's involvement at that point.

Three other points need to be mentioned before leaving the first circle. First, we may raise the question of when the circle should be stopped, that is, no further respondents added. Several criteria are useful in making this judgment, although none of them alone nor all of them together lead unfailingly to a "right" decision. One criterion is that of redundancy; when suceeding respondents add almost no new information it may be time to stop. Another criterion is that of consensus; when consensus is reached on a joint construction, there is little point in adding further respondents. Yet another criterion is that of irreconcilable differences; when it is apparent that members of the circle come to different conclusions and cannot be swayed from them on the basis of available information and preferred value systems, it may also be time to stop. In this case there may be coalescence around several constructions, each with its own group of adherents, rather than a consensual construction.

A second point relates to the credibility check. As a construction (or several competing ones) begins to emerge, respondents who were *early* contributors (R_1, R_2, and so on) may not find themselves in agreement with the joint construction but may have no further opportunity to influence it. It may be useful, therefore, to bring together all members of the circle to discuss the construction and to affirm its credibility—or to note continuing points of contention. Without such an overall check the evaluator must remain forever ignorant of whether convergence did occur.

Finally, we may note that circles can be made more than once: They can be recycled or spiraled. Whey they are recycled, the same respondents as before are involved, probably in the same order. One reason for recycling is to provide a second (or third or . . .) opportunity to respondents to critique and hone the emerging joint construction; multiple cyclings may obviate the need for a general credibility check as in the preceding paragraph. Circles may also be spiraled, in that the first group of respondents is replaced by another group of respondents selected so as to be very like the first. This group then continues with the refining/ honing process. The advantage of spiraling is that it brings fresh minds to the task, enlarges the group of persons who have input into the process (increases the base of ownership, some would say), and reduces the amount of time and effort any one respondent must provide. On the down side, spiraling also implies extra effort of the part of the evaluator, who must start at ground zero with the second group instead of being able to build on their prior experience.

At the end of this step, then, the evaluator will emerge with a joint— hopefully consensual—construction from a group of respondents who reflect a particular stakeholder group. While each respondent may have started with a somewhat different personal (emic) construction, the process is such as to expose each such personal construction to the criticism of others, and to require each respondent to take account of the constructions of others, having to come to terms with them. The evaluator is able to say, "This stakeholder group now sees the evaluand as being of thus-and-so nature and having thus-and-so characteristics, and raises the following claims, concerns, and issues about it."

Testing and Enlarging Joint Stakeholder Constructions

In the previous step, stakeholder hermeneutic circles were established, which facilitated the emergence of joint constructions for that stakeholder group, developed virtually entirely from the emic constructions originally entertained by the individual circle participants. But a variety of other information is available that can and probably will have material impact on these constructions. It is the purpose of this step to systematically introduce such material into a further "making" of the circles in order to inform the constructions further and raise them to a higher level of sophistication. Again, consensus is the aim, but because in this step we will be introducing the constructions and CC&I of what may be contending parties, consensus is far less likely. Later, as we shall see, it is the points of *difference* on which the evaluation will focus; points on which consensus can be reached can be eliminated from further consideration (as we shall do in the next step). Additional information can be drawn from all of the following sources:

(1) *Documents and records.* We made the point in *Effective Evaluation* that documents and records are among the most available, accessible, and rich sources of information, but also among the least used. Evaluations always occur in a context; undocumented contexts no longer exist in our society. Every school, juvenile center, social service agency, hospital, retirement home, government agency, in short, every conceivable kind of context systematically amasses a variety of documents and records that can be of use. Systematically tapping into documents and records provides a variety of cues for questions that can be asked during an interview; many of the CC&I that emerge during an interview can be further illuminated by reference to existing documents and records. There is thus a synergism between interviewing and document/record analysis that needs to be exploited.

(2) *Observation.* The kind of synergism we have noted between interviews carried on in hermeneutic circles and documents and records exists

even more strongly with observation. Early on, evaluators ought to do a lot of free observation, if for no other reason than in the interest of prior ethnography or gaining personal experience with the context. Such observation, while apparently casual, can lead to useful questions: "Yesterday while I sat in Ms. Jones's classroom I saw two boys who seemed not to be listening to her but worked at a computer keyboard instead. It seemed to be behavior condoned by Ms. Jones but I couldn't tell why. Can you help me with that? Doesn't that seeming permissiveness detract from time-on-task?" Similarly, apparently casual remarks during the course of an interview can lead to productive observation. "You know, Ms. Jones has a unique way of keeping children on task. When they don't seem to be responding to her direct teaching, she excuses them to pursue parallel computer assisted instruction instead. For some of her children whom no other teacher in earlier grades was able to reach, that approach seems to be really working."

(3) *The professional literature.* Positivists often denigrate constructivist approaches because they seem to be unconcerned with the existing professional literature. That literature is, after all, the repository for knowledge that has so far been achieved; it is the basis on which future studies are built and the foundation to which newly discovered knowledge is aggregated. (Think of the metaphor of the "edifice of knowledge," with each new study being yet another "brick" used to build its foundations and walls.) But with few exceptions that literature is intended to accumulate generalizations, a goal that simply does not square with constructivist ontology. It is a rare constructivist study report that begins with a review of the literature (unless that requirement is enforced by a journal editor or a dissertation committee).

But it would be shortsighted indeed for constructivists to ignore the literature on the grounds that it can be of no use, simply because it is intended to aggregate knowledge. Whatever the implementors of those studies may have had in mind, their results can provide useful inputs for constructors to consider. Indeed, as we have already suggested in several places, if the naturalist has a moral imperative, it is to be always open to new knowledge and to consider how such knowledge ought to impinge on his or her existing constructions. Thus, while the constructivist well rejects the proposition, "So-and-so has been found to be generally true and hence will be true in your situation," he or she ought to take very seriously the proposition, "So-and-so is believed by some people to have efficacy in situations like yours. Does it seem that way to you? Would this assertion be meaningful here, in this place, at this time, in your view?"

Now, for most people in our society, socialized as they are to positivism, and, therefore, to the belief that reports of science should be taken literally, to suggest that they critique *literature findings* on their own terms may be more than a little overwhelming. Many would find it hard to resist the apparent authority and legitimation that such findings enjoy. Hence our advice is not to introduce materials to a circle with the preface, "The research literature suggests . . ." But one can surely introduce it with the more disarming preface, "Some people believe that . . . ," or "It is sometimes asserted that . . . " followed by the question, "Does that make sense to you in terms of your experience here?" Such findings are likely to be treated in more skeptical fashion. They are also likely to be taken more seriously in terms of personal reconstructions.

We have found the phrase "literature analects" useful for describing "snippets" of findings or assertions from the professional literature that can be introduced into hermeneutic circles for consideration. They deserve to be treated no differently from information gleaned from local documents and records, or from local observations (or from any of the sources yet to be discussed). They are units of information that bear upon the emergent construction and need to be dealt with. But they need not be given special status. They are not ultimate truths, however scientific the process by which they were obtained.

(4) *Other stakeholder circles.* Quite possibly the most important, and most conflicting, material that can be introduced into a circle is parallel material from other circles. There will always be multiple circles, one for each stakeholding group involved, and typically the constructions that emerge in these groups are rather different, in terms both of descriptions of the evaluand and the CC&I that surface.

"I find the claims, concerns, and the issues that you parents have brought to my attention very interesting."

"But I've been talking to other groups too, and I find them mentioning things that I haven't heard here. I wonder if you'd mind reacting to some of them. For instance, the teachers seem to feel that. . . . "

And later:

"I've been mentioning some of the things coming out of this group in other groups that we've been working with, and there seems to be some objection to the ways in which you have formulated some of them. I wonder what you think about that. For instance, principals seem to object to. . . . "

Of course the aim here, as it is in all circle activity, is to come to some consensus, some joint or shared construction about state of affairs. Ideally, at the end all groups would concur in a common description of the evaluand, would have handled many of the CC&I by common consent (for example, resolving them by bringing their now mutual knowledge to bear), and would have agreed on a list of CC&I that required further work. Those CC&I would not require further evaluation but an action plan for dealing with them. Only those CC&I on which there is no agreement call for further evaluation activity and negotiation.

(5) *The evaluator's etic construction.* It would be silly to suppose that the evaluator has no a priori knowledge and opinions that bear upon the evaluand and its context. Indeed, if one were to propose hiring an evaluator of such pristine mind, it is likely that the proposal would be thought whimsical and mindless. Empty-headedness, as we have said in multiple contexts, is not tantamount to open-mindedness.   Now positivists would be immediately concerned that inviting the evaluator to introduce his or her etic (outsider) construction would be grossly prejudicial, illustrating subjectivity in its worst form. The issue, however, is not whether the evaluator has some opinion or not, but how that opinion surfaces. We contend that it is ludicrous to expect, as positivists do, that evaluators will somehow be able to maintain an objective stance, or that positivist methodology, by interpolating a layer of so-called objective instrumentation between evaluator and evaluand, will guarantee that only true states of affairs will emerge. We see no problem with introducing the evaluator's *construction* (and we think that *is* the proper word, in

contrast to *bias,* which seems to suggest something nefarious in the evaluator's intent) *if*—and it is a *big* if—that construction is laid on the table alongside all other inputs to suffer the same kind and degree of criticism as must they. We hope that the evaluator will restrain him- or herself during Step 4, in which the individuals' joint stakeholder constructions are hammered out. But in this Step 5 we urge the evaluator to join in the fun, so long as his or her constructions receive no more weight than that to which they are entitled. Parallel to the case of the professional literature, we think that the evaluator's construction would be invested with too much weight if it were announced to be that. However, if the evaluator's construction is introduced again in some low-key way— "Some people believe that ... "—it is open to critique without fear of reprisal or embarrassment.

These five sources—available documents and records, observations, the professional literature, inputs from other circles' constructions, and the evaluator's own etic construction—are legitimate sources for information bearing on existing constructions. Whatever information can be gleaned from them deserves attention. It must either, on reflection and for good reason, be rejected, or it must be accommodated within the accepted construction. Sometimes such accommodation must be very radical; it may change the existing construction to such a degree as to deserve the appellation "revolution." (The paradigm revolution we have discussed so extensively in relation to positivism is an interesting illustration of just such a dramatic change.)

When all this information has been exposed and dealt with, the end of the hermeneutic interaction is essentially reached (although as we shall see below, the hermeneutic circle may be profitably used in several other places yet to come).

Sorting Out Resolved Claims, Concerns, and Issues

This sorting step is perhaps the simplest of the 13 involved in carrying out a fourth generation evaluation. After the hermeneutic circles of Steps 4 and 5 have been completed, it is likely that a good number of the claims, concerns, and issues that surfaced within individual stakeholder circles vanished as further information was input to that group. For example, the parents who were at first concerned that their children, while learning a lot about number systems, did not seem to be learning practical skills like estimation or checkbook balancing, might, after hearing from the teacher circle, discover that those practical matters were reserved for consideration in the second semester. And so on. And while these CC&I may no longer be of local import, they may nevertheless be useful either as of historical interest or as items that might be considered in other settings (but see theorems 11-14 of Chapter 3). Thus these CC&I ought not to be eliminated but set aside for consideration when the final case report is written.

Prioritizing Unresolved Items

While many CC&I will have been resolved in the hermeneutic process, particularly as information from contending stakeholder groups is introduced and considered, others will continue to be problematic and will require further attention. Without such unresolved items, the evaluation would end with Step 5. But is unlikely that such a level of consensus could be reached, particularly in situations in which various stakeholder groups differ rather sharply in the values they bring to bear. It should be noted that certain characteristics or outcomes may be highly valued by one group and utterly rejected by another. An evaluand might well be judged totally effective in one construction and totally ineffective in another—while displaying the same performance in each! Thus the probability of continued disagreement—lack of consensus—is high.

Indeed, it is likely that the number of unresolved CC&I may be sufficiently large that the resources available for evaluation may not stretch sufficiently to make dealing with all of them possible. Under such circumstances it will be necessary to prioritize the items, determining how resources should be spread to deal with those thought most salient. In the spirit of hermeneuticism and the educational and empowerment themes that underlie fourth generation evaluation, this prioritization task should be carried out in a participatory way that provides opportunity for input and control to each of the stakeholding audiences. Given that, at this point in the process, the stakeholders (and especially their representatives) will have had ample experience with the hermeneutic circle and its associated dialectic, and will have already witnessed the power of the approach in leading to at least some consensus, it will probably be most useful to carry out prioritization within another such hermeneutic circle constituted particularly for this purpose, but one whose members *cut across* the several stakeholder groups. Stakeholders should be encouraged to devise their own means for selecting their representatives so that the outcomes will be thought to be binding by each group (although in cases of extremely conflictual items some ratification process may be needed).

This hermeneutic circle must be at liberty to determine the criteria to be employed in the prioritization. There are at least three that ought to be considered, however:

- *Possible ease of resolution of a CC&I.* It may be obvious that some CC&I remain unresolved because certain information was lacking but might be made available without a great deal of difficulty.
- *Possibility of achieving an action compromise although dissensus might continue.* In many cases practical exigencies may demand some action decision ("After all, we can't just close the schools!"). What may be needed here is some information about and insight into the kinds of action mechanisms that might be employed which, while not wholly satisfactory, would allow life to go on while some more substantial consensus was sought (for example, in subsequent evaluations).
- *Centrality to the value system of one or more of the stakeholders.* Issues that rest upon major value positions will be the most sticky, but also the most important to deal with. Stakeholders whose constructed-to-be-central CC&I are not dealt with are likely to be intransigent on most others as well.

It may, finally, be the case that those items that are classified as of lowest priority are, nevertheless, not considered to be of little importance. They ought not to be discarded but set aside for inclusion in any subsequent evaluation activity (see Step 12—Recycling, below).

Collecting Information/Achieving Sophistication

To say that certain matters remain "unresolved" simply means that no joint (collaborative, shared) construction has as yet evolved. It may not be possible to come to a resolution because of value differences that are not open to negotiation. Presumably the stakeholding groups (including the client) who have agreed to work under the "Conditions for a Productive Hermeneutic Dialectic" understand that value differences are to be as open to negotiation as anything else; if groups do not agree to such conditions, or if they abrogate them at some point in the process, there is little chance that the hermeneutic dialectic will work. But for most practical purposes joint constructions *can* be evolved if enough information is available and if appropriate levels of sophistication can be reached.

The evaluator, having identified unresolved CC&I and worked through the prioritization process, is now ready to embark on the step that looks most like conventional evaluation: the collecting of information that will, when added to existing constructions, lead to *reconstruction*, and the determination of ways and means to make appreciation of that new information possible.

Now some information may already be available from the prior work of the hermeneutic circles in Steps 4 and 5 (Figure 7.1). While the information may have been insufficient to lead to reconstruction, it is nevertheless relevant. The evaluator ought now to identify that information and collect it from wherever it may have surfaced, that is, from whichever circle dealt with it. Under some circumstances, such as, if the unresolved item is of sufficient importance, it may be useful to reconstitute the original circle for the specific purpose of considering this item.

Some information may exist elsewhere and may be collectible. For example, evaluations done on similar evaluands in similar contexts may exist, and may shed light on the matter locally, although care must be taken *not* to treat those other evaluation data as generalizable. They may, however, extend experience vicariously, serve as a metaphoric springboard leading to new insights, or simply add information, which, when taken account of, leads more rapidly to the evolution of a local reconstruction. The existing professional literature may be usefully tapped again, as it was during Step 5 (Figure 7.1). Documents and records from other sources may be consulted, whether local (say, from some other similar situation) or more general (say, census data). The experience of the evaluator in other projects may also usefully be considered.

Some information may require the construction of new instrumentation which may include paper-and-pencil or even brass instrumentation;

similarly, existing instrumentation, such as published tests, may be used given a collaborative decision by stakeholders to do so. Such an approach is warranted if certain stakeholders pose a CC&I that, while perhaps foreign to the constructivist belief system, is important to those stakeholders and must be responded to. For example, parents who want to be convinced that their children are making a year's gain in reading, say, for the year's class time may insist that a standardized reading test be given "before and after." While the fourth generation evaluator might wish to point out the problems of such a way of dealing with their concern, he or she might nevertheless feel (in the spirit of empowerment) compelled to take that course anyway. If, however, *other* stakeholders object, for example, the parents of ethnic minority children who feel that reading tests are ethnically biased, further negotiation is called for.

In some cases, special studies may be needed. It may be the case that one or more of the CC&I deals with a matter not routinely considered in the context of the evaluation. Let us imagine that selected parents object to certain textbooks on the ground that their content is at variance with their religious beliefs. Their claim is that the use of these materials subverts the children's religious training and leads to their "falling away." It is unlikely that the local school has ever collected data on such a matter. The constructivist might well decide to set up a hermeneutic circle of such youngsters (assuming they are old enough to carry through such a process) to discuss the tensions they may feel between their curriculum and their religious beliefs. Some stakeholders may, on receiving inputs from such a group, decide that the curriculum is indeed more coercive than they had imagined. On the other hand, parents of these youngsters might be persuaded that their fears are relatively groundless—their children may have devised excellent defenses against the putative encroachment. Of course it is also possible, perhaps even likely, that this claim will not be settled (because it is founded on such fundamental value differences), but even in that eventuality all sides will have exhibited a willingness to entertain the others' constructions and to treat them fairly and openly. At the very least better feelings are likely to result.

It may, finally, be the case that the evaluator identifies a need not so much for new information as for a more appropriate level of sophistication. In such cases the search for information may take the form of materials and experiences that may be employed in lifting the sophistication levels of all concerned. For example, a relatively intransigent value position may be loosened once the holders become aware of value relativism. Understanding that the only viable alternative to relativism is absolutism, and that absolutism is not a position congruent with the American democratic ideal, those stakeholders may suddenly become much more open to alternatives.

Preparing the Agenda for Negotiation

The identification of unresolved CC&I and the collection of information relating to them makes it possible for the evaluator to prepare an agenda for negotiation among the stakeholders. It is useful to think of this step as analogous to the more usual drawing up of a set of conclusions and recommendations. Conventionally this is the task of the evaluator because he or she is the expert, is detached from and disinterested in the local setting ("objective"), and possesses the requisite technical expertise to deal with data and their interpretation. Of course the delegation of this task to the evaluator is meaningful and rational only on positivist assumptions: that the data represent a "real" state of affairs and that they have been obtained "from nature" directly without any possibility of evaluator bias, that is, without the evaluator's own values being determinative. But such a position is intolerable within constructivist assumptions. Data are never value-free, as we have seen, and they certainly do not "speak for themselves," that is, they do not carry their own meaning and interpretation is an unequivocal way. Evaluators, guided consciously or unconsciously by their own values, select *which* facts are to be determined and once obtained, *what they mean*. If that is the case, as constructivists aver, then the evaluator's values are very much at issue; they ought not to be solely determinative, especially in a pluralistic, multivalued (multiethnic, multigendered, multireligious, and so on) society. The negotiation session, representing the full array of stakeholders, is a mechanism intended to display and take account of the full range of values. If the earlier hermeneutic circles are determinative of *which* "facts" (note that the constructivist places this equivocal term in quotation marks) should be collected, this negotiation session decides *what they will mean.*

The preparation of the agenda for negotiation involves a series of activities on the part of the evaluator.

- Define each CC&I carefully, *in the terms of the stakeholding group(s)* that surface it. Translation into the terms of other groups may not be entirely satisfactory, a fact that suggests that each definition should be followed by enough discussion, with examples, to make it as plain as possible to everyone that the CC&I involves.
- Elucidate *competing* constructions, in the case of issues, or the *elements* of particular constructions, in the case of a concern or claim, that generate or account for the nonresolution. Recall that nonresolution may have occurred simply for lack of information or for some more fundamental reason, such as value differences. All parties must be clear *why* each unresolved CC&I appears on the agenda.
- Provide all available information that illuminates each unresolved CC&I. In the case of issues, information that supports or refutes *each* side of the issue should be clearly delineated. In the case of claims or concerns, information that supports or refutes each should be provided. The information should not be presented in a confrontational way ("the teachers are right after all"). The purpose of the hermeneutic process is not to attack or to justify but to *connect* different constructions. It is *engagement,* not confrontation, that leads to reconstruction.
- Provide for training, role-playing, practice, and whatever else may be required to build the respondent's level of sophistication to whatever level may be needed to facilitate connection. If some stakeholders are initially more sophisticated than others, steps should be taken to correct the inequality. If necessary, the evaluator him- or herself should be prepared to act as the lesser group's advocate, or, particularly in case of important issues, the lesser groups may be aided (but not replaced) by special advocates. If the information needed is beyond the level of stakeholders to appreciate, as might be the case with complex statistical materials, steps must be planned to deal with this deficiency. In all cases care must be taken to maintain, not destroy, the balance of power.
- Test the agenda with stakeholder surrogates to determine its acceptability as a basis of negotiation. Stakeholders who will not be involved in the actual negotiations may be used as "stand-ins," perhaps again in a hermeneutic circle arrangement, to critique the proposed agenda and aid in its refinement into final form.

Carrying Out the Negotiation

The negotiation is preferably carried out via the hermeneutic dialectic process using yet another circle. The circle may be the same one selected to test the agenda in the previous step. The advantage is that participants will be familiar with the agenda, have worked their way through it, and committed themselves to its acceptability. The disadvantage may be that the agenda-critiquing experience may determine and firm up the positions that the several participants may take, preventing the present session from being a "true" negotiation. Our own preference is to use a new group, but logistics, the availability of participants, and other factors may argue for use of the same circle.

The negotiating circle is selected in ways that honor the principle of participatory (empowering, educative) evaluation, but without being merely representative in the statistical sense. Representativeness in the participatory sense implies that the stakeholder groups select their own representatives in whatever ways they believe to be appropriate. The only constraint is that only such representatives be sent who are willing to work according to the "Conditions for a Productive Hermeneutic Dialectic." The persons elected as representatives must be empowered to act *on behalf of* their stakeholders. While the stakeholders *may* be asked to ratify the negotiation subsequently, the negotiation itself is the special province of the persons elected to do it. They thus play a very special role. They must be acutely conscious of the constructions held by the stakeholders they represent (and that means, particularly, the joint construction to which members of the stakeholding audience came as a result of the earlier circles). They must be clear about what, in the view of that audience, is critical to maintain and what can be accommodated. They cannot, however, be *instructed*; they must be free to negotiate in the best sense of that term. Finally, they must be completely trustworthy in the view of their constituents and, like Caesar's wife, they must be above suspicion.

The negotiation itself should also be a hermeneutic dialectic in form and process. The evaluator becomes the mediator and facilitator for the circle, as he or she was in earlier circles. The evaluator has no special license, elite status, or superior power, nor is he or she warranted in exerting any special control. Whatever emerges from the group must come as the result of their deliberation and decision. Indeed, if they choose, they may adopt some other process than the hermeneutic dialectic, even though, in our opinion, that would weaken the efficacy of the evaluation. While positivists may be unwilling to follow through on stakeholding principles on the grounds that to do so threatens the technical adequacy of the study, fourth generation evaluators *are* willing to proceed in whatever ways stakeholders decide even when it is believed that the efficacy of process is thereby decreased. In the final analysis the process is but the means; we are equally concerned with ends.

Negotiations end when some consensus is reached on each previously unresolved CC&I. In effect, a new joint construction is reached by consensus that supersedes previously developed constructions. Its test of adequacy is that it should be patently more informed and sophisticated than any of its predecessors—by common assent. Of course, that is an ideal. In many cases consensus will not be reached; competing constructions will remain. How long should negotiations go on in the face of likely continuing differences? We suggest that a criterion of "least constructions" be used.[1] Negotiation should go on until the smallest number of viable constructions has evolved. A major responsibility of the negotiators will be, in such a case, to delineate carefully the continuing differences that characterize these competing constructions as a basis for future efforts to achieve commonality.

Emergent joint constructions may, by common consent, be referred to the several stakeholder groups for ratification. It is conceivable that one or more stakeholder groups may have insisted on ratification a priori, as a condition for participating in the negotiation session. We frown on such a condition because, in effect, it provides the representatives of that group with extra power at the negotiating table. They are in a position to argue that, unless their construction is given priority, they will recommend nonratification to their constituents. We believe it is more consistent with the spirit of mutual empowerment to leave the ratification decision to the negotiators themselves.

One stakeholder likely to be particularly troublesome on this matter is the original client. The client may claim a legal need to retain veto power over the decisions of the negotiating group. Whether that is legally the case or not, such a priori insistence represents, in our judgment, an illegitimate use of power. If the negotiating group comes to a joint construction with which the client disagrees, full consensus is not possible, and some practical compromise must be reached instead. It is at this point that the client can exercise power more legitmately. We do *not* think it disempowering for the client to point out his or her legal obligations, and we would think it inappropriate for other stakeholders to reject such representations out of hand. The upshot of this entire argument is that we think it appropriate for all parties to negotiate their differences rather than to insist on their "rights" as legally defined or mandated.

In the end, the entire process ends more or less arbitrarily, when resources or time are exhausted, or when outcomes are agreed upon. It is unlikely that every previously unresolved CC&I will be resolved at this point. The basis is thus laid for future evaluation activity. This posture accords with the principle that every good evaluation is likely to raise more questions than it answers. Evaluation is indeed a continuous process.

We come finally to the question of action. Given that the CC&I have been considered by the negotiators, what determination is made with respect to the action to be taken in relation to each of them? Three possible outcomes come to mind; it is likely that all three will exist within the same evaluation as different outcomes are reached with respect to different CC&I:

- *Full resolution.* When some claim, concern, or issue is fully resolved, the action to be taken is self-evident. Some require no action; for example, the claim that a certain teaching strategy will produce a certain local result, when demonstrated, requires no further action, excepting perhaps a resolve to continue doing that "good thing." Others require some refinement or improvement: the teaching strategy was partly successful but fell short in these and other ways, and so we ought to do thus-and-so. Still others will suggest rejection or abandonment: the strategy didn't work at all and we probably ought not to use it again. *Resolution always implies action.* But notice that when full resolution occurs, it is because (in fourth generation evaluation) stakeholders have come to a shared construction. *By their agreement they commit themselves jointly to accept continuing responsibility and accountability for whatever action is taken.*

- *Incomplete or partial resolution.* For a variety of reasons, including inability to acquire all the information thought desirable, some CC&I will remain unresolved. Action is deferred pending further study and consideration. A mechanism for this additional study should be proposed and implemented. Some compromise, place-holding action may be implemented until the additional information becomes available.

- *No resolution.* Different, possibly conflicting constructions are retained—at least two, possibly more. Little can be done except to continue working on the problem (probably through further evaluation activity) and to attempt an accommodation to permit practical action. It would be unfortunate if a practical accommodation could not be reached, because the only alternatives in such a case are to take no action at all (usually a bad option) or to determine action arbitrarily (essentially a disempowering option).

Reporting

Conventional evaluation reports adhere to a more-or-less standard form. The questions that the evaluation was intended to answer are described, and the design for answering them is given. More often than not that design is delineated in terms of the instruments used to collect data and the statistical tools used to analyze the data obtained from them. A final section draws conclusions relevant to the questions and lays out a series of recommendations.

The report of a fourth generation evaluation takes a very different form. It is in the broadest sense a report that delineates the joint (shared, collaborative) construction that has emerged via the hermeneutic dialectic process. It is intended to render that construction not only in a "factual" sense but in ways that clarify the meaning and interpretations to be made of those "facts." The report cannot simply be *about* the evaluand and its context, but must enable readers to see *how the constructors make sense of it, and why.* The best way to do that, we feel, is via the case study report, which provides a vicarious experience of the situation, allowing the readers to "walk in the shoes" of the local actors.

We have used the term *understanding* to describe the state of mind that can be achieved through such *vicarious experience.* Readers can thereby make their own sense of the situation. They can appreciate the nature of the joint construction that emerged from the evaluation process, *but are not obligated to fall into agreement with it.* The case study helps readers to assimilate the joint construction into their own constructions, thereby generating personal *reconstructions* different from either the negotiated joint construction or their own prior constructions.

Elsewhere (Lincoln & Guba, 1988) we have supported a variety of criteria that the good case report should meet. These are *not* criteria for the evaluation as such—those will be discussed in Chapter 8 to follow. The report itself must, however, exhibit certain qualities, which we have categorized into a fourfold classification:

- *Axiomatic criteria,* by which we mean that the study must resonate with the axiomatic assumptions (the basic belief system) that underlie its guiding paradigm. It must, for example, reflect multiple rather than single realities.
- *Rhetorical criteria,* by which we mean those relating to form and structure, including (following Zeller, 1987) unity, overall organization, simplicity or clarity, and craftmanship. The latter is characterized in a case study that displays power and elegance, creativity, openness, independence, commitment, courage, and egalitarianism.
- *Action criteria,* by which we mean the ability of the case study to evoke and facilitate action on the part of readers. These criteria include fairness, educativeness, and actionability or empowerment.
- *Application or transferability criteria,* by which we mean the extent to that the case study facilitates the drawing of inferences by the reader which may apply in his or her own context or situation. These criteria include the presence of thick description, provision of vicarious experience, metaphoric power, and personal reconstructability.

The reader is referred to the noted reference for details concerning the meaning and utility of these terms.

The writing of a case report is a process difficult to communicate. In many ways it resembles creative writing—it is more novelesque than technical in format and intent. It is said that Sigmund Freud was disappointed in the fact that his case studies read more like short stories than like technical reports; because he was a scientific marginal man he would have much preferred to have it otherwise. But one cannot have it both ways. Case reports by their nature require case writing. A generalized format will not fit.

Nancy Zeller (1987), in her dissertation, undertook the task of analyzing available writing forms to find that one that seemed most appropriate, on certain criteria she developed, to case reporting. Her conclusion was that what has come to be called the "New Journalism," as exemplified in the writing of Tom Wolfe, provided the best model. She provides numerous examples of such techniques as scene-by-scene construction, character through dialogue, the third-person subjective view, full detailing of status life indicators, and interior monologue and composite characterization, drawing on a case study that she herself carried out in order to provide "raw material." The reader is referred to her excellent work for guidance.

It may be good practice for the evaluator to make reports individually to each of the stakeholding audiences, in the spirit of empowerment and to provide some basis for their continuing growth in information and sophistication. These reports, which may be oral and sometimes accompanied by a special written report, should be made in language appropriate to that audience, taking its level of sophistication into account. However, we would now quarrel with advice we have given in several earlier works that each audience should receive a separate report, which might in some cases be very different from those received by others. We no longer condone such a practice because it detracts from the commitment made to the emergent joint construction, continues to emphasize separateness rather than togetherness, and runs the risk of creating further conflicts among stakeholders. However reports are presented, the common core must be the joint construction emerging from the negotiation process.

For some audiences there may only be one credible source from which to receive the report, and that is that stakeholding group's representatives on the negotiating team. In such cases the evaluator should cooperate fully with the team members and assist them in whatever ways they believe appropriate to making an effective presentation. Finally, a report ought not be forced onto an audience that may not wish to receive one (for example, in order to maintain a low profile for political reasons). It is reasonable to assume that any audience represented on the negotiating team will know what is going on. Informal channels continue to function well.

Recycling

Fourth generation evaluations are by their nature divergent—they tend to raise more questions than they answer. There are always unresolved CC&I, and the emergent construction is likely to hold only for a brief time. New information or increased sophistication may suddenly become available, reopening the cases of even those CC&I that had been thought to be settled. A reconsideration may be in order at almost any time. Fourth generation evaluations never stop; they merely pause.

Postscript

The methodology of fourth generation evaluation is not simple. Indeed, a casual reading of this chapter may easily lead to the conclusion that "it can't be done." We would be the last to want readers to underestimate the complexity of the task that confronts any fourth generation evaluator. Moreover, the skills required to carry out such an evaluation are very different from those mostly technical skills that have characterized evaluators operating within the conventional mode. But, while it is certainly not easy, it is certainly possible, and when it is successful it is very powerful indeed. It is powerful because it creates a dynamic for action that is almost impossible to achieve in any other way.

So often evaluands turn out to be interventions that someone has concocted in order to remedy some condition or meet some need. Persons charged with the responsibility for carrying out those interventions are rarely involved in their development in any meaningful way. They are, however, held accountable. If their performance turns out to be anything short of excellent—however excellence is defined by the designers and adopters of the intervention—it is they who are held at fault and they who suffer the consequences.

It is certainly possible to coerce people into compliance, but it is impossible to coerce them into excellence—by anyone's definition. Only empowerment can invest people with a sense of self-efficacy, which enables them to act in productive ways. Only empowerment can encourage risk-taking, unleash energy, stimulate creativity, instill pride, build commitment, prompt the taking of responsibility, and evoke a sense of investment and ownership.

Empowerment means the sharing of power tools and the sharing of leadership. Empowered people make organizational contributions because their empowerment continuously leads them to "figuring out about the place," to productive "sense-making." They do not need a special institutional dynamic to get things done, a kind of bureaucratic hierarchy that sees to it that each lower level does things "by the book." The person-organization distinction disappears.

Fourth generation evaluation is a means to empowerment, both because of its process aspects and because it shares information (which is itself power). It may be a difficult and cumbersome process, and may take much longer than we are accustomed to thinking evaluations should take. More resources may be required. But in the end, it works, and when it works, things happen. We will no longer need to argue about who is to blame for the shortfalls; instead we can all glory in our mutual accomplishments.

Note

1. We are indebted to Dr. Thomas Schwen of Indiana University for this criterion.

8 Judging the Quality of Fourth Generation Evaluation

If we accept the definition of disciplined inquiry as set forth by Cronbach and Suppes (1969), it seems clear that standards for judging the quality of such inquiry are essential. The Cronbach and Suppes definition (1969, pp. 15-16) suggests that disciplined inquiry "has a texture that displays the raw materials entering into the arguments and the local processes by which they were compressed and rearranged to make the conclusions credible." Thus a disciplined inquiry process must be publicly acceptable and open to judgments about the "compression and rearrangement" processes involved.

We have, in another context, argued that evaluation is properly construed as one form of disciplined inquiry (Lincoln & Guba, 1985, 1986b) along with two other forms of such inquiry: research and policy analysis. Neither of the two latter, however, should be confused with evaluation, which has its own intended products, audiences, and outcomes (Lincoln & Guba, 1985, 1986b).

It is, as a result, incumbent on us to deal with the question of the nature of quality criteria that may be appropriate primarily to evaluation, particularly in view of the fact that we have proposed a form of evaluation that differs in such dramatic ways from the first three generations' predecessors. A useful beginning is to consider those standards and criteria that have been devised for conventional evaluation.

Standards and Criteria for Conventional Evaluation

Not surprisingly, the first such criteria took the form of *test* standards, which exist currently in the form of the 1974 revision of the *Standards for Educational and Psychological Tests*. These standards were developed by a joint committee of the American Educational Research Association, the American Psychological Association, and the National Council on Measurement in Education (American Psychological Association, 1974).

This committee early on recognized the importance of tests used in program evaluations and intended to devote a section of their standards to this topic. For a variety of reasons—for instance, lack of time and necessity to limit the scope of the test standards document (see Joint Committee, 1981, p. 142)—the Joint Committee on Test Standards decided not to proceed along these lines, but instead recommended to the parent groups that a new joint committee devoted especially to this task be appointed. Responsive action was taken in 1975, with the establishment of the Joint Committee on Standards for Educational Evaluation, under the directorship of Dr. Daniel Stufflebeam.

The Joint Committee on Standards for Educational Evaluation undertook its task with enthusiasm, believing that there would be

> several benefits from the development of sound standards: a common language to facilitate communication and collaboration in evaluation; a set of general rules for dealing with a variety of specific evaluation problems; a conceptual framework by which to study the oft-confusing world of evaluation; a set of working definitions to guide research and development on the evaluation process; a public statement of the state of the art in educational evaluation; a basis for self-regulation and

accountability by professional evaluators; and an aid to developing public credibility for the educational evaluation field. (1981, p. 5)

The Joint Committee did not intend to devise criteria standards that would in any way inhibit the growth of evaluation as a field of professional activity. The committee, for example, disclaimed having a particular view of what constitutes good education. They claimed that they attempted to recognize in the standards all types of studies used in evaluation. They wanted to encourage the sound use of a variety of evaluation methods (both quantitative and qualitative, whenever and wherever appropriate). And because the members of the Joint Committee were themselves experienced evaluators, they wrote the standards in ways that would help evaluators identify and confront political realities in and around the projects that they evaluated (Joint Committee, 1981, pp. 5-7).

It is our best judgment that, while the *Standards*[1] devised by the Joint Committee are not especially congenial to the posture of fourth generation evaluation, neither are they destructive of its aims and processes. The interested reader is invited to study the *Standards* from this perspective. Our position is that we can live with these standards although they are by no means very powerful for judging the quality of a given evaluation on those matters that are of central importance to fourth generation evaluation. Quality criteria are, of course, the central focus of this chapter, and we shall shortly take up the question of how one judges the processes and products of a fourth generation evaluation. But another word is in order regarding standards.

The *Standards for Evaluation Practice* (Rossi, 1982), developed by a committee of the Evaluation Research Society, on the other hand, are absolutely unacceptable from the standpoint of the fourth generation evaluator. (In 1987, the Evaluation Research Society joined with the Evaluation Network to form the American Evaluation Association. Currently, the American Evaluation Association operates with two sets of standards; the organization has been quite open about accepting either set as a guide to professional practice. For reasons that will become clear, we believe it is impossible to move in the direction some have suggested to merge the two sets of standards.) The *ERS Standards* are divided into six sections, felt to be "roughly in order of typical occurrence" (p. 11):

formulation and negotiation, structure and design, data collection and preparation, data analysis and interpretation, communication and disclosure, and utilization. The *ERS Standards* embody a series of assumptions—especially with respect to the evaluator role, and to some extent, the relative power of the client—that are not acceptable to fourth generation evaluators, and that, furthermore, make their merger with the Joint Committee's *Standards* unlikely to impossible (Lincoln, 1985). Some analysis of why that is so will make the issue clearer.

First, it is assumed that interaction between client and evaluator is likely to be limited to those contacts needed to "formulate and negotiate" (Rossi, 1982, p.12) and to "communicate and disclose" (p. 15). But fourth generation evaluators argue that negotiation occurs continuously throughout an evaluation, as does data analysis and the interpretation process. (Experienced evaluators who are not themselves fourth generation evaluators intuitively understand this to be the case in many instances.) Evaluation activities, they say, are cyclic, feedback-feedforward in nature, and iterative, whereas the *ERS Standards* paint them as linear and highly sequenced, implying that there are cutoff times for each activity beyond which no more of that activity actually occurs.

Second, strong emphasis is placed on the quantitative and experimental aspects of evaluation. Words like "treatment," "sampling," "reliability," "validity," "generalizability," "replicability," and "cause-effect" relations leave little doubt about which methods are believed to possess the most power. In fact, the preface to the "Structure and Design" standards itself specifies that evaluation *case* studies are "as subject to specification as the design of an experimental study" (Rossi, 1982, p. 13). Nowhere are qualitative methods (in the service of *any* paradigm) given direct approval. In the discussion of the adequacy of methodologies, no attempt is made to specify criteria appropriate to more constructivist/responsive evaluation efforts. Case studies are treated simply as looser variants of scientific technical reports.

Third, the emphasis on uncovering cause-effect dimensions or relationships flies in the face of constructivism's denial of the efficacy of that concept. No mention is made of the fact that often no satisfactory "cause" *can* be isolated for a given "effect." The mandated search for statistically significant cause-effect relationships often blinds evaluators and clients alike to more diffuse but also more powerful social forces operating within a given context, program, project, or site. And, most certainly, ascertaining what people think exists and why they think so is at least as important as verification of some a priori postulate about cause-effect relationships *that the evaluator thinks exists.*

Fourth, the *ERS Standards* call, both explicitly and implicitly, for the evaluation to be "shaped" in such a way as to meet the information and decision making needs of the "client," who is, typically, the person or agency that both has the power to commission the evaluation (the legal authority) and is the agent who is to contract and pay for it. There is, of course, nothing inherently wrong in ensuring that an evaluation meets a client's information or decision-making needs. In fact, that is why many of them are mounted. But the fourth generation evaluator has a much expanded idea of who ought to have access to information, who ought to have to power to withhold it (certainly not the "client" or funder), and who ought to be involved in decision making. Servicing decision-making or information needs, particularly for a single person or agency, serves only to concentrate power in the hands of those who already possess inordinate power relative to program participants, targets, or stakeholders. Having such limited foci for evaluations typically is disenfranchising and disempowering to the many other stakeholders who are invariably involved. The fourth generation evaluator typically refuses to accept a contract in which information is released only at the discretion of the "client" (funder). To try to fulfill such a criterion, given constructivist methodology, would be impossible in any event. The fourth generation evaluator considers decision making only one of the many objectives to be served in any given evaluation effort. Thus this emphasis on shaping the evaluation with the client's information and decision-making needs in mind would not only unnaturally but also unnecessarily and unethically limit the range of activity of the fourth generation evaluator.

Finally, the *ERS Standards* also fail to recognize the role that values play not only in evaluation (a process based, after all, on the root premise of values, which might properly be *expected* to pay attention to values) but in inquiry more broadly and generally. The continuing emphasis in this set of standards on objectivity and freedom from bias—criteria that are, after all, grounded in positivist ontological and epistemological assumptions—ignores mounting recognition by even the conventional scientific community that all science, and certainly social science, is value-bound (Bahm, 1971; Baumrind, 1979, 1985). In retrospect, the possibility of acting to "value" a project (program, curriculum, and so on) while acting as though values were unimportant or corrupting to the valuing (evaluation) effort should have struck us long ago as bizarre, if not contradictory, behavior. Hindsight is always 20–20.

Our overall conclusion, then, is that, while certain existing standards may be usefully applied to fourth generation evaluations, others are not only not useful but are actually destructive of the aims of fourth generation evaluation. Specifically, the Joint Committee's *Standards* may be applied, and would do no harm, but those of the ERS are contradictory to and exclusive of the goals of the fourth generation. Even those that are useful, however, are probably not as powerful as others that we will shortly suggest.

Criteria for Judging the Adequacy of Fourth Generation Evaluation

Is it possible to identify standards that seem more appropriate to fourth generation evaluation? Are there standards that are also more powerful than the all-purpose professional standards currently available, such as the Joint Committee *Standards*? We believe that there are three different approaches to considering the quality of goodness of a fourth generation evaluation (or, for that matter, any constructivist inquiry): invoking the so-called *parallel* or quasi-foundational criteria, which we have typically termed the *trustworthiness* criteria; considering the unique contribution made to goodness or quality by the *nature of the hermeneutic process itself*; and invoking a new set of non-foundational criteria—but criteria embedded in the basic belief system of constructivism itself—which we have termed the *authenticity* criteria. We shall take up each in turn.

The Parallel Criteria (Trustworthiness)

These criteria for judging adequacy (goodness, quality) are called the *parallel*, or *foundational*, criteria because they are intended to parallel the rigor criteria that have been used within the conventional paradigm for many years. Typically, conventional criteria for judging the rigor of inquiries include internal validity, external validity, reliability, and objectivity.

Internal validity is defined *conventionally* within the *positivist* paradigm as the extent to which variations in an outcome or dependent variable can be attributed to controlled variation in an independent variable (Lincoln & Guba, 1985, p. 290); or, as Cook and Campbell (1979, p. 37) put it, the "approximate validity with which we infer that a relationship between two variables is causal or that the absence of a relationship implies the absence of cause." Assessing internal validity is the central means for ascertaining the "truth value" of a given inquiry, that is, the extent to which it establishes how things really are and really work. Establishing truth value involves asking the question, "How can one establish confidence in the 'truth' of the findings of a particular inquiry for the subjects [sic] with whom and the context in which the inquiry was carried out?" There are a number of putative threats to the internal validity of any inquiry—including history, maturation, testing, instrumentation, statistical regression, differential selection, experimental mortality, and selection—for which the inquiry design must compensate, either by controlling and/or randomizing processes.

External validity can be defined (positivistically) as "the approximate validity with which we infer that the presumed causal relationship can be generalized to and across alternate measures of the cause and effect and across different types of persons, settings and times" (Cook & Campbell, 1979, p. 37). External validity has as its purpose a response to the applicability (or generalizability) question: "How can one determine the extent to which the findings of a particular inquiry have applicability in other contexts or with other subjects [sic]?" Just as there are threats to internal validity, there are, in conventional inquiry, threats to external validity, including selection effects, setting effects, history effects and construct effects (Guba & Lincoln, 1985, pp. 291-92; Lecompte & Goetz, 1982). When these threats are taken care of, then a given study should have applicability to the larger population from which the smaller sample was drawn.

Reliability (in positivist terms) responds to questions about the consistency of a given inquiry and is typically a precondition for validity, because a study that is unreliable cannot possess validity (Lincoln &

Guba, 1985, p. 292). Reliability refers to a given study's (or instrument's) consistency, predictability, dependability, stability, and/or accuracy, and the establishment of reliability for a given study typically rests on replication, assuming that every repetition of the same, or equivalent, instruments to the same phenomena will yield similar measurements. In conventional inquiry, reliability can be threatened by several factors, including any careless act in the measurement or assessment process, by instrumental decay (including "decay" of the human instrument), by assessments that are insufficiently long (or intense), by ambiguities of various sorts, and by others. The question that determines consistency is usually some variation of this one: "How can an inquirer decide whether the findings of a given inquiry would be repeated if the inquiry were replicated with the same (or similar) subjects [*sic*] in the same (or a similar) setting or context?"

Objectivity responds to the positivist demand for neutrality, and requires a demonstration that a given inquiry is free of bias, values, and/ or prejudice. The guiding question is this: "How can an inquirer establish the degree to which the findings of a given inquiry are determined only by the subjects [*sic*] of the inquiry and the conditions of the inquiry, and not by the biases, motivations, interests, values, prejudices, and/or perspectives of the inquirer (or his/her client)?" Typically, freedom from the contamination of values or bias in a study is warranted in either of two ways: intersubjective agreement, or the utilization of a methodology and a set of methods that are thought to render the study impervious to human bias or distortion. The experiment is believed to be such a method by adherents of positivism. Other, lesser methods threaten objectivity by permitting inquirer (and others') values to reflect or distort the "natural" data, by creating the possibility that openly ideological inquiry (e.g., feminist or neo-Marxist) may be pursued, or by legitimating the data and information generated by a single "subjective" observer.

Within the framework of logical positivism, the foregoing criteria are perfectly reasonable and appropriate. This is the case because internal validity, external validity, reliability, and objectivity are grounded—that is, have their foundational assumptions rooted in—the ontological and epistemological framework of that paradigm (model, worldview) for inquiry. But the traditional criteria are unworkable for constructivist, responsive approaches on axiomatic grounds (Guba & Lincoln, 1981; Lincoln & Guba, 1985).

It is clear that internal validity, which is nothing more than an assessment of the degree of isomorphism between a study's findings and the "real" world, cannot have meaning as a criterion in a paradigm that rejects a realist ontology. If realities are instead assumed to exist only in mentally constructed form, what sense could it make to look for isomorphisms? External validity, a concept that embodies the very essence of generalizability, likewise can have little meaning if the "realities" to which one might wish to generalize exist in different forms in different minds, depending on different encountered circumstances and history, based on different experiences, interpreted within different value systems. Reliability is essentially an assessment of stability—of the phenomena being assessed and of the instruments used to assess them. Ordinarily it is assumed that phenomena are unchanging (at least in the short haul), so that any instrument that assesses them ought, on replicated readings, provide essentially the same assessment (otherwise it is judged unreliable). But if the phenomenon can also change—and change is central to the growth and refinement of constructions—then reliability is useless as a goodness criterion. Finally, objectivity clearly reflects the positivist epistemological position that subject/object dualism is possible, but if a rival paradigm asserts that interaction (monism) is inevitable, what can objectivity mean? As Morgan (1983) has noted so well, goodness criteria are themselves rooted in the assumptions of the paradigm for which they are designed; one cannot expect positivist criteria to apply *in any sense* to constructivist studies, including fourth generation evaluation.

What then might be criteria that *are* meaningful within a constructivist inquiry? As a first approximation to answering this question we set about to develop a set parallel to those conventional four, staying as close as possible to them conceptually while adjusting for the changed requirements posed by substituting constructivist for positivist ontology and epistemology. This process—trying to understand what might be criteria appropriate to the axioms themselves—gave rise to the following criteria (Lincoln & Guba, 1986a).

Credibility. The credibility criterion is parallel to internal validity in that the idea of isomorphism between findings and an objective reality is replaced by isomorphism between constructed realities of respondents and the reconstructions attributed to them. That is, instead of focusing on a presumed "real" reality, "out there," the focus has moved to establishing the match between the constructed realities of respondents (or stakeholders) and those realities as represented by the evaluator and attributed to various stakeholders. There are several techniques for increasing the probability that such isomorphism will be verified, or for actually verifying it. Included among those techniques (widely recognized by anthropologists, sociologists, and others who engage in field-work) are the following:

(1) *Prolonged engagement:* Substantial involvement at the site of the inquiry, in order to overcome the effects of misinformation, distortion, or presented "fronts," to establish the rapport and build the trust necessary to uncover constructions, and to facilitate immersing oneself in and understanding the context's culture (Lincoln & Guba, 1986a, pp. 303-304).

(2) *Persistent observation:* Sufficient observation to enable the evaluator to "identify those characteristics and elements in the situation that are most relevant to the problem or issue being pursued and [to focus] on them in detail" (Lincoln & Guba, 1986a, p. 304). The object of persistent observation is to add depth to the scope which prolonged engagement affords.

(3) *Peer debriefing:* The process of engaging, with a disinterested peer, in extended and extensive discussions of one's findings, conclusions, tentative analyses, and, occasionally, field stresses, the purpose of which is both "testing out" the findings with someone who has no contractual interest in the situation and also helping to make propositional that tacit and implicit information that the evaluator might possess. The disinterested peer poses searching questions in order to help the evaluator understand his or her own posture and values and their role in the inquiry; to facilitate testing working hypotheses outside the context; to provide an opportunity to search out and try next methodological steps in an emergent design; and as a means of reducing the psychological stress that normally comes with fieldwork—a means of catharsis within a confidential, professsional relationship.

(4) *Negative case analysis:* The process of revising working hypotheses in the light of hindsight, with an eye toward developing and refining a

given hypothesis (or set of them) until it accounts for all known cases. Negative case analysis may be thought of as parallel or analogous to statistical tests for quantitative data (Kidder, 1981) and should be treated in the same way. That is, just as no one achieves statistical significance at the .000 level, so probably the qualitative data analyst ought not to expect that *all* cases would fit into appropriate categories. But when some reasonable number do, then negative case analysis provides confidence that the evaluator has tried and rejected all rival hypotheses save the appropriate one.

(5) *Progressive subjectivity:* The process of monitoring the evaluator's (or any inquirer's) own developing construction. It is obvious that no inquirer engages in an inquiry with a blank mind, a tabula rasa. It is precisely because the inquirer's mind is not blank that we find him or her engaged in the particular investigation. But it is equally obvious that any construction that emerges from an inquiry must, to be true to constructivist principles, be a *joint* one. The inquirer's construction cannot be given privilege over that of anyone else (except insofar as he or she may be able to introduce a wider range of information and a higher level of sophistication than may any other single respondent). The technique of progressive subjectivism is designed to provide a check on the degree of privilege. And it is simple to execute. Prior to engaging in *any* activity at the site or in the context in which the investigation is to proceed, the inquirer records his or her a priori construction—what he or she expects to find once the study is under way—and archives that record. A most useful archivist is the debriefer, whom we have already discussed. At regular intervals throughout the study the inquirer *again* records his or her developing construction. If the inquirer affords too much privilege to the original constructions (or to earlier constructions as time progresses), it is safe to assume that he or she is not paying as much attention to the constructions offered by other participants as they deserve. The debriefer is in a sensitive position to note such a tendency and to challenge the inquirer about it. If the inquirer "finds" only what he or she expected to find, initially, or seems to become "stuck" or "frozen" on some intermediate construction, credibility suffers.

(6) *Member checks:* The process of testing hypotheses, data, preliminary categories, and interpretations with members of the stakeholding

groups from whom the original constructions were collected. This is the single most crucial technique for establishing credibility. If the evaluator wants to establish that the multiple realities he or she presents are those that stakeholders have provided, the most certain test is verifying those multiple constructions with those who provided them. This process occurs continuously, both during the data collection and analysis stage, and, again, when (and if) a narrative case study is prepared. Member checks can be formal and informal, and with individuals (for instance, after interviews, in order to verify that what was written down is what was intended to be communicated) or with groups (for instance, as portions of the case study are written, members of stakeholding groups are asked to react to what has been presented as representing their construction).

Member checking serves a number of functions, including the following:

- It allows the evaluator to assess the intent of a given action—what it is that a given respondent intended by acting in a certain way or by proffering certain information;
- it gives the respondent (*member* of stakeholding group) the chance to correct errors of fact or errors of interpretation;
- it provides interviewees (informants, respondents) the chance to offer additional information, especially by allowing them to "understand" the situation as a stranger understands it; this often stimulates a respondent to think about information, which further illuminates a given construction and can bring out information that might have been forgotten if the opportunity to review the interview had not occurred;
- it puts the respondent "on record" as having said certain things and as having agreed that the interviewer "got it right";
- it allows a chance for the inquirer to summarize, not only for the respondent but as a first step toward analysis of a given interview; and
- it gives the respondent a chance to judge overall adequacy of the interview itself in addition to providing the opportunity to confirm individual data items (Lincoln & Guba, 1985, p. 314).

Claims to adequacy of the overall inquiry most often are made by means of a formal member check, usually just prior to submitting a final agenda for negotiation of the case study (the purpose of which is to lay out the contextual particulars relevant to this negotiation). This member check session, involving knowledgeable and articulate individuals from each stakeholding group, has as its focus an inspection of the case study, the purpose of which is to correct errors of fact and/or interpretation. Of course, there are sometimes problems with the member-check process. We should note, however, that upon completion of five extensive case studies of five widely disparate sites across the United States—in the Special Education in Rural America Project (Skrtic et al., 1985)—the final formal member-check process failed to turn up a single suggestion for correction *of interpretation.* Several errors of fact were noted on several of the sites' case studies, but of the hundreds of persons interviewed, not one single person felt compelled to challenge the interpretations finally written into case study form. This is a powerful example of the kind of trust the hermeneutic process, carried out with integrity, can engender. No person, no matter how powerful or remote from power, at any site, felt that her or his construction had been misrepresented.

Sometimes, stakeholding groups brought together for the final member check may be adversarial. Some among the groups may feel that deliberate confrontation is in their best interests (much as the decades of the 1960s and 1970s brought forth a particular kind of social confrontation—called "mau-mauing"—with a definitive social end: recognition and funding for local minority groups). Member-checking processes can also be misleading, in the event that all members of a stakeholding group share a common myth, decide that they will maintain an organizational front, or even deliberately conspire to withhold information. If a conspiracy is afoot, being naive is no help, and nothing short of wide experience (and occasionally being "taken" by shrewd clients) can overcome naiveté. But the process itself is an enormous help to avoiding conspiracies, because the openness of the process, and the free flow of information, serve to counteract the secrecy needed to maintain myths, fronts, and deliberate deception.

The reader who is familiar with our earlier work will notice that we have avoided a discussion of triangulation as a credibility check. In part, we have done so because triangulation itself carries too positivist an implication, to wit, that there exist unchanging phenomena so that triangulation can logically *be* a check. For those readers who have found the idea of triangulation a useful one, we would offer the following caveat: Member-checking processes ought to be dedicated to verifying that the *constructions* collected are those that have been offered by respondents, while triangulation should be thought of as referring to cross-checking specific data items of a factual nature (number of target persons served, number of children enrolled in a school-lunch program, number of handicapped elementary children in Foster School District who are in self-contained classrooms, number of fourth-grade mathematics textbooks purchased by the district for the 1987–1988 school year, number of high school English teachers employed, and the like).

Transferability. Transferability may be thought of as parallel to external validity or generalizability. Rigorously speaking, the positivist paradigm requires both sending and receiving contexts to be at least random samples from the same population. In the constructivist paradigm, external validity is replaced by an empirical process for checking the degree of similarity between sending and receiving contexts. Further, the burden of proof for claimed generalizability is on the *inquirer,* while the burden of proof for claimed transferability is on the *receiver.*

Generalization, in the conventional paradigm, is absolute, at least when conditions for randomization and sampling are met. But transferability is always relative and depends entirely on the degree to which salient conditions overlap or match. The major technique for establishing the degree of transferability is thick description, a term first attributed to anthropologist Gilbert Ryle and elaborated by Clifford Geertz (1973). Just what constitutes " 'proper' thick description is . . . still not completely resolved" (Lincoln & Guba, 1985, p. 316). Furthermore, it may never be, since the conditions that need to obtain to declare transferability between Context A and Context B may in fact change with the nature of the inquiry; the "criteria that separate relevant from irrelevant descriptors are still largely undefined" (Lincoln & Guba, 1985, p. 316). But the constructivist works with very different types of "confidence limits"; the hypotheses relevant to naturalistic inquiries are only "working" and, therefore, are liable to disconfirmation or to assessments of nonutility, even in the same context, at a later period of time. The object of the game in making transferability judgments is to set out all the working hypotheses for *this* study, and to provide an extensive and careful description of the time, the place, the context, the culture in which those hypotheses were found to be salient. The constructivist does not provide the confidence limits of the study. Rather, what he or she does is to provide as complete a data base as humanly possible in order to facilitate transferability judgments on the part of others who may wish to apply the study to their own situations (or situations in which they have an interest).

Dependability. Dependability is parallel to the conventional criterion of reliability, in that it is concerned with the stability of the data over time. Often such instability occurs because inquirers are bored, are exhausted, or are under considerable psychological stress from the intensity of the process. But dependability specifically excludes changes that occur because of overt methodological decisions by the evaluator or because of maturing reconstructions. In conventional inquiry, of course, alterations in methodology (design) of the study would render reliability greatly suspect, if not totally meaningless (unstable). Likewise, shifts in hypotheses, constructs, and the like are thought to expose studies to unreliability.

But methodological changes and shifts in constructions are expected products of an emergent design dedicated to increasingly sophisticated constructions. Far from being threats to dependability, such changes and shifts are hallmarks of a maturing—and successful—inquiry. But such changes and shifts need to be both tracked and trackable (publicly inspectable), so that outside reviewers of such an evaluation can explore the process, judge the decisions that were made, and understand what salient factors in the context led the evaluator to the decisions and interpretations made. The technique for documenting the logic of process and method decisions is the dependability audit.

The inquiry audit is a procedure based on the metaphor (and actual process) of the fiscal audit. In a fiscal audit, two kinds of issues are explored: First, to what extent is the *process* an established, trackable, and documentable process, and, second, to what extent are various data in the bookkeeping system actually confirmable? The dependability audit relies on the first, or process, judgment. The other half of the auditing process rests in the fourth trustworthiness criterion, confirmability. We shall discuss both of these forms of auditing together in the following section.

Confirmability. Confirmability may be thought of as parallel to the conventional criterion of objectivity. Like objectivity, confirmability is concerned with assuring that data, interpretations, and outcomes of inquiries are rooted in contexts and persons apart from the evaluator and are not simply figments of the evaluator's imagination. Unlike the conventional paradigm, which roots its assurances of objectivity in *method*—that is, follow the process correctly and you will have findings that are divorced from the values, motives, biases, or political persuasions of the inquirer—the constructivist paradigm's assurances of integrity of the findings are rooted in the data themselves. This means that data (constructions, assertions, facts, and so on) can be tracked to their sources, and that the logic used to assemble the interpretations into structurally coherent and corroborating wholes is both explicit and implicit in the narrative of a case study. Thus both the "raw products" and the "processes used to compress them," as Cronbach and Suppes (1969) put it, are available to be inspected and confirmed by outside reviewers of the study. The usual technique for confirming the data and interpretations of a given study is the confirmability audit.

This audit and the dependability audit alluded to above can be carried out together (and probably should be). As we mentioned earlier, the concept of an inquiry audit is rooted in the metaphor of the fiscal audit. The fiscal auditor is concerned with attesting to the quality and appropriateness of the *accounting process,* and in similar fashion the inquiry auditor is concerned with attesting to the quality and appropriateness of the *inquiry process.* That examination is effectively the *dependability audit.* But a fiscal auditor is also concerned with the "bottom line," that is, can entries in the accounts ledgers be verified and do the numbers add up right? In similar fashion the inquiry auditor attests to the fact that the "data" (facts, figures, and constructions) can all be traced to original sources, and the process by which they were converted to the "bottom line" ("compressed and rearranged to make the conclusions credible," to use Cronbach & Suppes's terminology) can be confirmed. This effectively is the confirmability audit to which we alluded. Algorithms for setting up an "audit trail" and for carrying out an inquiry audit are described in detail in Schwandt and Halpern (1988). An abbreviated discussion of the process can also be found in Lincoln and Guba (1985).

The Hermeneutic Process as Its Own Quality Control

Another way of judging the quality of evaluations conducted as fourth generational is to look within the process itself. Conventional evaluation, for example, is dependent virtually entirely on external, objective assessments of its quality for confirmation of goodness. But fourth generation evaluation is conducted via a hermeneutic, dialectic process. Data inputs are analyzed immediately on receipt. They may be "fed back" for comment, elaboration, correction, revision, expansion, or whatever to the very respondents who provided them only a moment ago. But those data inputs will also surely be incorporated into the emerging joint, collaborative reconstruction that emerges as the process continues. The opportunities for error to go undetected and/or unchallenged are very small in such a process. It is the immediate and continuing interplay of information that militates against the possibility of noncredible outcomes. It is difficult to maintain false fronts, or support deliberate deception when information is subject to continuous and multiple challenges from a variety of stakeholders. The publicly inspectable and inspected nature of the hermeneutic process itself prevents much of the kinds of secrecy and information poverty that have characterized client-focused evaluations of other generations.

Further, the possibility that the so-called biases or prejudices of the evaluator can shape the results is virtually zero, provided only that the evaluation is conducted in accordance with hermeneutic dialectic principles. (The argument that not all evaluators will "play the game" honorably and honestly is unconvincing. The same observation can be made of inquiry conducted within *any* paradigm, as recent experience so well attests.) So long as the evaluator's constructions (to which she or he is entitled as is any other constructor; calling them biases may have persuasive value but is hardly compelling) are laid on the table along with all the others and are made to withstand the same barrage of challenge, criticism, and counterexample as any others, there is no basis for according them any special influence, for better or worse.

The Authenticity Criteria

The above two approaches to the problem of criteria of goodness of fourth generation evaluations, while useful, are not entirely satisfying (either to us or to our critics). The first are, after all, *parallel* criteria. They have their roots and origins in positivist assumptions, and while adjustments have been made for the different assumptions of the naturalist paradigm, there remains a feeling of constraint, a feeling of continuing to play "in the friendly confines" of the opposition's home court.

In addition to their positivist ring, they share a second characteristic that leaves an uncomfortable feeling: they are primarily *methodological* criteria. That is, they speak to *methods* that can ensure one has carried out the process correctly. In the positivist paradigm, method has primacy. Method is critical for ensuring that the results are trustworthy. But method is only one consideration in constructivist inquiry or fourth generation evaluation. Outcome, product, and negotiation criteria are equally important in judging a given inquiry. Relying solely on criteria that speak to methods, as do the parallel criteria, leaves an inquiry vulnerable to questions regarding whether stakeholder rights were in fact honored. To put the point more bluntly, prolonged engagement and persistent observation (or any other *methods* one might choose) do not ensure that stakeholder constructions have been collected and faithfully represented. So reliance on pure or pristine method alone is insufficient to guarantee that the intent of the inquiry effort was achieved.

The second approach, while rooted in constructivism, suffers from being implicit to the process, and hence is not very persuasive to those who wish to see explicit evidence. We were moved as a result (and at the gentle critical prompting of our caring critic, John K. Smith) to devise what we have now called "authenticity criteria," which spring directly from constructivism's own basic assumptions. That is, they could have been invented by someone who had never heard of positivism or its claims for rigor. These criteria can be explicitly confirmed and would be addressed in any case study emerging from a constructivist evaluation. The authenticity criteria include the following (Lincoln & Guba, 1986a):

Fairness. Fairness refers to the extent to which different constructions and their underlying value structures are solicited and honored within the evaluation process. These different constructions must be presented, clarified, checked (as in the member-checking process), and taken into account in a balanced and evenhanded way. Since inquiry (and evaluations) are value-bound and value-situated, and evaluators inevitably confront a situation of value pluralism, then multiple constructions resting on differing value systems will emerge from stakeholders in and around the evaluation effort. The role of the evaluator is to seek out, and communicate, all such constructions and to explicate the ways in which such constructions—and their underlying value systems—are in conflict.

There are two techniques for achieving fairness. The first involves stakeholder identification and the solicitation of within-group constructions. The process of identifying all potential stakeholders and seeking out their constructions should become a part of the permanent audit trail completed for each evaluation case study. The presentation of constructions will be most clearly displayed in the identification of conflict over claims, concerns, and issues. Explicating the differences between belief and value systems is "not always an easy task, but exploration of values when clear conflict is evident should be a part of the data-gathering and data-analysis processes (especially during, for instance, the content analysis of individual interviews)" (Lincoln & Guba, 1986a, p. 79).

The second step in achieving this criterion is the open negotiation of recommendations and of the agenda for subsequent action. This process is especially visible in the methodological steps of prioritizing unresolved claims, concerns, and issues, collecting information relevant to them as well as adding a level of sophistication that may be required, preparing the agenda for negotiation, and carrying out the negotiation itself, as carried out by equally skilled bargainers, from approximately equal positions of power, and with the same (equal) information available to all. The open negotiation is modeled on labor negotiation and arbitration (and, indeed, our rules were devised from a study of that literature). Negotiations that are true to fourth generation evaluations have the following characteristics:

(1) They must be open, carried out in full view of the parties or the parties' representatives; closed sessions, secret codicils, or the like are not permitted.

(2) The negotiations must be carried out with equally skilled bargainers. While it is hardly ever the case that all stakeholders will be equally skilled bargainers, all sides should *have access* to skilled bargainers. When it is necessary, the evaluator will act as adviser and educator to the less skilled. We are aware that this appears to be an advocacy role, which some will resist, but we have already argued earlier that the proper and appropriate province of the evaluator is the empowerment of previously disenfranchised stakeholders, so this does not breach the assumptions or goals of fourth generation evaluation.

(3) The negotiation must be carried out from approximately equal positions of power, not just in principle but also in practice.

(4) The negotiation must be carried out under circumstances where all parties are in possession of the same level of information; in some instances, this may mean that stakeholders may require assistance in understanding what the information means for their interests, but providing such assistance is also a legitimate role of the evaluator.

(5) The negotiation itself must focus on matters that are known to be relevant.

(6) Finally, the negotiation must be conducted in accordance with rules that the stakeholders themselves devised and to which all have assented.

Fairness also requires the creation of an appellate mechanism should any negotiating party feel that the rules are not observed. It also mandates fully informed consent with respect to any process that is part of the evaluation procedures. Consent is obtained not only prior to opening the evaluation effort but as information is uncovered and shared; as power relationships shift, this consent must be renegotiated continuously. And last, fairness requires the constant use of the member-check process, not only for the purpose of commenting on whether the constructions have been received "as sent" but for the purpose of commenting on the fairness process (adapted, Lincoln & Guba, 1986a).

Since discussions of fairness are fairly straightforward in other literatures, it is reasonably clear what this criterion might mean if achieved, and it is reasonably documentable when it has been achieved. The next criteria are more ambiguous, although, clearly, documentation as to their achievement needs to be provided.

Ontological authenticity. This criterion refers to the extent to which individual respondents' own emic constructions are improved, matured, expanded, and elaborated, in that they now possess more information and have become more sophisticated in its use. It is, literally, "improvement in the individual's (or group's) conscious experiencing of the world" (Lincoln & Guba, 1986a, p. 81).

Ontological authenticity can be enhanced through the provision of vicarious experience, which enhances the opportunity for individual respondents (stakeholders and others) to apprehend their own "worlds" in more informed and sophisticated ways. Insofar as the evaluator can make available examples, cases, or other material that aids participants to reassess their own experience—seeing how it is the same as or different from the experience of others—it may serve to enhance their own awareness of the context in which they find themselves. While vicarious experience may not be enough, it is nevertheless a powerful tool for expanding respondents' own awareness or consciousness, particularly of structural aspects of a given context or community.

There are two techniques for demonstrating that the criterion of ontological authenticity has been achieved. First, there is the testimony of selected respondents. When individual stakeholders can attest to the fact that they now understand a broader range of issues, or that they can appreciate (understand, comprehend) issues that they previously failed to understand—that is evidence of ontological authenticity. Second, the audit trail for the case study should have entries of individual constructions recorded at different points in the evaluation process. Those entries ought to include those of the evaluator as well, in order to document "progressive subjectivity."

Educative authenticity. Educative authenticity represents the extent to which individual respondents' understanding of and appreciation for the constructions of *others* outside their stakeholding group are enhanced.

> It is not enough that the actors in some contexts achieve, individually, more sophisticated or mature constructions, or those that are more ontologically authentic. It is also *essential* that they come to appreciate (apprehend, discern, understand)—not necessarily like or agree with—

the constructions that are made by others and to understand how those constructions are rooted in the different values systems of those others. (Lincoln & Guba, 1986a, p. 81)

Stakeholders should at least have the opportunity to be confronted with the constructions of others very different from themselves, for, among other things, the chance to see how different value systems evoke very different solutions to issues surrounding the evaluand.

There are two techniques for establishing whether or not educative authenticity has been achieved. First, testimony of selected participants in the process will attest to the fact that they have comprehended and understood the constructions of others different from themselves. This testimony will often emerge in the negotiation process, and so will be not only documentable but publicly available. Second, at the end of the process, the audit trail should contain entries related to the developing understanding or appreciation as seen through exchanges during the hermeneutic circles process.

Catalytic authenticity. This criterion may be defined as the extent to which action is stimulated and facilitated by the evaluation processes. Reaching new and more sophisticated constructions, and achieving some appreciation of the positions of others, even achieved within a system of consummate fairness, is simply not enough. The purpose of evaluation is some form of action and/or decision making. Thus no fourth generation evaluation is complete without action being prompted on the part of participants.

Any number of clues lead us to observe that *action* is singularly lacking in most evaluations: the call for getting "theory into action"; the preoccupation in recent decades with "dissemination" at the national level; the creation and maintenance of federal laboratories, centers, and dissemination networks; the non-utilization of evaluations, and the general disenchantment with evaluation efforts at the federal level, together with the concomitant lowering of funding levels for such activity. This form of evaluation, with its heavy involvement of stakeholders, participants, and targets promises to stimulate action in a manner and at a level unheard of in the first three generations.

There are three techniques for assuring that this criterion has been met. First, there should be available testimony of participants from all stakeholding groups, including not only testimony of their interest in acting on the evaluation but their willingness to become involved in doing so. Second, we can rely on resolutions issuing from the negotiating sessions themselves. When action is jointly negotiated, it should follow that action is "owned" by participants and, therefore, as the research has shown, more willingly carried out. And third, there is, of course, systematic follow-up within some given time period to assess the extent of action and change revolving about the evaluation effort.

Tactical authenticity. It is not enough to be stimulated to action. It is quite possible to want, and even to need, to act, but to lack the power to do so in any meaningful way. Thus tactical authenticity refers to the degree to which stakeholders and participants are empowered to act. The first step in empowerment, of course, is taken when all stakeholders and others at risk are provided with the opportunity to contribute inputs to the evaluation and to have a hand in shaping its focus and its strategies. But this process of empowerment must be continued throughout the process for participants to be *fully* empowered to act at the consummation of the negotiation process.

There are three ways in which tactical authenticity may be demonstrated. First, testimony of selected participants and stakeholders from all groups is solicited. (It is clearly not enough simply to survey the clients and funders.) Second, some follow-up has to be undertaken in order to determine which groups do in fact participate and to examine the ways in which they participate. And, finally, some judgment can be rendered, usually by participants and evaluator alike, as to the degree of empowerment during the evaluation process itself. Was it participatory? Have all stakeholders felt that they or their representatives have had a significant role in the process? Are all participants more skilled than previously in understanding and utilizing power and negotiation techniques? If the answers to those questions are uniformly yes, then tactical authenticity has probably been achieved.

Summary

It is apparent that there are many ways to assess the goodness of a fourth generation evaluation. It is not and need not be the case that such evaluations are sloppy, corner-cutting, or unmindful of standards. Quite the opposite. It ought to be evident that the most basic question is this: "*What* standards ought apply?" We have described several ways to respond to this question in this chapter, and have tried to indicate where the proposed standards come from and/or how they have been derived. Each set has utility for certain purposes. The trick is not to confuse the purposes. It is also important to keep in mind that goodness criteria, like paradigms, are rooted in certain assumptions. Thus it is not appropriate to judge constructivist evaluations by positivistic criteria or standards, or vice versa. To each its proper and appropriate set.

Note

1. The *Standards* devised by the Joint Committee in 1981 are intended to apply to evaluations of educational programs, projects, and materials. A reconstituted Joint Committee has recently published (Joint Comittee, 1988) a second set of standards that apply to the evaluation of educational personnel; these standards are not covered in the present discussion.

9 Putting It All Together so That It Spells E-V-A-L-U-A-T-I-O-N

The construction of fourth generation evaluation has embedded within it certain consequences for the process of evaluation and for the role of the evaluator. New principles are needed in order to guide its implementation. In this chapter we shall try to pull those principles together (insofar as we have been able to derive them) in summary fashion. We want to make clear the ways in which fourth generation evaluation stands in stark relief to earlier generations of evaluation, and the ways in which the roles of the evaluator have been dramatically altered and enlarged. As a result, evaluation must now be viewed in very different ways. We will try to capture some of these basic differences between evaluation as it has been practiced in the previous three generations, and evaluation that may be characterized as fourth generation, and we shall indicate what kinds of roles the evaluator must play now as opposed to those evaluators played in earlier generations.

Views of Evaluation in Its Fourth Generation

First and foremost, evaluation is a *sociopolitical* process. Social, cultural, and political factors should not be viewed as unattractive nuisances (to coin a phrase) that threaten validity, but as integral and meaningful components of the process, without which the evaluation effort would be sterile, useless, and meaningless. Evaluation, like democracy, is a process that, to be at its best, depends upon the application of enlightened and informed self-interest.

Far from viewing cultural and political elements as hazards that impede the evaluation effort, fourth generation evaluation recognizes that all human activity—including all forms of inquiry—is bounded and framed by elements of culture and politics. Rather than attempting to circumscribe or negate such elements with the artifice of method, constructivist evaluation treats social, cultural, and political features as elementary properties of human circumstance and incorporates them into the inquiry process. The *conscious* awareness of such elements does not compromise the evaluation activity; rather, it enhances it, because values themselves become a part of what is investigated and inquired into.

Second, evaluation is a *joint, collaborative process.* It is a process that aims at the evolution of consensual constructions about the evaluand (that which is being evaluated). That aim cannot be fulfilled unless it is jointly pursued by all stakeholders. Unless individual stakeholder constructions are solicited and honored, there can be no hope of consensus. Similarly, the process must be pursued in collaborative ways, for, without collaboration, there can be no hope of honoring individual constructions.

That is not to say that all evaluations will end in consensus. Quite the opposite. Some evaluations may end with actions being undertaken via a negotiation where honorable and responsible people simply "agree to disagree." But a fair and deliberate effort must be made to help all stakeholding parties arrive at least at the point where such agreement (to disagree) can be reached. That in itself is a form of joint, consensual construction. Areas of the disagreement likewise become a part of the construction(s) presented in the case study.

Third, evaluation is a *teaching/learning process*. Everyone—and most assuredly this includes the evaluator—serves as both learner and teacher as the evaluation pursues its course. The stakeholders teach the evaluator—and one another—about their constructions, and the evaluator assists in communicating those constructions from one individual and one group to another. Evaluators help each group clarify its own construction, while at the same time learning from it yet another view of which account must be taken. The process is clearly mutually educative.

This stance represents a major break with the past in that typically the evaluator, usually along with the client or funder, has informed stakeholders of his, her, or their concerns and questions of interest. Issues that held salience for stakeholders were not typically part of the evaluation effort unless the stakeholders had chanced on some issue of interest to evaluators and clients. The evaluator who enters a setting willing to be taught by all stakeholders and participants is undoubtedly a new species in the ecosystem.

Fourth, evaluation is a *continuous, recursive, and highly divergent process*. All reconstructions that emerge from an evaluation continue to be problematic; that is, they are not taken as "truth," or even as the best approximations of "truth" that may exist, but simply as the most informed and sophisticated constructions that it has been possible to evolve. They remain open to challenge and may, depending on the nature of new information or increased sophistication that may become available, be entirely replaced and abandoned. Such an evaluation effort cannot converge on "truth" but continually expands as it forms reconstruction after reconstruction. Thus evaluations have no "natural" end point—a point at which the "truth" is finally known—but merely pause as new information and increased sophistication are sought. In fact, fourth generation evaluations typically "end" for exactly the same reasons as other evaluations end: It is time for action, stakeholders and clients must arrive at a decision, or the contract is ended. Evaluations are thus theoretically infinite, but logistically, fiscally, or practically, they do typically have an end point.

Fifth, evaluation is an *emergent process*. It is impossible to design an evaluation except in a general way (for example, by deciding to follow the methodology—strategy—of Figure 5.1). The process is *substantively* unpredictable because one cannot know what constructions will be introduced by the several stakeholders, or what those stakeholders will find persuasive in leading to reconstructions and approaches to consensus. An evaluator cannot know or predict beforehand what claims, concerns, and issues stakeholders will find troubling or compelling. Every step, therefore, is contingent on the previous steps and can be unfolded only serially.

One logical consequence of emergent design is that the entire set of design features, methodological decisions, and issue identification processes can only be specified *when the evaluation has been declared terminated*. While the evaluation is ongoing, as new information emerges, the evaluator is duty-bound to follow wherever it leads. Hence, the design unfolds as information is proffered or as new constructions are located and analyzed.

Sixth, evaluation is a *process with unpredictable outcomes*. In view of points four and five above, it is not possible to say with any confidence what the outcomes of an evaluation will be—what we will "know" when it is completed or what value position we will take. Since there is no guarantee that consensus in reconstruction will in fact occur, there may be *multiple* outcomes. So, for example, one construction may lead to the belief that the evaluand is "successful" or "effective" while another construction may lead to the opposite view. (Please notice that definitions of "successful" and "effective" themselves militate against the possibility of *always* achieving consensus. Perfectly reasonable people can readily agree that what is effective for one child in school, for instance, may be quite ineffective for another. Traditional, self-contained classrooms versus open classrooms is a simple example of how parents may disagree about what is "right" or "effective" for their child.) We would simply stress again that the question, "But which view is right?" is inappropriate. Views are neither right nor wrong but different, depending on how the construction is formed, the context in which it is formed, and the values that undergird the construction in the first place. It is not more research that is needed but more negotiation. It is not less politics in evaluation that is needed but a finer-grained understanding of the values that underlie the various political and policy positions.

Seventh, evaluation is a *process that creates reality*. The term *findings* has to be discarded, since it suggests the existence of objective "truths," which the evaluation has, through its methodology, uncovered. The reconstruction(s) that emerge from an evaluation are the literal *creation* of the participants and stakeholders who construct them, as were the constructions each group originally introduced into the negotiation.

If the foregoing seven characteristics are descriptors of the new goals of evaluation, then it is appropriate to ask what might be the consequences of acting on such views of evaluation. Following the fourth generation model has what seem to us to be several very desirable consequences.

The Consequences of Fourth Generation Evaluation

One consequence of this model is that *parochial absolutism yields to ecumenical relativism*. The world is no longer viewed as a closed system operating by immutable laws, which, once discovered, lay an inescapable mandate for behavior on us all. No longer can the discoverers and manipulators of those laws be viewed as a special priesthood. Instead, the world becomes relative, with a variety of views not only tolerated but sanctioned. There is no special priesthood, only groups who, by virtue of the knowledge they have acquired and their sophistication in using it, are entitled to offer constructions and to have their constructions respected. Everyone is empowered in the process. The implication is that scientists (e.g., inquirers, evaluators) cannot stand aside from their constructions as though Nature herself had handed down "findings." Scientists, especially social scientists, must take as much responsibility as stakeholders and participants for the manner in which their constructions are used—or misused—unable to hide behind the cloak of "science."

Let us note again that this conclusion does not mean that "anything goes." The opposite of absolutism is not anarchy. And it is not the case that being a relativist means that one has no power to criticize ideas or constructions. All ideas may be subjected to critique within some framework. All that taking a position of relativism implies is that the framework within which any critique of ideas occurs is relative and may change from context to context, given the particulars of that context.

The second consequence of following the fourth generation model is that *accountability yields to shared responsibility*. It is so often the case that evaluations are conducted not only to determine a state of affairs but also (and especially when the existing state of affairs is judged a priori to be unacceptable) to determine who or what is accountable. So, for instance, it is fashionable these days to hold teachers accountable for the (putative) sorry state of our schools. Much so-called evaluation is directed to making this accountability manifest, for instance, statewide testing programs to determine which schools are doing their jobs or teacher competency tests to determine which teachers are below "minimal standards." But such an approach implies a simplistic, causal, push-pull, mechanistic view of the world, rather than recognizing the shared responsibility and accountability implied by a "mutual simultaneous shaping" view of the world.

We find that we increasingly agree with Cronbach's assertion that the demand for accountability is a sign of pathology in the organization (Cronbach et al., 1980, p. 4). *Accountability* has traditionally meant stewardship, particularly with respect to a public trust. But as the term is used today, it has come to mean that someone is about to have "the blame" laid on him or her, and typically the blame comes to rest on the least powerful stakeholders and participants in a given context. The idea of *shared* responsibility comes closer to the original meaning of accountability as stewardship, and we are persuaded that—to continue our earlier example—we should cease "blaming" teachers for the failure of children to learn in school and begin sharing responsibility for those learning outcomes.

A third consequence of following the fourth generation model is that *exploitation yields to empowerment.* Existing evaluations tend simply to ignore stakeholders, often with the caution that "interesting data were obtained from participants, but were ultimately found to be difficult to process." The translation for that disclaimer is that stakeholder claims, concerns, and issues were not congruent with evaluator-identified issues, so were ignored. Or, those evaluators who make some effort to determine and respond to stakeholder views nevertheless feel free to reject them if they "threaten the technical adequacy" of the evaluation design. Cozy managerial relationships in which only clients, sponsors, and evaluators are empowered to raise the questions to be addressed, and where information is shared only with them, clearly disempower and disenfranchise other stakeholders. Indeed, in many cases, clients and sponsors retain the right to determine whether information shall be released, and, if so, to whom, by what means, and at what times. Stakeholder groups are often exploited in the sense that they are forced to yield to data collection procedures that produce data that will be used *against* the very group from whom they are collected. A good example is teacher competency tests. Fourth generation evaluation with its insistence on collaborative design and implementation obviates these problems.

A fourth consequence of following the fourth generation model is that *ignorance yields to comprehension and appreciation.* Any given construction can be no better than the information on which it is based and the sophistication the constructor can bring to bear in appreciating and understanding that information. Conventional evaluations do virtually nothing to improve either knowledge or sophistication for any except a few privileged stakeholder groups, mainly clients and sponsors. But fourth generation evaluation shares knowledge and works at improvement of sophistication for all. A good fourth generation evaluation leaves *everyone* more informed and sophisticated than before. It is an educative experience for all.

The fifth consequence of following the fourth generation model is that *immobilization yields to action.* Conventional evaluations tend not to be used. Indeed, discussions of means to induce clients and others to use evaluation results are among the "hottest" sessions at meetings of evaluators today. Clients may (believe they) know whom to hold accountable, what factors (interventions) have failed, and what resistances have been met, but they gain precious little insight into what to do next. Evaluations as now conducted may be problem identifiers, but they are certainly not solution identifiers. (In fact, it may well be that they are not even problem identifiers, since nomination of what is considered a "problem" is left to a relatively small number of powerful persons. And one cannot devise a solution to the unworkableness of a program if one has not identified and framed its problems correctly. This is another benefit of high participation of stakeholders—the increased likelihood of finding what all construct to be problems, not just what clients believe they might be.)

Moreover, because of evaluation's history of blaming and exploiting most stakeholders (people other than clients and sponsors), evaluation is distrusted and resisted. But fourth generation evaluation, both because of its open stance that is empowering and enfranchising and because its formulations lead to constructions in which shared responsibility is featured, is catalytic in producing action. Evaluation and action are part and parcel of the same process rather than being two different processes separated in time (and often space, given that traditional evaluation tends to separate the evaluation context from the locus of decision making).

There may be other consequences of which we are unaware, but this set has emerged from our own practice, and we believe it is a compelling rationale for at least additional exploration of fourth generation evaluation. But likewise, the practice of fourth generation evaluation also has significant consequences for the roles that the evaluator assumes.

New Evaluator Roles

The characteristic roles of the evaluators—technician, describer, and judge—in each of the preceding three generations of evaluation are retained, but with some reinterpretation, expansion, and elaboration as befits their incorporation into the "new" evaluation.

One, the first generation role of technician (measurement specialist, test-maker, and statistician) is converted into that of the human instrument and human data analyst. These new roles, one should note, also demand certain technical proficiencies and skills, including a good deal of knowledge about conventional measurement instruments and approaches and conventional data analysis. We have argued often (although we have not always been heard) that evaluators who operate in a constructivist, responsive, and, now, fourth generation mode, will use primarily, *although not exclusively,* qualitative methods. But there will be times when quantitative methods—tests or other measurement instruments, or numeric displays—will be, and should be, used. The single limitation that a constructivist, responsive, fourth generation evaluator would put on the use of quantitative methods is that no *causally inferential* statistics would be employed, since the causal linkages implied by such statistics are contrary to the position on causality that phenomenologically oriented and constructivist inquiry takes. Thus the fourth generation evaluator must have technical skills equal to those of a first, second, or third generation evaluator, including skills in tests, measurements, quantitative analysis, *and* qualitative methods and analyses.

Two, the second generation role of describer is converted into that of illuminator and historian. The role of the original describer was to detail patterns of strengths and weaknesses in the attainment of specified objectives. The task of the fourth generation evaluator is much broader. Whereas the describer was to relate only characteristics of achievement and nonachievement of objectives, the fourth generation describer is responsible for providing "thick description" of the context and the factors found to be salient in it, illuminating the stage on which the evaluation drama is unfolding and providing a vicarious experience of what it is like to be a major or minor actor there.

Three, the third generation role of judge revolved around the necessity for drawing conclusions about the evaluand's success, effectiveness, or utility and about making recommendations on how to improve the evaluand so that it might be more successful. In this fourth generation, however, the role of judge is converted into that of mediator of the judgmental process. The central task is to enable stakeholders to reach consensus on one or more constructions that embody such conclusions and recommendations; that is, to facilitate the rendering of judgments, conclusions, and recommendations by participants and stakeholders who are operating from a jointly developed agenda for negotiation.

Thus fourth generation evaluation takes on the roles of evaluators in the previous three generations, redefines and expands them, and incorporates them all into an even more highly skilled practitioner than formerly. But fourth generation evaluation approaches also require—and define—several *new elements in the evaluator's role.* The new elements that are indicated by the political, ethical, and methodological ramifications of the hermeneutic, dialectic process are four in number.

First, fourth generation evaluation mandates that the evaluator move from the role of controller to that of collaborator. The evaluator must share control, however much that appears to threaten the "technical adequacy" of the evaluation. That is, the evaluator must solicit and honor stakeholder inputs not only about the *substance* of constructions but also with respect to the *methodology* of the evaluation itself. In a participative process a major role of the evaluator must be to attain the conditions of participation for all—a *political* role, it should be noted.

Second, the evaluator must now assume the role of learner and teacher rather than that of investigator. The evaluator cannot simply test certain a priori hypotheses or answer certain questions but must learn what the various stakeholders' competing constructions are and teach them all to all of the stakeholders. This teaching/learning process is basic to the hermeneutic mode. It is the evaluator's responsibility in this role to be *stage manager* for the process, setting the stage in such a way that all stakeholders can learn from one another as well as teach one another (evaluator included). In some views of learning, teachers cannot so much teach as they must set the stage within which learners can learn and teach themselves. It is in this sense that the evaluator is a teacher. But such evaluations are also an advanced course; teachers also learn.

Third, a new role for the evaluator is that of reality shaper rather than mere discoverer. In conventional evaluations, evaluators can sidestep taking responsibility for their "discoveries" because of the claim to value-freedom and the presumption of a search for a single reality "out there." The data appear to "speak for themselves"—without intervention from the scientist, who has merely put questions to "nature"—and those data represent "the way things really are and really work." The evaluator in conventional evaluation is little more than a midwife who knows the techniques for wresting from Nature the answers to the important questions that evaluators know how to raise. He or she is but the messenger and not responsible for what some persons might think to be bad news. But the fourth generation evaluator must recognize the leadership role he or she plays in assisting the emergent reconstructions to see the light of day; to act not only as the technician who facilitates the process but as an active participant who shapes the product as well. In the spirit of shared mutual responsibility the evaluator can no more escape the consequences of the reconstruction that is achieved—whatever that turns out to be—than can any other participant.

Fourth, the evaluator divests him- or herself of the role of passive observer and recognizes and embraces the role of change agent. Conventional evaluation may see the evaluator as an "instrument of change" but not as a change agent directly, since taking the overt posture of change

FOUR GENERATION EVALUATION

agent would be a violation of the criterion of objectivity mandated by conventional inquiry and evaluation. But in fourth generation evaluation, the evaluator is a key figure in a process that creates a new and more sophisticated "reality" (the reconstruction or reconstructions of the hermeneutic process) that has built into it direct and immediate implications for action (see the earlier discussion in this chapter on the consequences of this type of evaluation). The evaluator is charged to teach stakeholders the constructions of others and also to introduce other information such as that from a documentary analysis, from similar evaluations in similar contexts (to afford vicarious learning), from the professional literature, and so on. Thus the evaluator is a leading agent in the process of reconstruction of existing reality constructions. If it is the case that people act in accordance with their constructions (and on what other basis could they act?), then the evaluator is a leading agent in the process of changing action and action for change.

There may be other roles that have not yet become manifest. We ourselves are just beginning to explore this form of evaluation, and our experience is nearly as limited as the readers'. But we believe that evaluators who move to enact these roles will find that they encompass much of what the fourth generation evaluator must do. We did.

"Some Warnings and Advice" on Doing Fourth Generation Evaluation

With all due respect to Rosalie Wax (1971), who first offered fieldworkers warnings and advice, we'd like to offer our own list of advice on carrying out the process. It is easy to forget the implications we have just discussed, especially if one has been socialized (as most of us were) to conventional ways of doing inquiry in general and evaluations in particular. We would urge all evaluators who think they want to do their work in accordance with the fourth generation model to post the principles displayed in Table 9.1 over their desks, where they can be constantly reminded how novel, how contrary to conventional practice, and how powerful, this new approach can be.

Table 9.1 Some Principles for Fourth Generation Evaluators

1. Evaluation is a process whereby evaluators and stakeholders jointly and collaboratively create (or move toward) a consensual valuing construction of some evaluand. It does *not* necessarily yield irrefutable (i.e., empirically confirmable) information (although that may be a side product).
   COROLLARY 1A: Evaluation *creates* reality.
   COROLLARY 1B: The consensual valuing construction that is the outcome of the evaluation is subject to continuous reconstruction (change) including refinement, revision, and, if necessary, replacement.

2. Evaluation is a process that subsumes data collection and data valuing (interpretation) into one inseparable and simultaneous whole.
   COROLLARY 2A: No portion of the evaluation process can be considered to be value-free.

3. Evaluation is a local process. Its outcomes depend on local contexts, local stakeholders, and local values and cannot be generalized to other settings.
   COROLLARY 3A: Evaluation data from other settings cannot be applied to local settings, although they may be adapted, or learned from, in the sense of vicarious experience.

4. Evaluation is a sociopolitical process. Social, cultural and political aspects, far from being merely distracting or distorting nuisances, are integral to the process, at least as important as are considerations of technical adequacy.

5. Evaluation is a teaching/learning process. Evaluators, clients, sponsors, and all stakeholders both teach and learn from one another; indeed, such teaching/learning is an absolute prerequisite to the meaningful reconstruction of emic views.

6. Evaluation is a continuous, recursive, and divergent process, because its "findings" are created social constructions that are subject to reconstruction. Evaluations must be continuously recycled and updated.
   COROLLARY 6A: A good evaluation raises more questions than it answers.
   COROLLARY 6B: A good evaluation has no "natural" end point.

7. Evaluation is an emergent process. It cannot be fully designed in advance for its focus (or foci) depends on inputs from stakeholders and its activities are serially contingent.
   COROLLARY 7A: Evaluation is a process with *in-principle* unpredictable outcomes.

8. Evaluation is a process for sharing accountability rather than assigning it.

9. Evaluation is a process that involves evaluators and stakeholders in a hermeneutic dialectic relationship.

Table 9.1 continued

> COROLLARY 9A: Evaluation is a *joint* process in that it integrates the constructions of stakeholder groups *and* the constructions that the evaluator brings to the evaluation in an emergent emic/etic blend. It aims toward consensus but requires, at a minimum, the clarification of competing constructions. Evaluation thus implemented is an *educative* activity for all.

> COROLLARY 9B: Evaluation is a *collaborative* process in that the several stakeholder groups share control with the evaluator over the methodological and interpretative decisions that are made. Evaluation thus implemented is an *empowering* activity for all.

> COROLLARY 9C: Evaluation is a process that eliminates the distinction between basic and applied inquiry. Evaluation thus implemented *simultaneously* aids understanding and clarifies the nature of needed action.

> COROLLARY 9D: Evaluation is a process the proper conduct of which requires the evaluator to engage in face-to-face *interactions* with individual stakeholders; effective evaluation cannot be accomplished at a distance.

10. Evaluators play many conventional (but reinterpreted) and unconventional roles in carrying out fourth generation evaluation.

> COROLLARY 10A: The evaluator remains a technician, but as a human instrument and data analyst; a describer, but as a historian and illuminator; and a judge, but as an orchestrator of the judgmental process.

> COROLLARY 10B: The evaluator becomes a political collaborator, a stage manager, a reality shaper, and a change agent, sharing in the responsibility for the outcomes of the fourth generation process in each of those ways.

11. Evaluators must possess not only technical expertise but also relevant interpersonal qualities. Perhaps chief among these are patience, humility, openness, adaptability, and a sense of humor.

A Final Word

The model of fourth generation evaluation—indeed, this entire book—is a construction with precisely those characteristics that we have been inputing to constructions throughout this volume. That is, it is a social construction, built on the stuff of experience—our own and that of others, which we have absorbed in the form of vicarious learning—values, beliefs, the particular settings and contexts in which we have worked and been asked to work, and the influence of others' constructions, from which we have tried to draw meaning and possibility. Thus this book, as is any construction, is problematic, subject to reconstruction wherever and whenever new information and/or increased sophistication can be brought to bear. We are inclined to believe that the best construction is one that most quickly leads to its own reconstruction. As a result, we would welcome comments, suggestions, and challenges, so long as they are offered in the spirit of the hermeneutic dialectic and are accompanied by a commitment from the offerer to enter into a genuine dialogue and negotiation. We believe it is through such continuing negotiation that the hope for an accommodation lies, not because the several views of the world will be found to be compatible after all, for they will not, but because through negotiation we can all rise to more informed and sophisticated constructions than we now enjoy.

An Agenda for Negotiation

In the spirit in which this book is offered, we would like to volunteer what could be the start of an agenda for negotiation. We thought it might be of some utility if we listed here some of the major issues that distinguish fourth generation and more conventional models of evaluation. This set of topics might well be the earliest issues that may need to be resolved—and reconstructed—in the process of beginning a new generation. The following have proven to be the most intractable of issues we have faced. The reader is invited to confront them with us.

(1) How can one square the notion of constructed realities with the common-sense experience of reality? We have tried often to explain that while each of us experiences a *physical* world that is quite similar (or coterminous, in the same setting), the "stuff" of which realities are made rarely lies in the rooms, tables, chairs, automobiles, blackboards, or backstops that fill up our space. Rather, the stuff of our realities is *what we make of that physical world, and the social constructs we utilize to make sense of it and to impose order on it.* And *that* stuff comprises the

fears, hopes, beliefs, values, prejudices, dreams, ambitions, frustrations, and possibilities brought to the physical realities we inhabit.

An example: One of us has been individually responsible for each of the chapters, and one of us is sitting here, late at night, working at a computer terminal putting the finishing touches on this, the last chapter. The computer on which I work is most assuredly a physical presence which, with its associated printer, file cases of disks, monitor, keyboard, and special desk, takes up no small amount of room in my study. The computer is most assuredly "real" in the physical sense. But until you know that I could not make it "work" for two years, that it sat, useless and unused, because I could not make the printer work in conjunction with it, you could not understand my "constructed reality" of this computer. Thousands of dollars, down the drain, or so I thought. I was so little interested in it, intrinsically, that I never bothered to go back to the store that sold it to me to ask them for a consult. Rather, I used this machine as an increasingly funny story about myself and technology for nearly two years, until one of my computer-whiz students took it upon himself to get the machines working in tandem, and me over my technophobia. It took about three hours, and ever after, I have accomplished my scholarly writing—and letters to my mother—at this keyboard. But readers could not "know" about computers and one of the authors until they understood my "construction" of computers and technology in my life. That one author has a computer is of little interest to the reader, until he or she inquires into exactly what the *history* of the machine is, and the constructions and reconstructions surrounding it. The move from hostile terrain to wondrous admiration and a joyous cybernetic relationship would never be chronicled without my "construction": the values, beliefs, fears—indeed, phobias—and finally, sense of cooperation, sympathy, understanding, mastery and triumph.

The point we wish to make is that it is not the physical reality of objects, contexts, and events that are of interest, either to us or to most human beings, it is the *meanings* we attach to them. Those meanings are the stuff of a constructed reality. We are willing to leave moot the question of a "real" physical reality in any event; certainly with respect to the kind of inquiry that is of interest to social and behavioral scientists. Still, many of our critics, and of our students, stumble on the issue of the nature of reality;

it is obviously one that has not yet been evolved to such an informed and sophisticated level that consensus can be safely assumed.

(2) How can one manage fourth generation evaluation in the real world of power? Isn't it naive to believe that any group in power would willingly divest itself of that power in order to empower some other group? Certainly this is a problem, and it bears no small resemblance to the question of why the rich would consent to be taxed at a higher rate in order that the poor would have more food stamps, have better access to adequate health care or day care for their children, or to be able to achieve higher levels of job training.

When stakeholders are articulate professionals who already feel empowered in many ways, and sponsors—those who commission and fund the evaluation—are themselves merely "first among equals," there is not much of a problem. But in situations where there are vast power and information disparities, and where those in power prefer things to remain that way, the situation is quite different. Those who argue that fourth generation evaluation "won't work in the real world" are not being merely obstructionist. We do not know the answer to this dilemma, but would willingly listen to any compelling rationale that could be used to convince those with disproportionate power that it is in their best interests and the best interests of those whom they presumably serve, to enfranchise their stakeholders. One opening wedge may lie in a redefinition of power. Rather than to regard it as a fixed-sum commodity, for example, so that the only way to acquire some of it is to take it away from someone who already has it, we may wish to regard it as (potentially) ever growing and enlarging, as in the case of love. To love does not require depriving someone else of love; love can be continuously created. Can power?

(3) How can one hope to gain support for an evaluation in the face of the acknowledged inability to specify a design beforehand, and so have some sense of what will be involved (for example, who's at risk and how much it will cost)? In part, the question of time and money costs is answerable, if not entirely satisfactorily. No evaluation ever appears to have enough money attached to it, and most evaluation efforts must report results by some date, even an arbitrary one (usually linked to a new funding period or to some decision that must be made). Thus the issue of

how much an evaluation will cost is linked to an arbitrary cutoff date by which some set of issues must be resolved and some decision reached regarding future directions of the program, project, and so on. So fourth generation evaluators should be prepared to live within the same kinds of time and fiscal constraints to which their brethren of the first three generations adhered.

With respect to design considerations, Dobbert (1982) has included a useful discussion in her very fine book on how one makes an argument for funding when all design specifications cannot be made in advance. We would recommend a reading of this work to analyze in what ways an unspecified design can nevertheless be laid out in broad-brush terms. Clearly, an evaluation contract will have to specify the *types* of activities in which the evaluator will engage and the *types* of persons with whom he or she will be engaged, rather than specifying individuals, tests, specific measurements, or exact timelines. Equally clearly, there will be some clients for whom this is not enough, and the evaluator will have to make a choice: to do the evaluation the client's way or not at all.

It is also the case that, since outcomes are theoretically unpredictable in a fourth generation evaluation, they cannot be specified in the evaluation contract. But it is not unreasonable to expect that the *process*—a negotiation over a stakeholder-identified evaluation—can be described and potential outcomes—such as decisions about how to proceed from a given point, developed jointly by stakeholders—can be estimated. Unlike a conventional evaluation, the exact decision points cannot be preordinately determined, but it is not unreasonable to expect the evaluator to have facilitated some kind of agreements and consensus at *approximately a given time.* Thus contracting can be modestly specific on certain timelines and events, although not as sharply drawn as a conventional evaluation contract.

It might be noted, too, that, in conventional evaluations, those at risk are rarely identified beforehand. In part, this has been because of the posture of the positivist paradigm that the search for truth ought—to mix metaphors—to allow the chips fall where they may. Therefore, risk, save as outlined in federal law (a limiting posture on risk, we believe), was rarely considered. Fourth generation evaluation takes a much longer and broader view of risk, and defines it as having something, however small, to lose in the evaluation effort. As a result, the usual regulations regarding risk to human participants are merely the tip of the iceberg. How do we go about specifying risk? We cannot, of course, in any a priori way; nor will we be cognizant of who is at risk, or what the level of risk is, until the evaluation effort is nearly completed. But this does put such evaluators in a bind, morally and contractually. And this poses a problem that needs much additional discussion.

Our sense is that this kind of evaluation will depend heavily on the skills of the evaluation contractor to be persuasive, on her or his reputation, and on the willingness of the client to purchase the time of a *specific person*, or persons.

(4) Can you really expect support for a position that denies the general applicability (generalizability) of results? We believe this to be the case but have a hard time arguing it. The commonsense, everyday experience of evaluators (and clients alike) is that evaluation results (in the broadest sense) rarely possess generalizability in any meaningful (i.e., scientific) sense. When the findings from one site are transplanted to another, second site, they rarely exhibit much "fit" and, typically, are set aside in favor of "local knowledge" anyway. The generalizability criterion is, as a result, honored more in the breach than the observance; it is the ritual of making generalizability statements that is more respected than the hope that findings will prove generalizable. But funders balk at funding efforts that do not, at the very least, make some claim to widespread applicability (whether or not it is the intent of the evaluators to make strenuous efforts at fulfilling this criterion). Nevertheless, we have here again the process that Mitch Brickell in a memorable phrase labeled "biting the hand that feeds you while all the time appearing to lick it." Perhaps the answer lies in helping clients realize that applicability and generalizability are never attained anyway, and that claiming to provide for them merely wastes their time and money.

The foregoing issues are some of the more intractable ones that we have faced, both from clients and from critics. In the best constructivist sense, we would like to open a dialogue revolving around sensible postures we and others might take on these problems. We would welcome any and all arguments offered in a sense of enriching the constructions of all stakeholders.

References

American Psychological Association. (1974). *Standards for educational and psychological tests* (rev. ed.). Washington, DC: Author.

Arendt, Hannah. (1963). *On revolution.* New York: Viking Press.

Bahm, A.J. (1971). Science is not value-free. *Policy Sciences, 2,* 391-396.

Baumrind, Diana. (1979). IRBs and social science research: The costs of deception. *IRB, 1*(6), 1-4.

Baumrind, Diana. (1985). Research using intentional deception: Ethical issues revisited. *American Psychologist, 40,* 165-174.

Belenky, Mary F., Clinchy, Blythe McVicker, Goldberger, Nancy Rule, & Tarule, Jill Mattuck. (1986). *Women's ways of knowing.* New York: Basic Books.

Biklen, Sari K., & Bogdan, Robert. (1986). On your own with naturalistic evaluation. In monograph by David O. Williams (Ed.), *Naturalistic evaluation* (New directions for program evaluation, no. 3). San Francisco: Jossey-Bass.

271

Bleier, Ruth (Ed.). (1986). *Feminist approaches to science*. New York: Pergamon Press.

Bogdan, R., Brown, M.A., & Foster, S.B. (1984). Be honest but not cruel: Staff-parent communication on a neo-natal unit. In S.J. Taylor & R. Bogdan (Eds.), *Introduction to qualitative research methods* (2nd Ed.) New York: John Wiley.

Bok, Sissela. (1982). *Secrets*. New York: Pantheon.

Boruch, Robert F. (1974). Bibliography: Illustrated randomized field experiments for program planning and evaluation. *Evaluation, 2*, 83-87.

Boruch, Robert. (1986, October). *What have we learned about randomized social experiments over the last decade?* Keynote address at the American Evaluation Association Annual Meeting, Kansas City, MO.

Campbell, Donald T. (1969). Reforms as experiments. *American Psychologist, 24*, 409-429.

Campbell, Donald T., & Stanley, Julian C. (1963). Experimental and quasi-experimental designs for research on teaching. In N.L. Gage (Ed.), *Handbook of research on teaching*. Chicago: Rand McNally.

Cook, Thomas D. (1985). Postpositivist critical multiplism. In L. Shotland & M.M. Mark (Eds.), *Social science and social policy*. Beverly Hills, CA: Sage.

Cook, Thomas D., & Campbell, Donald T. (1979). *Quasi experimentation: Design and analysis issues for field settings*. Chicago: Rand McNally.

Cook, Thomas D., & Reichardt, Charles S. (Eds.). (1979). *Qualitative and quantitative methods in evaluation research*. Beverly Hills, CA: Sage.

Cronbach, Lee J. (1963). Course improvement through evaluation. *Teachers College Record, 64*, 672-683.

Cronbach, Lee J. (1975). Beyond the two disciplines of scientific psychology. *American Psychologist, 30*, 116-127.

Cronbach, Lee J. & Suppes, Patrick. (1969). *Research for tomorrow's schools: Disciplined inquiry in education*. New York: Macmillan.

Cronbach, Lee J. and associates. (1980). *Toward reform of program evaluation*. San Francisco: Jossey-Bass.

Davies, P.C.W., & Brown, J.R. (1986). *The ghost in the atom*. Cambridge: Cambridge University Press.

Index

team evaluation and, 196
Exploitation, protection against, 65-66,
   160-161

Facts
   constructivist methodology and, 44
   mastery of, 23
   reporting, 223-225
   theories and, 63-64, 105
   values and, 64-66, 105-106, 123-125
Fairness, judging evaluation and, 245-
   247
Federal regulations, 120-123, 133-134,
   268
Field excursions, 200
First generation evaluation, 22-26, 31
   evaluator's role, 259
   focusing elements, 39-40
Fiscal audit, 242
Follow-up, action assessment using, 250
Foundational criteria, for judging
   evaluation, 233-236
Fourth generation evaluation
   carrying out negotiations and, 220-
      223, 246-247
   claims, concerns, and issues, 213-214
   collecting information, 215-217
   consequences of, 256-259
   constructions in, see Constructions
   constructivist paradigm and, 79-116
   definitions of, 90
   flow of, 185-187
   goals of, 253
   judging quality of, 228-251
   methodology of, 184-227
   negotiation agenda, 218-219, 265
   organizing, 195-201
   principles for, 263-264
   prioritizing unresolved items, 214-215
   purpose, 71-74
   recycling in, 226
   reporting, 223-225
   stakeholder identification, 201-204
   warnings about, 262-264
   See also Constructivist inquiry
Functional relationships, causal
   relationships vs., 96

Gatekeepers, cooperation with evaluation
   and, 151, 191, 198-199
Generalizations, 241
   applicability of, 172
   context-stripping and, 36-37
   legitimate, 169
   scientific method and, 61, 94-96
   usefulness of findings and, 234
Godel's Incompleteness Theorem, 66

Harm, guarding subjects from, 120-121
Hawthorne experiments, 25, 146
Hermeneutic dialectic process, 72-73,
   149-155
   broadened inquiry and, 54-56
   carrying out negotiation and, 220-223
   client's agreement with, 191
   conditions for, 191
   evaluator's role, 41, 260-262
   developing joint constructions and,
      204-209
   high-salience issues and, 153
   interacting elements, 177-180
   methodology, 44, 89-90
   political input and, 65
   privacy and, 132-133
   quality control in, 244
   three-dimensional form of, 173
   unresolved items and, 215
History
   ambiguous nature of, 69-70
   generalizations and, 95-96
Humanistic paradigm, 36
Humans, as instruments, 175-176
Hunches, 164
Hypotheses
   confidence in, 237-238
   conclusions relevant to, 171
   controllable, 130
   effect on observation, 99
   falsification of, 171
   propositional form, 167
   testing, 162, 166-167

If-then relationships, 85
Indeterminacy phenomena, 92, 99

Scientific management movement, 25-26
Scientific paradigm
  abuses of omission, 119
  applying to all forms of inquiry, 103-
    109
  epistemology, 87-88, 98-103
  Kuhnian revolution in, 84, 172
  male influence on, 128
  objectivity, 66-67, 110, 127-128, 168
  ontology, 85-98, 119
  overcommitment to, 35-38
  reactive posture of, 131
  reasons for rejecting, 43, 57-68, 90-103
  values and, 62, 64, 100-103
Scientists, as stakeholders, 256
Second generation evaluation, 27, 31
  evaluator's role, 260
  focusing elements, 39-40
Self-esteem, loss of, 121
Sensitive cases, sampling, 178
Shaping, mutual simultaneous, 97-98,
  110
Social experimentation, 30
Social factors, becoming acquainted with,
  200-201
Socialization, 43
  belief in scientific method and, 76-77
  of evaluator, 197-198
Social problems, solutions to, 46-47
Social sciences
  first generation evaluation and, 24-25
  scientific paradigm and, 35
Sociopolitical process, evaluation as, 253
Sophistication
  case reports and, 225
  changing constructions and, 87, 145,
    147-148, 180, 219
  communicating constructions and, 86,
    150
  in fourth generation evaluation, 217-218
  relativity of truth and, 104
  stakeholder inclusion and, 203
  vicarious experience and, 181
Sponsor, contractual identification of, 188
Staff, written specification of, 194
Stakeholders
  adversarial, 240

as groups at risk, 51-52
broadened inquiry and, 54-56
claims, concerns, and issues of, see
  Claims, concerns, and issues
classes of, 40-41
constructions of, see Constructions
empowerment of, see Empowerment
emerging, 202
evaluation information and, 53
exploitation of, 52
formal organizational lines and, 199
gatekeepers and, 151, 191, 198-199
identification of, 58-59, 72, 201-204,
  246
member checks and, 238-240
parallel circles, 211-212
relative stake of, 203
scientists as, 256
types of, 201-202
written statement to, 191-192
Standards, 30
  for conventional evaluation, 229-233
  for fourth generation evaluation, 233-
    251
  for tests, 220
Stanford-Binet intelligence test, 24
Statement of purpose, 189-190
Status quo
  constructivism and, 139
  science's maintenance of, 124
Subjectivity
  human instruments and, 169, 196-197
  objectivity vs., 112-113
  progressive, 238
  tacit knowledge and, 177
  values and, 88
Subject-object dualism, 44, 66-67
Subjects, ethical treatment of, 120-123
Summative merit evaluation, 190

Tables, dummy, 171
Tactical authenticity, 250
Team evaluation, 196
Technical adequacy, 129, 203-204
Technical reports, scientific paradigm
  and, 171-172

About the Authors

EGON G. GUBA is Professor Emeritus, School of Education, Indiana University, where he served for 23 years prior to his retirement in 1989. He received the doctorate in quantitative inquiry from the Department of Education, University of Chicago, in 1952, having studied with, among others, Ralph W. Tyler, widely acclaimed as the "Father of Evaluation." He remained on the faculty there, teaching statistics and measurement, until moving on in 1957 for a year's appointment at the [then] University of Kansas City and Community Studies, Inc.

In 1958, he accepted an appointment at the Ohio State University, where he served, first, as Head, Division of Educational Research, and subsequently as the Director of the Bureau of Educational Research and Service. It was during this period that he undertook to evaluate "Project Discovery," a joint venture of Encyclopedia Britannica Films and Bell and Howell Corporation, which called for an ethnographic approach. This experience persuaded him that conventional modes of evaluation,

293

and, indeed, of inquiry generally, were beset by serious problems. Following a move to Indiana University in 1966, he set these doubts aside for a period of ten years, during which he was associated with two projects and served as Associate Dean for Academic Affairs of the School of Education. But when he returned to full-time teaching in 1976, his doubts recurred. He took advantage of the opportunity afforded by UCLA to serve as Visiting Scholar at its Center for the Study of Evaluation to sort out some of the questions he was posing to himself. A monograph, "Toward a Methodology of Naturalistic Inquiry in Educational Evaluation," represented a primitive attempt to carve out a new direction.

He joined forces with Yvonna Lincoln shortly thereafter; their joint efforts have since resulted in *Effective Evaluation* (1981) and *Naturalistic Inquiry* (1985). The present volume updates their earlier thinking and moves it to a more informed and sophisticated level—the fourth generation of evaluation.

YVONNA SESSIONS LINCOLN is currently Associate Professor of Higher Education at Vanderbilt University. Prior to coming to Vanderbilt, she taught at the University of Kansas, at Indiana University, and at Stephens College. She holds the doctorate in education from Indiana University (1977) and degrees from the University of Illinois and Michigan State University. She is the coauthor, with Egon G. Guba, of *Effective Evaluation* and *Naturalistic Inquiry*, and is the editor of *Organizational Theory and Inquiry: The Paradigm Revolution.* She has published numerous journal articles and presented papers at conferences nationally, many of them in the program evaluation field. Her special interests are program review processes in higher education, program evaluation, and the effect on the academic disciplines in higher education of the growing discontent with conventional models for carrying out scientific inquiry. She serves on the Executive Boards of the Association for the Study of Higher Education and of Division J (Postsecondary Education) of the American Educational Research Association, and is President-elect of the American Evaluation Association. She and Egon Guba shared the 1987 Paul Lazarsfeld Award of the American Evaluation Association for "significant contributions to evaluation research and theory."